APR 2 0 2000

ELK GROVE VILLAGE PUBLIC

3 1250 00537 4257

P9-CEC-944

DISCARDED BY
ELK GROVE VILLAGE PUBLIC LIBRARY

DISCARDED BY
ELK GROVE VILLAGE PUBLIC LIBRARY

ELK GROVE VILLAGE PUBLIC LIBRARY
1001 WELLINGTON AVE.
ELK GROVE VILLAGE, IL 60007
(847) 439-0447

Understanding
JEWISH HOLIDAYS
and CUSTOMS
Historical and Contemporary

by Sol Scharfstein

KTAV PUBLISHING HOUSE INC.
Hoboken, N.J.

296.4 SCH
Scharfstein, Sol, 1921-
Understanding Jewish
holidays and customs

This book is lovingly dedicated to
my
grandchildren
Alyissa
Danielle
David
Jeffrey
Lauren
Matthew
Zachary

Copyright © 1999
KTAV Publishing House, Inc.
Library of Congress Cataloging–in–Publication Data

Scharfstein, Sol. 1921–
    Understanding Jewish Holidays and Custom : historical and
contemporary / Sol Scharfstein; design & graphics by Tom Costagliola ;
artwork by Dorcas Gelabert.
        p. cm.
Summary: A historical and contemporary overview of customs and
ceremonies as practiced by Jews from Biblical times to the present,
discussing the changes that have taken place through the centuries.
    Includes Index.
    ISBN 0-88125-626-9 (pbk.) -- ISBN 0-88125-634-X (cloth)
1. Fasts and feasts-Judaism-Juvenile literature. 2. Judaism-Customs and
practices-Juvenile literature. [1. Fasts and feasts-Judaism. 2. Judaism-
Customs and practices.] I. Title.
    BM690.S3176 1999
    296.4--dc21   98-55100
                                                   CIP
                                                   AC

Printed in Hong Kong

Distributed by
KTAV Publishing House, Inc.
900 Jefferson St.
Hoboken, NJ 07030

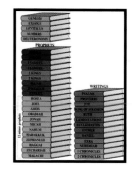

TABLE OF CONTENTS

INTRODUCTION

Jewish holidays and ceremonies are highlights which illuminate and add substance to our meaningful journey through life.

Understanding Jewish Holidays and Customs is a book about the beliefs, practices, and customs that make up the historic faith of Judaism. The rich traditions it documents have been a mighty force in the lives of Jews for many thousands of years.

As you will see, Jewish holidays and customs began thousands of years ago, but they are not carved in stone. In every era of history and every part of the world, rituals and ideas have changed, in accordance with the needs of the day. Despite the changes, the timeless Torah core has always been retained.

THE DEVELOPMENT OF JEWISH FESTIVALS AND CEREMONIES

The very first Jewish holiday celebrations go back to the Torah, the Five Books of Moses. The solemn holidays of Rosh Hashanah and Yom Kippur, and the joyous festivals of Passover, Shavuot and Sukkot, were all described and observed in biblical times.

Jewish life-cycle ceremonies also go back to the time of the Bible. Circumcision, marriage and the rituals of death and burial are all mentioned in the Torah. Other customs, according to the Talmud, were instituted by the prophets. Among these were the Hakafot procession on Sukkot, when the worshipers, carrying lulavim, march around the bimah in the synagogue.

Additional rituals were developed during the Babylonian Exile which saw the beginning of the synagogue as a Jewish institution. The process continued in the time of the Second Temple. One of the important innovations, introduced by Ezra the Scribe, was the public reading from the Torah on Mondays and Thursdays. In the years that followed, the sages known as the Men of the Great Assembly, contributed some of the basic prayers which are still at the center of Jewish worship in synagogues around the world, whether Reform, Conservative, Reconstructionist or Orthodox.

The era of the Second Temple also saw the development of some new holidays. One was Purim, the other was Chanukah. With these as precedents, several holidays have been added in recent decades to commemorate important events in modern Jewish history: Yom Ha-Shoah, or Holocaust Memorial Day; Yom Ha-Atzma'ut, or Israel Independence Day; and Yom Yerushalayim, or Jerusalem Day.

HOLIDAYS AND LIFE–CYCLE EVENTS

Meanwhile, each of the holidays and life-cycle events was accumulating its own collection of customs and practices. Many ceremonies begun as individual practices, were gradually adopted by other people, and eventually spread throughout the Jewish world. Some unknown individual, for instance, living in a time and place no longer remembered, invented or adopted a spinning toy to amuse his or her children at Chanukah time. This eventually became the draydel with which we are all familiar. Other such customs are the Purim masquerade, the use of noisemakers during the Purim service and the flags displayed on Simchat Torah.

Local customs developed in Jewish communities all over the world, sometimes connected with events in those specific communities or adopted from non-Jewish neighbors. This process also gave us many of the traditional "Jewish" foods, such as blintzes, latkes, hamantashen, gefilte fish, stuffed cabbage, honey cake, knishes and the like.

Although Jewish communities throughout the world followed the same religion each community developed its own ways of celebrating holidays and life-cycle events. Customs in Eastern Europe differed from those in North Africa. Moroccan Jews had their own customs, so did Yemenite, Dutch and German Jews. The descendants of these communities in Israel and North America very often still follow the customs of their ancestors.

NEW CUSTOMS AND CEREMONIES

In the nineteenth century, with the growth of Reform, Conservative and Reconstructionist Judaism, many ancient ceremonies and customs were abandoned, and new ceremonies were created to emphasize the importance of women's role in Judaism. Bat Mitzvah was one of the first. Another is Simchat Ha-Bat. In the years and centuries to come, as new needs are felt, new ceremonies and customs will continue to be added.

To understand the present practice in Reform, Conservative and Reconstructionist movements, it is essential to have an understanding of earlier traditions.

Our rabbis say *tzay ulemad*, "go and learn". Learning about the many customs and practices of Judaism will help you feel closer to your ancestors, closer to your fellow Jews, and most of all, closer to your God.

You can't hear God
    but you can learn about God's ideas.
You can't shake God's hand,
    but you can be touched by God.
You can't see God,
    but God's light is in your prayers,
        and in your customs and ceremonies.

ACKNOWLEDGEMENTS

Numerous multitalented people have worked hard to bring *Understanding Jewish Holidays and Customs* to life. They labored long and hard, critiquing, editing, and researching.

I wish to thank the following for their expert assistance. It is their scholarship and sensitivity that have helped shaped the text

Yaakov Elman
Robert Milch
Bernard Scharfstein
Herbert Stavsky
Shirley Stern

The final responsibility for any omissions, errors and mistakes is my own.

Everything Starts With a Calendar

How accustomed we are to the conveniences of civilization! Is it too cold? Fix the thermostat. Do we have to get up early? Set the electric alarm. Want to know when to buy Purim gifts? Consult the Jewish calendar. It tells us the date of every festival. Knowing how to read it yields a great deal of information, as you will soon see.

But what did people do before there was a printed calendar? How did they manage without a calendar?

In Early Days

In the earliest days of our history, in the days of the patriarchs Abraham, Isaac, and Jacob, the Jewish people were shepherds who wandered in search of green pastures for their flocks. They had no lamps. They often went to bed at sunset and got up at sunrise. Men, women, and children thought of the sun as a wonderful friend. They knew that without the sun it would always be dark and cold.

But then they learned to plant crops, and they found that they had to do more than just divide the year into seasons of winter and summer. Watching the sun rise and set did not help them.

Then someone said, "While you have been sleeping at night, I have been watching the moon and the stars. Sometimes the moon is full and round, sometimes it is only half its size, and sometimes I can't find it at all. It seems to disappear."

The shepherds of ancient Palestine were filled with wonder by the moon's changes. They did not know that the moon has no light of its own but is lighted like the earth itself only by the rays of the sun.

The Gezer Calendar Stone was discovered by R. Macalister in 1908. This 10th–century B.C.E. limestone plaque is inscribed with the planting schedule of the ancient Palestinian farmer.

1. *2 months of sowing.*
2. *2 months of late sowing.*
3. *The month of pulling flax.*
4. *The month of the barley harvest.*
5. *The month when everything else is harvested.*
6. *2 months of vine pruning.*
7. *The month of summer fruit.*

Nor did they know that the changes in the size of the moon, its "waxing" and "waning," are caused by the moon's traveling around the earth.

Legend of the Moon

A legend even grew up about the moon. In the beginning (says the Talmud) the Almighty created the sun and the moon equal in size. But the moon was not satisfied to share her glory with the sun. She complained. To punish her for being jealous, the Almighty shrank the moon down to her present size. But then He took pity on her and promised that someday the Israelites would celebrate the new moon and build their calendar based on her movements.

Report to the Sanhedrin

Committees were appointed to watch the moon to see how often these changes happened. Special observers were placed at stations to wait for the appearance of the new moon. As soon as the slightest crescent showed in the sky, the observers rushed to Jerusalem. They rushed to the Sanhedrin, the High Court of the Jewish people. "We testify that we have seen the new moon," they swore. They stated the moment it had made its appearance.

It was a moment of high excitement. Once the Sanhedrin had proclaimed the new month, runners were dispatched to light fires on the highest hills ringing the capital city. As soon as these signals were seen by the inhabitants of the next town, they in turn lit a fire on their highest hill. At last the signals reached the farthermost communities. The new month had officially begun.

But what about the settlements that lay beyond the shimmering ocean? Jews of far-off countries like Persia and Italy and Egypt could not rely on messages which sometimes arrived very late. "We will observe the thirtieth day and the day after it as the new month," they decided. "In that way, we will be certain not to go astray." That is why, according to tradition, our forefathers who lived too far from Judea to be reached by signals and messages added an extra day to the Passover, Shavuot, Sukkot, and Rosh Hashanah holidays. It meant a great deal to them to keep the customs of our people properly. In that way they were certain to do so.

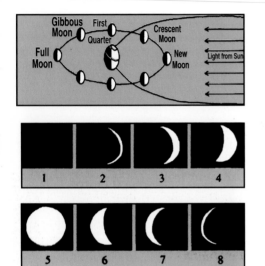

This diagram shows stages in the moon's journey around the earth. The diagram shows how the moon looks to us at each stage of its journey.

8

The Sun and the Moon

Now a new problem arose to plague these pioneer calendar-makers. From the moon they had arrived at a month of 29 1/2 days. Twelve moon-months added up to 354 days. But if they had followed the moon-calendar, they would at times have been celebrating Passover in the winter instead of the spring, and planting seasons would have been utterly confused.

Then the people watched the sun more closely than before. With remarkable wisdom, they discovered that a year calculated by the sun has 365 days. (We know the reason for this is that the earth, revolving once daily on its axis, takes 365 days to go completely around the sun.) "We must devise a plan to keep the moon-month in step with the sun-year," the astronomers said.

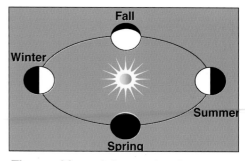

The position of the earth relevant to the sun gives us our seasons. Seasons are named here as they are in the Northern Hemisphere. In the Southern Hemisphere the seasons are opposite.

Leap Year

There is a new moon every twenty-nine or thirty days. Twelve such months make up the normal Jewish year. This method of figuring, as we have seen, created differences between the solar, or sun year, of 365 days, and the Jewish, or lunar year of 354 days. To make up for this difference, the Jewish leap year has an additional month after Adar, called Adar Sheni (Second Adar). The second Adar month comes every third, sixth, eighth, eleventh, fourteenth, seventeenth, and nineteenth year.

"Now we have it," the people said. "A calendar arranged in a cycle of nineteen years, and seven of the nineteen years are leap years."

Now you will understand what we mean when we describe the Jewish calendar as both a lunar (moon) and solar (sun) calendar. The months of the Jewish calendar are moon-months, but the year is a sun-year.

All this was accomplished and still there was no written calendar. Partly this was because there was a close-knit Jewish community and the known world occupied only a small part of the globe. Partly it was due to the fact that Jews were accustomed to hand down laws and traditions by word of mouth, from father to son and from generation to generation. The passing of time brought important changes. Our people were driven out of the Jewish homeland. Jews were scattered to the four corners of the earth. There was no central Jewish com-

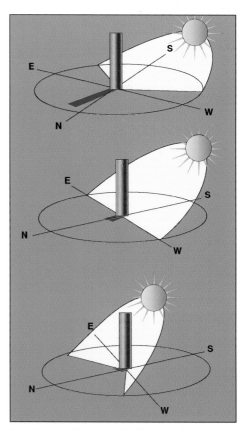

In winter, the sun follows a lower path across the sky than in the summer. In spring and fall, it follows a path in-between.

9

If you wish to figure out the number of the Hebrew year, there is an easy formula. Subtract 1240 from the civil year. Then add 5000. The Hebrew year of 1981 would be:

```
    1981
   -1240
     741
   +5000
    5741
```

That is the year if you are figuring it between January 1 and Rosh Hashanah. If you are figuring it between Rosh Hashanah and December 31, add one more year.

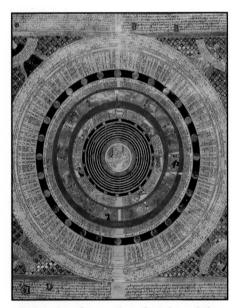

Calendar from the Catalan Atlas (1375-77), illuminated by Abraham Cresques and his son Jafuda (Judah). Abraham Cresques was known as the "Master of Maps and Compasses." He was the cartographer to the king of Aragon. In 1376 he made the famous Catalan Atlas which he sent as a gift to the king of France. His son Jafuda was nicknamed the "Map Jew." In the persecutions of 1391 Jafuda was forced to convert to Christianity.

munity and no chief authority with regard to religious laws and customs. So it became necessary to have a written calendar, and a great scholar who lived about 1600 years ago prepared one.

A Written Calendar

In the year 359 C.E., Hillel II so called to set him apart from the famed Hillel who lived in the days of the Second Temple, set the rules for making a calendar.

Taking quill in hand, he wrote that the length of the Jewish month is the time it takes the moon to go around the earth. This month is 29 days, 12 hours, and 44 minutes. "We must be practical," said Hillel. "We will reckon the months by full days." So the law was laid down that some months should have 30 days and others 29. From that day Jews everywhere could determine the calendar for themselves and observe the festivals on the same day.

Now we know about the way our calendar began, but that does not explain how we number our years. Why is the Jewish year called 5718 instead of 1958, or 5719 rather than 1959? The answer to this question lies, as is very often the case, in the lap of Jewish tradition.

From the beginning of recorded time, calendar makers have used events great and small as starting points for their date guides. The Romans, for example, counted time from the founding of their capital city. Early Christians dated events from the birth of Jesus, which they called "the year 1." (Later calculations show that he was actually born about three years before that time.) Our everyday calendar follows that rule. It is called the Gregorian calendar, because it was revised by Pope Gregory XIII in 1582, and was adopted by England for herself and her American colonies in 1752. Jews, however, number the years from the time of the Creation of the world as accounted for in the Bible. And, in place of B.C. and A.D., which mean "Before Christ" and "Anno Domini" (the year of our Lord), we use B.C.E. and C.E., which mean "Before the Common Era" and "Common Era." The latter abbreviations are used in this book.

Names of the Months

You have just seen the months Adar, Nisan, and Tishrei mentioned, and you probably know the names of at least some of the other months of our calendar. Where did the months get their names?

Originally, the Israelites used numerals to distinguish one month from another. The month in which the spring season began was the first month; the other months were called accordingly the second, third, and so on.

The Hebrew names of the months, as we know them, were adopted when our people lived in the Babylonian exile after the destruction of the First Temple in 586 B.C.E. The names were derived from the Babylonian calendar.

Now Read the Calendar

We are now ready to greet our Jewish calendar as an old friend and to read it with ease and speed. At this point, it would be helpful if you were to take a Jewish calendar, or *luach*, as it is known in Hebrew, and place it before you. Glance at a few pages. Do you see that it is a guide to our religious observances as well as a date-reminder?

ASTROLOGICAL SYMBOLS FOR THE JEWISH MONTHS

CHESHVAN	IYAR	SIVAN
TISHREI	AV	NISAN
ELUL	TEVET	ADAR
TAMMUZ	SHEVAT	KISLEV

Jewish Year **Hebrew Months**
5758 Elul **September 1998** **Tishrei 5759**

Sunday	Monday	Tuesday	Wednesday	Thursday	Friday	Saturday
	Hebrew Dates	**1**	**2**	**3**	7:06PM **4**	Ki Tetze **5**
		10 Elul	11 Elul	12 Elul	13 Elul	14 Elul
6	Labor Day **7**	**8**	**9**	**10**	6:55PM **11**	Ki Tavo SELICHOT **12**
15 Elul	16 Elul	17 Elul	18 Elul	19 Elul	20 Elul	21 Elul
13	**14**	**15**	**16**	**17**	6:43PM **18**	Nitzavim **19**
22 Elul	23 Elul	24 Elul	25 Elul	26 Elul	27 Elul	28 Elul
EREV ROSH HASHANAH **20**	ROSH HASHANAH DAY 1 **21**	ROSH HASHANAH DAY 2 **22**	FEAST OF GEDALIAH **23**	**24**	6:31PM **25**	Vayelech SHABBAT SHUVAH **26**
29 Elul	1 Tishrei	2 Tishrei	3 Tishrei	4 Tishrei	5 Tishrei	6 Tishrei
27	**28**	**29**	YOM KIPPUR (YIZKOR) **30**	Jewish Holiday	CANDLE LIGHTING TIME	SHABBAT TORAH READING
7 Tishrei	8 Tishrei	9 Tishrei	10 Tishrei			

A page from a Jewish calendar. Notice the variety of information.

HEBREW MONTHS and HOLIDAYS	
TISHREI	Rosh Hashanah, Yom Kippur, Sukkot Simchat Torah
CHESVAN	
KISLEV	Chanukah
TEVET	
SHEVAT	Tu Bi-Shevat
ADAR	Purim
NISAN	Passover, Yom Ha Shoah
IYAR	Yom Ha–Zikkaron, Yom Ha–Atzma'ut, Lag Ba-Omer
SIVAN	Shavuot
TAMMUZ	
AV	Tisha B'Av
ELUL	

The Mosaic floor of the synagogue at Bet Alpha. The round panels shows the symbols of the zodiac. The names are in Hebrew. This mosaic is about 1500 years old. A mosaic is a picture made by placing small pieces of colored glass or stone in cement.

The Hebrew Days

The Jewish week begins on Sunday. It ends on Saturday, or Shabbat. The names of the days are really numbers. They tell what day of the week it is. This is how the days are named in Hebrew:

Sunday-Yom Rishon (The First Day)
Monday-Yom Sheni (The Second Day)
Tuesday-Yom Shlishi (The Third Day)
Wednesday-Yom Revi'i (The Fourth Day)
Thursday-Yom Chamishi (The Fifth Day)
Friday-Yom Shishi (The Sixth Day)

Saturday-Shabbat (The Sabbath)

Observe that the day, in Jewish reckoning, begins at sunset. Saturday, which is the seventh day of the week, begins on Friday evening. That is because the Bible tells us, in the story of the Creation, that "there was evening and there was morning, one day." The very first day, the day of Creation, began not with daybreak but with sunset. All our holidays follow this order and begin at sunset of the day before.

A detailed Jewish calendar tells us when the sun sets on the eve of a Sabbath or holiday; it informs us to light candles about 18 minutes before sunset.

Look again at the calendar. It will tell you which portion of the Torah and Prophets will be read in the synagogue next Saturday.

Rosh Chodesh

When does the new Jewish month begin? Your calendar knows, and points to the first day of the new month, called Rosh Chodesh, and even to the exact second when the new moon is "born." In olden days special celebrations were held throughout Palestine to greet the new month. The custom of "blessing the new month" has come down to us. It is recited in the synagogue on the preceding Sabbath. In this prayer we ask that we may be granted a month of good health and happiness. On Rosh Chodesh day, prayers of thanksgiving are read at services. Jews also observe the custom of blessing the new moon–*Kiddush L'vanah*. In this ancient ceremony, Jews gather in groups outdoors. When the moon is visible to all, each says to his neighbor: "Blessed be the Almighty, Who renews the months. *Shalom Aleichem!*" and everyone replies: "Peace be unto you . . . may this month bring *Mazal Tov* . . . good fortune to us and to all mankind!"

That is the story of the Jewish calendar. It reminds us of happy occasions such as festivals and of sad ones such as fast and memorial days. It is as old as written history and as timely as tomorrow's newspaper.

"New Moon Prayers," painting by A. Bender, late 19th century.

Rosh Chodesh in Ancient Times

In ancient times, at the time of the First Temple (*Bet ha–Mikdash*), the beginning of the new month was celebrated with great festivity. The shofar was blown. People did not go to work. They came to Jerusalem. There they sacrificed a special new-month offering. Afterwards, a family feast was held. A special feature of the day was that women were released from all their chores. This was a reward for them because long before, after leaving Egypt, when the Jews were wandering in the desert, the women had refused to contribute their jewelry to help build an idol. After the First Temple was destroyed, many of these customs were no longer practiced. But other customs developed. Special prayers were said in honor of the new moon. One of the prayers was *Hallel*. It is a special prayer of praise to God that is recited only on holidays. But an exception is made for the new moon, when half-*Hallel* is recited.

In Modern Times

The beginning of the new month is still celebrated with special prayers and customs in many modern temples. Usually the new moon is blessed following the *Havdalah* service on the Saturday night following its appearance. Often this lovely ceremony is held in the open air where the new moon could be seen.

Learning More About: Two-Day Holidays

Most reform Jews celebrate the holidays of the Jewish year for one day, the same as some of the ancient Jews did in the time of the Bible. Orthodox and Conservative Jews, however, celebrate some of the holidays for two days.

Long ago the Jews lived in the Land of Israel. At that time they observed each holiday for only one day. They did not have written calendars the way we do today.

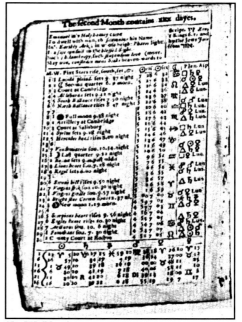
A calendar based on the Bible was introduced by the Pilgrims in Massachusetts, in 1666. The Pilgrims studied and revered the Bible. They used the Hebrew names of the months in this early American calendar.

Tab ecliptis luminariu3 et primo de fole								
nnmer⁹ annorn3	nomina menfin3	dies	digiti	feria	hore	minut	finis ecliptis hore	minu
1403	octob	1c	9	5	0	0	1	20
1c02	fepteb	30	8	6	17	28	19	12
1c06	Julii	20	3	2	1	40	3	3
1c 13	martii	7	4	1	23	40	1	9
15 18	Junii	7	10	2	18	22	19	17
1c24	lannar	23	9	2	3	12	4	6

Tabla de eclipfib⁹ lune								
1404	feptcb	14	17	1	17	5	2	33
140⁷	lannar	18	1	6	3	50	7	18
1500	noneb	5	13	5	10	17	13	30
1c01	maii	2	10	1	1c	33	19	6
1c02	octob	15	14	7	10	1c	12	9
1c04	februa	20	16	1	10	47	14	13
1c0f	ang⁹	14	1c	5	5	62	9	6
1c08	Junii	12	23	2	1c	21	19	0
1c09	Junii	2	7	7	9	29	2	3
1c 11	octob	6	13	2	9	11	2	2c
15 14	lannar	29	1c	2	14	20	16	3
1c 1c	lannar	10	1c	7	5	0	6	42
1c 16	Julii	13	14	1	10	0	12	30
1c 19	noneb	6	20	2	5	50	6	48

A chart from the Perpetual Almanac of Abraham Zacuto, Spanish astronomer whose books were studied by Columbus. The eclipse of the moon on February 29, 1504, is listed.

It was easy for them to figure out the dates of the holidays. All they had to do was look at the sky. If there was a new full moon, they knew that a new month had started. Then they would count the days until the date of the next holiday.

But then powerful enemies conquered Israel. Many Jews were forced to leave their country and live all over the world. They continued to celebrate all their holidays as before, even though they no longer lived in their homeland. Since they did not know exactly when the new moon could be seen in Israel, they were not always certain when a new month had begun. In order to make sure that they did not celebrate the holidays on the wrong day, they started the custom of celebrating for two days.

The Jews who remained in Israel, of course, continued to celebrate the holidays for only one day. Nowadays this applies to us too. We have written calendars that tell us exactly when the new moon appears, even though we may not see it ourselves. Thus we always know when a new month begins, and we always know the dates of the holidays. Since we no longer have the problem the two-day custom was meant to solve, it is really not needed anymore. That is why Reform Judaism decided to observe the holidays for only one day.

Israeli stamp with the Zodiac signs for all the months of the year. The quotation is from the Talmud and reads: "I created 12 constellations in the firmament."

The Sabbath

Shabbat in the Bible

We first learn about Shabbat at the very beginning of the Bible, in the book of Genesis. There, the story of the creation of the world is told. God created the world in six days. First God created the heaven and the earth. Next, God created water and dry land. Then, God made the sun, the moon, and the stars, fish, and birds, and animals. Finally, God created people. On the seventh day, when all the work was finished, God rested. God blessed the seventh day, making it special because it was the day of resting from all the work of creation.

Only one Jewish holiday is observed every week throughout the year. It is the Sabbath, the day of peace and rest.

Shabbat and the Ten Commandments

The Ten Commandments, the cornerstone of the Jewish faith, mention only one Jewish holiday–the Sabbath. The Fourth Commandment says, in part:

Remember the Sabbath day to keep it holy. Six days shall you labor and do all your work. But the seventh day is the Sabbath of the Almighty your God: on it you shall not do any work, you, or your son or your daughter, your manservant or your maidservant, or your cattle, or the stranger that is within your gates.

This commandment gave something to the world that it had never had before: a weekly day of rest. From the beginning of time, farmers tilled the soil, servants cleaned the house, potters sat at their wheels, and shepherds grazed their flocks from morning till night, every day, without taking time off to rest.

Then Moses, who led the Jews out of slavery in Egypt, ascended Mount Sinai and, at God's command, brought down the Ten Commandments. Among them was the Fourth

Shabbat is ushered in with the lighting of the candles and recitation of the *Kiddush*.

This ancient block of stone was a part of the wall of a building in the Temple compound in Jerusalem. The Hebrew inscription reads, "To the place of trumpeting."

In Temple days a priest would stand on a roof and announce by shofar blasts the approach and end of Shabbat. This inscription illustrates one of the ancient modes of communication between the priest in the Temple and the people of Jerusalem. Today in some heavily populated Orthodox communities a siren is used to announce Shabbat.

TWO *CHALLOT*
Jews from central and eastern Europe, known as Ashkenazim, regard *challah* as an absolute necessity for celebrating the Sabbath. In fact, tradition mandates that if one cannot afford both wine and *challah* for the Sabbath, the choice must be *challah*. Customarily, Ashkenazic Jews put two *challot* on the Sabbath table. The number two has many meanings. Here it is symbolic of the double portion of manna that the Israelites collected each Friday, while wandering in the Sinai Desert, after their escape from Egypt. One portion was for Friday, the other for the Sabbath. It also refers to the sacred Sabbath breads of the Bible: the *challah* gift–offering to the priests, and the Showbreads.

Commandment, establishing a day of rest for the Israelites, and later, for all people.

Shabbat in Ancient Times

As the centuries passed, different Sabbath customs developed. In ancient Israel, Shabbat was announced by blowing six blasts on the shofar. When the first blast was blown, all the farmers who were working in the fields stopped work and started for home. When the second blast was heard, all the shops were closed. At the third blast, Shabbat candles were lit and blessed in homes across the country. The last three blasts announced that the Sabbath had actually started.

Preparing for the Queen

Since the Jewish day is measured from sunset to sunset, the Sabbath arrives on Friday evening. The house is neat as a pin. The Sabbath is considered the queen of all our holidays, and one is happy to work very hard to welcome the Sabbath Queen.

Now the table is set. A silver *Kiddush* cup and candlesticks have a place of honor. Two *challot*–the twisted loaves of Sabbath bread–are placed at the head of the table and covered with a white cloth.

Why the Twist-Bread (*Challah*)?

The two *challot* are known as *lechem mishneh* (double bread). They remind us that when the Israelites were in the wilderness on their way to the Promised Land they gathered a double portion of manna on Fridays, because on the Sabbath they were not permitted to gather manna, the food that descended to them from the skies. The cloth covering the *challot* recalls the dew which covered the manna every morning.

In many homes, the old custom of dropping coins into a charity box before Shabbat begins is still followed. This is the moment for it. And now a family member steps up to the table and recites the age-old prayer: "Blessed are You, O Almighty, our God, Ruler of the Universe, Who has made us holy with commandments, and commanded us to kindle the Sabbath lights."

Now the parents bless the children by placing their hands over the bowed heads of each child. They recite the prayer for a boy: *"May God make you like Ephraim and Manasseh"*; and for a girl: *"May God make you like Sarah, Rebekah, Rachel, and Leah."*

No one saw her enter, but she is here. Silently, invisibly, the Sabbath Queen has come into the home.

Welcoming the Sabbath

The Friday evening service in the Orthodox and Conservative synagogues is usually short. The prayers include a song with the words: "Come, my friend, let us welcome Sabbath the Bride!" *Kiddush* over wine is recited in the synagogue just as it was in medieval days when strangers often spent the entire Sabbath in the house of prayer. In Reform congregations the late Friday Night Service is the major service of the week. It is held after the Sabbath meal when the congregation gathers to pray together and honor the Sabbath. In many synagogues candles are lit and Kiddush is recited. Almost always a sermon is preached by the rabbi of the congregation or there's a lecture by a guest speaker.

The service is generally followed by an *Oneg Shabbat* at which refreshments are served and congregants join in fellowship. Most Reform congregations have a Family Worship Service once a month which is generally held early in the evening so that children may more easily attend.

The ceremony of *Kabbalat Shabbat,* the greeting of the Sabbath on Friday evening, was first introduced at the end of the sixteenth century. It was begun by the Kabbalists, the religious mystics of the city of Safed in the Land of Israel, of whom the greatest was Rabbi Isaac Luria.

The Kabbalists had read in the Talmud that sages in the third century would dress in their Shabbat clothes on Friday evening and say, "Come, let us go out and meet the Sabbath Queen!" The Kabbalists revived this custom. Late on Friday afternoons, they marched in a procession outside the town to greet the Sabbath as queen and bride. They sang psalms and ended with, "Come, bride; come, bride!" One of the Kabbalists composed a poem called *Lecha Dodi* ("Come, my friend, to meet the bride"). This poem by Solomon Alkabetz is the one mentioned above which is still chanted at our Friday evening services.

In many Jewish homes it is traditional for the parents to bless the children on Friday night. For boys the blessing is, "May God make you like Ephraim and Manasseh." For girls it is, "May God make you like Sarah, Rebekah, Rachel, and Leah." This painting by the artist Moritz Oppenheim illustrates a blessing scene in a German–Jewish home. This picture was painted around 1850.

Page from a woman's ritual, showing two women making *challah* (loaves) for the Sabbath. Austria, 1751.

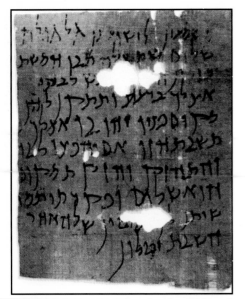

There is a quotation in the Talmud which says: "Sabbath observance balances all the commandments of the Torah." Pictured above is a letter from Simeon Bar Kochba to one of his commanders, Joshua ben Galgula. It expresses his concern for the holiness of the Sabbath.

In some European countries, a lamp such as this was used in place of Sabbath candles. It used oil and burned for a much longer period of time.

In Olden Times

Even in ancient times the Sabbath was a day of celebration as well as of rest. Work was halted and the Temple was crowded. When the Jews were exiled to Babylonia after the destruction of the First Temple, the Sabbath took on a deeper meaning for we had no Temple there and prayers took the place of sacrifices. The synagogue now began to play a vital role both as a house of prayer and a house of study. Here the Jew could hear the Torah read, follow a portion of the Prophets, and listen to a sermon.

Slowly, Sabbath customs and interpretations of laws for the Sabbath developed and grew. The Talmud, that great treasury of Jewish law and lore, devotes the closely printed pages of two volumes solely to the Sabbath.

To Honor the Sabbath

Shabbat has been honored by the Jewish people throughout history. The sages of the Talmud say that the prophet Ezra, upon returning from the exile in Babylonia in 459 B.C.E., made many laws for the good of our nation. One of these laws ordered Jewish women to rise early on Friday morning and bake bread to supply poor people with *challot* for the Sabbath.

In those days, too, it was declared that every Jew, no matter how great or how rich, must honor the Sabbath personally. Even the most famous scholars of talmudic times made certain to do something, some special bit of work, to usher in Shabbat with reverence.

In Jerusalem a priest, standing on a high tower of the Temple blew the shofar as a signal to put away all work and begin the Sabbath. This custom has been revived in modern Israel. Sirens are sounded prior to the beginning of the Sabbath. In many towns of Eastern Europe, the *shammash* or sexton announced in the marketplace that it was time to close and prepare for services in the synagogue.

Sabbath and Song

The whole of the Sabbath day is spent in happiness and relaxation. Shabbat meals are feasts, and they are accompanied by the singing of *zemirot*, special songs composed by rabbis and poets in different periods of our history in honor of the day of rest. These songs express the joy of the Sabbath.

One of the most famous *zemirot* is called *Yoh Ribbon Olam*. It was composed in the sixteenth century by Rabbi Israel Najara, who wrote more than 300 songs. This song, chanted on Friday evenings all over the world, describes the wonders of God's creation and ends with a prayer that God may rebuild Jerusalem, the city of beauty.

Here are two stanzas of *Yoh Ribbon Olam*, translated into English.

Welcoming the Shabbat by lighting the candles. Notice the artistic *Mizrach* on the wall.

Almighty, O Ruler of all the world,
You are the Ruler of Rulers.
Your majesty is e'er unfurled,
We see Your wondrous deeds.

Return to Your most holy shrine,
There all souls rejoice
In chanting hymns of lasting praise;
To You we raise our voice.

After the meal, *Birchat ha-Mazon*, or Grace, is said, and then the family chats, entertains Sabbath guests, reads, or perhaps goes to temple to enjoy a late Friday service or a forum.

Shabbat morning is taken up by services in the temple, which include the Torah reading and junior congregation for boys and girls. Then, another sunny Sabbath meal, more *zemirot*, and the blessing after the food.

This tiny Sabbath Queen is dressed and ready for her entrance.

Shabbat in Modern Times

In our own time Shabbat is celebrated in many Jewish homes with festivity and joy.

The celebration of Shabbat begins early on Friday with many special preparations. The entire house is specially cleaned for Shabbat and the table is beautifully set with the prettiest tablecloth and the best dishes. On the table are placed candlesticks with candles, two loaves of *challah* covered with a special cloth, and a *Kiddush* cup filled with wine.

On Friday evening mother traditionally lights the Shabbat candles. In some families each daughter lights a candle as well. Then mother covers her eyes and recites the blessing. According to Jewish law, men and boys may also light

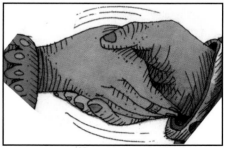
SHABBAT GREETINGS
When you meet acquaintances on Shabbat, whether in a synagogue or outside, you greet them by saying "Shabbat Shalom."

At the conclusion of the Torah reading, the Scroll is held aloft (*hagbah*) for all to see. At least three columns should be exposed.

A Shabbat meal in a kibbutz dining room. Notice the words *Shabbat Shalom* on the dining room wall.

The two Hasidim wrapped in their *tallits* are hurrying to the synagogue in Meah Shearim in Jerusalem.

Shabbat candles.

Order of Prayer

There are three daily services in the synagogue: morning (*Shacharit*), late afternoon (*Minchah*), and evening (*Ma'ariv*). On Sabbaths, new moons, and festivals, there is a fourth, known as the additional (*Musaf*) service, which follows the reading from the Torah after *Shacharit*. *Kiddush*, *Havdalah*, and *Birchat ha-Mazon* are outstanding examples of prayers for the home.

Torah Readings

Every Sabbath a *sidrah*, or Torah portion, is read aloud in the temple. (Torah readings are also held on new moons, holidays, and fast-day afternoon services.) Congregants are honored by being called up to the reading. This act of going up is called an *aliyah*.

The section from the Prophets recited after the reading from the Torah is called the Haftarah, or "conclusion." Each portion of the Torah has a specific Haftarah of its own; there is always a connection of some kind between the Torah reading and the Haftarah. Some Sabbath days are named after the Haftarah reading, such as *Shabbat Chazon* ("Sabbath of Vision"), when the first chapter of Isaiah (beginning with the words "The vision") is read.

From the Talmud we learn that the practice of Haftarah readings on Shabbat goes back to the first century C.E. Today, boys and girls who are celebrating their Bar and Bat Mitzvah, and young men about to be married, are honored by being called up for the reading of the Haftarah.

Sabbath in Israel

Shabbat is welcomed in Israel with great ceremony and joy. School ends early so that children can be at home to help with the preparations. Banks and public offices also close early in honor of Shabbat. By noon on Friday, a special feeling can be observed in the entire country. On many street corners in the business areas small stalls are set up and vendors sell lovely fresh flowers.

Since Israel is a Jewish country and most of the people who live there are Jewish, things can be done to celebrate

Shabbat that are not possible elsewhere. Buses do not run. Government offices are closed. And the country comes almost to a standstill. Only workers in essential jobs, such as police officers and fire-fighters, work on Shabbat.

The entire mood of the country is one of peace and contentment. The usual bustle of activity is gone. People stroll lazily along the street and in parks. Families share common experiences and troubles are forgotten.

In Me'ah She'arim ("One Hundred Gates"), an old very Orthodox section of Jerusalem, men and boys dressed in long cloaks, or caftans, many with fur hats (*streimlach*) hurry to the synagogue. There are many tiny synagogues in this quarter of Jerusalem. Each is frequented by a group of worshipers who have been praying together for many years. From these synagogues comes the chant of fervent praying.

Synagogue at the Mount Scopus campus of the Hebrew University. The large books on the desks are volumes of the Talmud.

Oneg Shabbat

On Saturday afternoons it has become the custom in Israel for people to gather for Sabbath discussions, visiting, and refreshments. This beautiful tradition is only a few generations old. It was originated by the outstanding Hebrew poet of modern times, Chayyim Nachman Bialik, and is called *Oneg Shabbat* ("Sabbath Joy"). The custom has also taken root in America, and in some temples the *Oneg Shabbat* is a regular Sabbath feature, ending in the *se'udah shelishit* (the "third meal" of Shabbat), evening prayer, and *Havdalah*.

Farewell to the Sabbath

In the late afternoon the daylight begins to wane. The Sabbath is slipping away. Of course, we will not let the Queen leave without a suitable farewell. There is an afternoon service (*Minchah*), a third Sabbath meal (the *se'udah shelishit*), and the closing Sabbath service. Then we have a *Havdalah* ceremony. *Havdalah* means "separation," and it marks the close of a Sabbath (or other festival) and the beginning of the weekdays that follow.

When three stars appear in the sky, it is time for *Havdalah*. First, a family member brings out a small box of fragrant spices (*besamim*). A ceremonial *Havdalah* candle, used especially for this occasion, is lit. The leader recites a blessing over wine, spices, and light. The blessing over the light is to

We bid farewell to Shabbat at the *Havdalah* ceremony, using the spicebox, the braided candle, and the cup of wine.

***Havdalot* come in a variety of happy, festive and joyful colors.**

The *Havdalah* candle is lighted, the wine is sipped, and the blessings are recited. The beauty and the togetherness of the Sabbath are over. Now the work week begins and we wish each other: *Shavuah Tov*, have a safe successful, and creative week.

SABBATH AND FESTIVAL
PRAYER BOOK

with
A New Translation,
Supplementary Readings and Notes

THE RABBINICAL ASSEMBLY OF AMERICA
AND
THE UNITED SYNAGOGUE OF AMERICA

This *Sabbath and Festival Prayer Book* was published by the Rabbinical Assembly and the United Synagogue of Conservative Judaism.

remind us that light was the first thing God created. The spices have replaced the burning of incense which was customary at festive events in olden times. The spice box often resembles a tower, and in Hebrew is called a *migdal* ("tower").

The family inhales the aroma of the spices and silently prays for a week that will be as sweet as the delicate smell of the spices. Each person comes close enough to the lighted candle to hold his or her fingers near enough to throw great shadows on the ceiling.

The head of the family says solemnly:

Blessed are You, O Almighty our God, Ruler of the Universe, Who made a distinction between light and darkness, between the holy and the ordinary, between the Sabbath and the weekday.

The leader sips some of the wine and dips the tip of the candle into the wine that remains. The flame sputters out. The Sabbath is over.

We are a little saddened when the Sabbath Queen departs. One thought makes us happy, however. In six days she will return and our home will be filled with Shabbat warmth and gaiety once again.

Special Sabbaths
The Sabbaths preceding and following certain festivals or fasts have a special character.

Shabbat ha-Gadol
The Sabbath before Passover is known as *Shabbat ha-Gadol*, the Great Sabbath. We feel that the holiday is just around the corner. A Passover spirit fills the synagogue when we recite a portion of the *Haggadah*. In Orthodox synagogues, just before the afternoon services, the rabbi gives a holiday sermon in which he explains the complicated laws pertaining to the observance of Passover. The rabbi may also present rabbinical interpretations of the Exodus from Egypt, the Song of Songs, or of anything else associated with Passover.

Shabbat Chazon and Shabbat Nachamu
The Sabbath before Tishah B'Av is called *Shabbat Chazon*, and the following Sabbath is called *Shabbat Nachamu*. These names refer to the *Haftarah* portion read in the synagogue on each of these Sabbaths.

On *Shabbat Chazon*, the reader chants from the first chapter of Isaiah, which begins with the Hebrew word *chazon* ("vision" or "prophecy"). The chapter foretells the gloomy events which were to face Israel after the destruction of the Temple.

Tied up with the feeling of mourning was the hope for happier days to come. Therefore, on the Sabbath after Tishah B'Av, we mark *Shabbat Nachamu*, the Sabbath of Comfort. On that day, the fortieth chapter of Isaiah is chanted in the synagogue, the chapter beginning with *nachamu, nachamu, ami* ("Comfort ye, comfort ye, My people").

A page from a Grace After Meals prayerbook, Prague, 1514. The page has an illustration of a Sabbath table and the *Kiddush* text.

Sabbath Before Rosh Chodesh

To welcome in each new month we have a special ritual. There is a special prayer in some synagogues on the Sabbath before the new moon and there is a ceremony blessing the new moon which is recited outdoors when the new moon appears. The Sabbath before Rosh Chodesh is called the Sabbath of Blessing. After the reading from the Torah, the exact time of the forthcoming arrival of the new moon is announced, and the congregation recites a special prayer for health and happiness.

Shabbat Shuvah

The Sabbath between Rosh Hashanah and Yom Kippur is called *Shabbat Shuvah* (Sabbath of Return). It receives its name from the first word of the prophetic portion which is read on that day. Since we are in the midst of the Ten Days of Penitence at this time, *Shabbat Shuvah* takes on an especially holy air. In the afternoon, the rabbi delivers a sermon encouraging the congregation to repent and atone and to determine to live noble lives in the days to come.

Shabbat Zachor

The Sabbath before Purim is called *Shabbat Zachor* (Sabbath of Remembrance), because an extra passage from the Bible is read, which says, "Remember what Amalek did to you as you came forth out of Egypt." The Haftarah, the portion from the prophets that is recited, is from the book of Samuel. It tells of Saul's war against Agag, king of the Amalekites.

Israeli stamp with Sabbath theme. The quotation is from the Book of Exodus and reads: "The people of Israel shall keep the Sabbath, observing the Sabbath throughout their generations."

23

A Polish-Jewish woman blessing the Shabbat candles. This painting is by Isidor Kaufmann.

Shabbat Shirah

The Sabbath on which we read *Sidrah Be-Shalach* (about two months before Passover) is called *Shabbat Shirah* (Sabbath of Song). This is because the *sidrah* contains the Song of Moses, the description of how the Almighty helped our ancestors escape across the Red Sea to freedom.

Shabbat in the Shtetl

Shabbat in the East European shtetl had a special flavor. Preparations began on Thursday when people went to market to shop for food. Although most of the people who lived in the shtetl were very poor, and many ate sparingly all week, the very best they could afford was bought for Shabbat. Thursday evening the dough was prepared for challah and left to rise overnight so it could be baked early Friday morning.

On Friday morning, the loaves of dough were placed in large ovens. The Shabbat meal was also prepared. Since no cooking was permitted on Shabbat, all the food had to be prepared in advance. Usually a large pot of stew called cholent was prepared. It was made of meat, potatoes, and beans or other vegetables, and allowed to cook in a slow oven overnight. It smelled and tasted delicious.

The children of the shtetl were especially happy when the end of the week came. The schools closed at noon on Friday and did not open again until Sunday morning. The pupils looked forward to this free time. School hours were very long. The children went to school from early morning to evening and had very little time to play. Is it any wonder that they were so happy when Shabbat came and they could forget their hard life for a while?

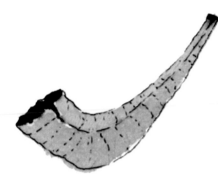

The High Holy Days

Summer has slipped away and autumn is in the air. Like candles flaring brightly before they go out, the leaves on the big maple out front have taken on brilliant hues of red and orange and yellow. "Take a last look," they seem to say. "Remember us when we are gone!"

And the Jewish calendar on the wall is almost down to its last page, for the Jewish year is drawing slowly to a close. Suppose we turn to that last page. The month is Elul, last in the Jewish year. It ends with the twenty-ninth day of the Hebrew month. This is the day before the Jewish New Year.

The New Year begins with a period of ten days, called the Ten Days of Repentance. This period is also known as the Solemn Days, the High Holy Days, and the Fearful Days. The first two of these days are called Rosh Hashanah.

The Month of *Elul*

The whole month preceding Rosh Hashanah has always held special meaning for Jews. In the little towns of Eastern Europe, the whole community would await the coming Holy Days with awe and excitement.

At daybreak, the *shammash*, or sexton, of the synagogue would march through the silent streets, a large wooden hammer in his hand.

"Knock, Knock!" went the hammer on the doors or shutters of the little houses. The shammash was calling the people to *Selichot,* special prayers said in the month of Elul.

When the High Holy Days came, every one was ready to greet the New Year.

TISHRE						תשרי
Sun.	Mon.	Tues.	Wed.	Thur.	Fri.	Sat.
	1	2	3	4	5	6
7	8	9	10	11	12	13
14	15	16	17	18	19	20
22	21	23	24	25	26	27
28	29	30				

The High Holy Days start with Rosh Hashanah on the first day of Tishrei and end ten days later with Yom Kippur on the 10th of Tishrei. Orthodox and Conservative Jews observe two days of Rosh Hashanah while Reform Jews observe one day. *Shabbat Shuvah* is on the 6th of Tishrei.

Preparing for blowing the shofar. The *machzor* is open to the *shofar* blowing prayers.

25

The day of the sounding of the shofar.

This Rosh Hashanah plate, used for *challah*, apples, and honey, was made in Delft, Holland, about 1700.

A New Year greeting card

The Seventh Month

The name Rosh Hashanah means "the beginning of the year," but it really is not that. For it comes on the first and second days of Tishrei, the seventh month of the Jewish calendar.

In the autumn, the first rains came in Palestine and the soil was plowed for the winter grain. So, in time, the first of Tishrei became the beginning of the year, and business dealings, sabbatical years (every seventh year), and jubilee years (every fiftieth year) were all counted from the first of Tishrei.

In the Bible

The Bible calls Rosh Hashanah the day of the sounding of the ram's horn. In the Bible we read, "In the seventh month, in the first day of the month, shall be a rest unto you, proclaimed with the blast of horns, a holy gathering."

As they do about all festivals and folkways, legends have clustered about Rosh Hashanah. It was said that this was the day on which Adam was created out of clay; it was also the birthday of Abraham and Isaac and Jacob; it was the day on which Joseph was released from prison in Egypt; and it was the day Moses appeared before Pharaoh, demanding that the Egyptian king let our people go.

On the Scales

Rosh Hashanah comes in the month of Tishrei, and in the Zodiac Tishrei is symbolized by scales. What does this interesting fact means?

The ancients, watching the skies, noticed different formations of stars. Their imaginations gave these twelve groupings, or constellations, various shapes and they called them by names: ram, bull, twins, crab, and so on. Later, these groups of stars became known as the signs of the Zodiac, which comes from the Greek word for "animal." The Zodiacal sign for the month in which Rosh Hashanah occurs is a pair of scales. This symbol reminds us that our deeds are weighed and judged in the Heavenly Book of Life on the New Year.

Le-Shanah Tovah Greetings

When Rosh Hashanah approaches, we like to wish our relatives and friends a happy, healthy, and joyous New Year. Since we cannot visit them all we follow the custom of sending greeting cards especially printed for the occasion.

Rosh Hashanah Food Customs

After the *Kiddush* for Rosh Hashanah we recite a blessing over apples dipped in honey. The blessing asks God to send us a "pleasant and sweet year." During the Rosh Hashanah period we also wish each other a *shanah tovah umtukah,* "a sweet and happy year."

Even the *challah* which we eat on Rosh Hashanah does not look like the usual braided challah we eat on Shabbat. Instead, it is a round and spiral shape. When we eat it we are saying that we hope our lives will be round and full and unending like the spiral *challah.*

Throughout Rosh Hashanah sweet foods are eaten. One of the Rosh Hashanah foods is *tzimmes* which is made with carrots, honey, yams and sometimes meat. It is also traditional to eat sweet noodle pudding, honey cakes, and *tayglach* which are pieces of dough cooked in honey.

Selichot

On the Saturday night before Rosh Hashanah, after the clock has struck twelve and the world has become very quiet, Jews the world over go to the temple to say *Selichot*. Services begin after midnight, and we are in a very grave mood. For this is a time to recite special prayers of repentance, and *Selichot* are prayers asking for forgiveness. Some of the prayers are beautiful poems composed by Jewish scholars and poets. They recall the hardships of exile, persecution, and martyrdom which our people have endured. *Selichot* are also said during the rest of the Ten Days of Repentance. When we recite *Selichot*, we ask God to forgive our sins and to send help when humankind needs it most.

Machzor

The weekday and Sabbath prayerbook is called a *Siddur*. The festival prayerbook is called a *Machzor*. The word *Machzor* comes from the word *chazor*, meaning "cycle." There are *Machzorim* with prayers for each main Jewish holiday: Rosh Hashanah, Yom Kippur, Sukkot, Passover, and Shavuot.

THE LADDER *CHALLAH*: FOR THE HIGH HOLY DAYS
The five runged ladder *Challah*, was designed for Rosh Hashanah and Yom Kippur. The ladder, *sulam* in Hebrew, with a numerical letter value of 130, refers to Moses's ascent of Mount *Sinai* to receive God's revelation of the Law. The name Sinai in Hebrew also has a numerical value of 130. The five rungs are symbolic of the ladderlike ascent of all prayers heavenward.

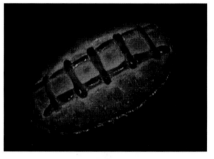

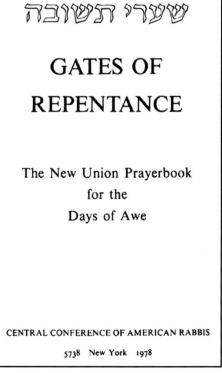

שַׁעֲרֵי תְשׁוּבָה

GATES OF REPENTANCE

The New Union Prayerbook
for the
Days of Awe

CENTRAL CONFERENCE OF AMERICAN RABBIS

5738   New York   1978

This High Holiday Prayerbook was published by the Central Conference of American Rabbis, a branch of the Reform movement.

A shofar maker tests his handiwork.

A class of enthusiastic novices learning to blow the shofar from a master teacher.

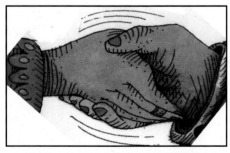
ROSH HASHANAH GREETINGS
On Rosh Hashanah it is customary to greet each other by saying, *L'Shanah Tovah Tikatevu*, "may you be written down for a happy new year."

The oldest *Machzor* is the *Machzor Vitry*, which was arranged by Rabbi Simchah of Vitry, a pupil of Rashi, in the Middle Ages.

Today there are a great variety of *Machzorim*, and each religious denomination has published its own version.

The Shofar

The shofar is blown every day in the month of Elul, except on the Sabbath. It provides the most impressive moment of the morning service of Rosh Hashanah.

How the Shofar Is Made

Usually the shofar is made from a ram's horn, although it may also be made from the horn of any other kosher animal except a cow or an ox. The horn is boiled in water until it gets soft. The inside is then hollowed out and the horn is flattened slightly. The mouthpiece is then carefully shaped and the horn is put aside to harden. Sometimes, particularly in lands of the Middle East, the shofar is long and very curved.

The Meaning of the Shofar's Call

In biblical times, the shofar was used to herald great moments. It proclaimed the ascent of a king upon the throne, it announced the Jubilee every fiftieth year and the beginning of Sabbaths and festivals. In wartime, it signaled the army.

The shofar has been so long associated with Jewish tradition that it has become a holy symbol. It recalls the offering of Isaac by Abraham, for at that time God, recognizing our people's devotion, ordered Abraham to substitute a ram for his son as a sacrifice on the altar.

It reminds us of the giving of the Ten Commandments to the accompaniment of shofar blasts on Mount Sinai.

Before the shofar is blown we recite Psalm 37, which says that the shofar will one day announce God's dominion over all peoples. Then the horn is sounded. There are three variations in the call: *Tekiah*, *Shevarim*, and *Teruah*. *Tekiah* is a long blast starting on a low note and rising nearly an octave; *Shevarim* consists of three shorter notes; *Teruah* is made up of nine quick, sharp calls ending with a high note.

The Prayer Called *Unetaneh Tokef*

One of the most important of the hymns and prayers read on Rosh Hashanah is also recited on Yom Kippur. It is called *Unetaneh Tokef* and was composed by Rabbi Amnon of Mayence.

According to the story that has been handed down from one generation to another, Rabbi Amnon was pressured by the local bishop to leave his faith and convert to Christianity. He always refused. Once, instead of refusing immediately, he requested a period of three days in which to think about it. When alone, he felt so guilty for not having simply said no, that when he was called to the bishop he asked that his tongue be cut out. Instead, the bishop had the rabbi's hands and feet amputated.

In this condition, Rabbi Amnon was carried to the synagogue for the High Holy Day services. As the cantor and congregation were about to begin the *Kedushah*, or sanctification service, Rabbi Amnon asked permission to offer a prayer he had composed. As soon as the last word had left his lips, the rabbi's life was mercifully ended.

Unetaneh Tokef expresses the idea of holiness and awe which fills the Rosh Hashanah service. It says, in part:

We will celebrate the mighty holiness of this day, a day of awe and terror. . . . You open the Book of Records . . . a great trumpet is sounded, and a still, small voice is heard. . . . The angels proclaim: This is the day of judgment and all who enter the world You cause to pass before You as a flock of sheep.

At Home

After Rosh Hashanah services, the family gathers for a festive meal. First, the blessing over wine is recited, then a family member says the *Ha-Motzi* over the *challah*. Often the *challot* are baked in the shape of a ladder, or a bird. The ladder symbolizes the wish that our Rosh Hashanah prayers may go upward and be heard by the Almighty. The bird is a symbol of mercy, for God has mercy even upon birds.

The members of the family dip a small piece of *challah* into honey and say to each other, as if it were a toast: "May it be Your will, O Almighty, to grant us a sweet and happy year!"

Blowing the shofar at the Western Wall.

A woodcut (Amsterdam, 1823) pictures the blowing of the *shofar*.

At a solemn moment in the service, the cantor kneels before the Holy Ark.

29

The Prophet Micah said, "You shall cast your sins into the depths of the sea." This *Tashlich* ceremony is being held on an ocean beach somewhere in the United States.

Youngsters "casting their tiny sins into the sea."

Day of Atonement in a Shtetl Synagogue. Oil painting by Maury—cy Gottlieb, 1878.

Throughout Rosh Hashanah sweet foods are eaten. One of the Rosh Hashanah foods is *tzimmes* which is made with carrots, honey, yams and sometimes meat. It is also traditional to eat sweet noodle pudding, honey cakes, and *tayglach* which are pieces of dough cooked in honey.

Tashlich

On the afternoon of the first day of Rosh Hashanah (or on the second day if the first is a Sabbath) many Jews gather near a flowing body of water to "cast all sins into the depths of the sea." *Tashlich* means "you will cast." Often crumbs of bread, symbol of sins and of broken promises, are thrown into the moving water.

There are many lessons that Rosh Hashanah teaches us. Perhaps all of them can be summed up in the saying of one of our rabbis of old. He said, "Live in such a way that you can truthfully say, `I have not yet wasted a single day of my life.'"

Fast of Gedaliah

The day after Rosh Hashanah is Tzom Gedaliah, the Fast of Gedaliah. Some 2,500 years ago, Nebuchadnezzar of Babylon conquered Jerusalem and destroyed the Temple. He appointed Gedaliah as governor of Judea. On this day, Gedaliah was assassinated and wicked Nebuchadnezzar instituted a reign of terror against the Jews. Tzom Gedaliah is one of the minor fast-days on the Jewish calendar and is observed by Orthodox Jews.

The Day Before Yom Kippur

After the New Year, the Days of Repentance continue. The Sabbath between Rosh Hashanah and Yom Kippur is a special Sabbath, called *Shabbat Shuvah*, or the Sabbath of Penitence. The rabbi usually delivers a sermon dealing with the subject of repentance on this Sabbath.

The ninth of the Ten Days is the day before Yom Kippur and an air of hush and expectancy is everywhere.

Why We Fast

In the late afternoon of the ninth day, we eat the feast that precedes the fast of Yom Kippur. The pre—fast meal must be eaten before sunset. After that, everyone except children under thirteen and sick persons, will fast until after sunset on the following day.

We do not fast in order to punish our bodies, but to enable us to concentrate on the meaning of Yom Kippur. By not touching food, we think only of the loftiness of this day–the holiest on the Jewish calendar.

A High Holiday service at a rapturous, enthusiastic prayer service at a Black Jewish synagogue.

Kol Nidrei

Before leaving home for the *Kol Nidrei* service, parents bless their children. This old custom dates back to the patriarchs and matriarchs: Abraham, Isaac, and Jacob; Sarah, Rebekah, Leah, and Rachel. The parents hold their hands over the heads of the children and say: "May God make you as Ephraim and Manasseh," or: "May God make you as Sarah, Rebekah, Leah and Rachel. May it be the will of our Parent in Heaven to plant love of God in your heart. May you wish to study the Torah and its commandments. May your lips speak the truth and your hands do good deeds. May you be inscribed for a long and happy life."

At dusk, men, women, and children gather in the synagogue. The Torah scrolls are taken out of the Holy Ark. The congregation rises. The cantor begins the famous *Kol Nidrei* prayer in the chant known round the world. Three times the cantor chants the prayer.

Israeli stamp in honor of Yom Kippur. The tab has a drawing of the scales. Yom Kippur comes in the month of Tishrei and the Zodiac symbol for the month is symbolized by scales.

In the Days of the Inquisition

Kol means "all," and *nidrei* means "vows." The words of the *Kol Nidrei* prayer state that all vows and oaths not carried out are hereby canceled and made void.

To understand the meaning of this prayer, we must know something of Jewish history. In the days of the Inquisition in fifteenth-century Spain and Portugal, Jews were often forced to give up their faith. Though they became Christians outwardly, these Jews, known as Marranos, secretly continued to observe Jewish customs.

In the *Kol Nidrei* prayer the Marranos begged God to forgive them for making vows they could not keep. *Kol Nidrei* released them from vows they had been forced to make when they were pretending to be Christians.

Kol Nidrei refers only to vows made to God. Promises to other persons which we make in the course of everyday life cannot be done away with by reciting a prayer.

Actually, the *Kol Nidrei* prayer goes back much farther than the Inquisition. In fact it is first mentioned in the ninth

This Yom Kippur *Machzor* was a mute witness to the cruel period of the Inquisition in Spain. It was designed in this elongated shape for a special purpose. In case of a surprise visit by officers of the government, Marrano Jews would drop the prayerbook into their wide sleeves, and thus escape detection.

31

JONAH AND THE GREAT FISH
The story of Jonah, who is shown, above, in an illumination from the Kennicott Bible, was probably written after the Exile. It is set in a time before the fall of Nineveh, when the city was a symbol of iniquity. The author chose the prophet Jonah, mentioned in 2 Kings 14:2, as the protagonist for his narrative.
Jonah lived in the eighth century B.C.E., when feeling in Israel ran high against Assyria. When God told Jonah to go to Nineveh and proclaim its imminent destruction. He rebelled and fled by ship in the opposite direction. During his journey a great storm arose and he was thrown overboard by the sailors to appease the wrath of God. But he was swallowed by a "great fish" (popularly identified as a whale), which eventually vomited him onto dry land. Jonah, now obedient to God, then journeyed to Nineveh. He delivered Yahweh's message to the inhabitants, who repented. The city was saved. The moral of the story is that God has mercy for all, even the hated Assyrians.

century. But it came to have a greater and deeper meaning in the evil days when Jews were forced to give up their faith.

Yom Kippur Day

Services begin early on Yom Kippur day and last until evening. Several times during the day the congregation makes a confession to every possible kind of sin and wrongdoing, just in case any of the sins has been committed unknowingly. This prayer of confession is called *Al Chet*. In it we ask forgiveness for such sins as dishonesty, disrespect for parents, cruelty, and the like. The confessions are made by the congregation as a whole, and forgiveness is asked for the congregation as a whole.

Memorial Prayer

An important part of the Yom Kippur service is the *Yizkor*, or memorial prayer for the dead. *Yizkor* is recited for the departed on several important holidays–Yom Kippur, Shemini Atzeret, the last day of Passover, and the second day of Shavuot. The soul being mourned is mentioned by name and the mourner pledges to give *tzedakah* as a memorial tribute.

Reading Jonah

At the afternoon service on Yom Kippur the *Haftarah* is the book of the prophet Jonah. In this book, we learn how Jonah fled to a distant country because he wanted to escape the presence of God. But his efforts were in vain, for he learned that God is everywhere. This reading teaches us that no matter where we live, in whatever age or country, God is with us and God's love embraces all the people on earth.

Ne'ilah

Weary as we are, we summon our strength for the last service of the day of Yom Kippur. It is called *Ne'ilah*, or "closing." The cantor and the congregation chant:

Open the gates for us, For the day is nearly past;
The sun is low, the day grows late–
Open Thy gates at last!

At the very end of the evening service the shofar is blown for the first and only time on Yom Kippur. The note is a long, steady one held as long as the breath holds out.

The Day of Atonement is over. People hurry home to break the fast that has lasted since sunset of the day before. The High Holy Days are at an end.

32

The Pilgrimage Festivals

The Torah mandates: *"Three times each year, every male among you must appear before God."* The three times referred to were the holidays of Sukkot, Passover, and Shavuot, known in Hebrew as the *Shalosh Regalim*, or "Three Pilgrimage Festivals."

According to the sages, everyone was required to appear before God except for women, minors, the infirm, and the aged. Even those who were not required to attend often participated in the pilgrimage. In practice, whole families made the pilgrimage together. Before Jerusalem became the capital, the pilgrimages were made to local shrines and to the Tabernacle in Shiloh.

A reconstruction of Solomon's Temple at the Bible Museum, Amsterdam.

The Pilgrims

Pilgrims were called *olei regel*, meaning "those who go up by foot." They were so called because Jerusalem is located high in the hills of Judea and the pilgrims had to climb up by foot to reach the Temple. Ancient sources state that hundreds of thousands made their way to the Temple during each of the *Shalosh Regalim*.

The Talmud describes, and so does the Christian New Testament, that Jews from as far as Babylon, Persia, Egypt, Ethiopia, Asia Minor, and Rome came to worship in the Temple on the Three Festivals.

The pilgrims traveled in large groups or caravans. They marched with flying banners announcing the names of their clan, town, or village. Many of the caravans were accompanied by musicians who played marching songs. Psalms 42, 82, and 122 are designated as Psalms of Ascent and were sung as the pilgrims ascended to Jerusalem.

Three times a year on Sukkot, Passover, and Shavuot, the Jews of ancient Israel would march on foot to the Holy Temple in Jerusalem. Today, in modern Israel the age–old pilgrimage ceremony is reenacted. Here pilgrims ascend Mount Zion to the blowing of shofars.

After they left Egypt, the Israelites wandered through the desert for 40 years. They traveled from one oasis to another for cool fresh water and shade from the hot desert sun.

A scale model of the city of Jerusalem and the Temple at the time of Herod the Great. All that now remains is a section of the gigantic wall which surrounded the city. The remaining part of the wall is known as the Western Wall. It is also known as the Wailing Wall.

Tilling the soil the old-fashioned way with a hand-held plow and a donkey. The ancient Israelites tended their farms in the same way.

Bikkurim

The object of the pilgrimage was to bring *bikkurim* ("first fruits") and offer a sacrifice at the Temple. The Torah also commands, "None shall appear empty-handed. Every person shall give as they are able." The sages decided that the minimum offering was to be three pieces of silver. The proceeds were to be used for the upkeep of the Temple and to care for the sick, aged, and infirm.

As the marching groups approached Jerusalem they were met by the priests and Levites, who welcomed them to the city and led the pilgrims to their designated tent grounds.

The Temple in Jerusalem

The gates to the city were a maze of stalls and shops selling food, clothing, shoes, medicines, and imported goods from all over the ancient world. Farmers and shepherds wandered through the streets, amazed at the variety of goods, the babel of languages, and the hubbub of business transactions. Outside the gates it was carnival time, with storytellers, magicians, and acrobats to entertain the children. Inside the gates the atmosphere was dominated by the Temple and its religious rituals.

At festival time, Jerusalem was a sea of color decorated with flowers and green branches. Crowds of pilgrims streamed toward the Holy Temple in the heart of the city. Silver trumpets sounded and choirs of Levites sang as the priests poured fresh spring water from golden pitchers onto the altar. The assemblage of thousands of voices joined the prayer, "We pray, O Lord, save us and make us prosperous." Day and night, long lines of worshipers snaked their way through the streets, bringing *bikkurim* and shekels to support the Temple.

The Necessity for Pilgrimages

Pilgrimages were a cultural, political, and religious weapon in the battle for the survival of the Jewish state. The pilgrimage reunions helped mold the separate tribes into a single cultural, political, and military entity.

Israel was surrounded by idol-worshiping nations whose religious rituals during the harvest seasons were enticing to isolated Israelite farmers and shepherds. The pilgrimages to Jerusalem helped combat the pagan rites of the idol worshipers and kept the ancient Jewish traditions alive. They reinforced the faith and reaffirmed the covenant with God that was made at Mount Sinai. In the city squares, priests and Levites lectured the pilgrims on Jewish law and on the teachings of the Torah.

Israelite farmers and shepherds lived dull, hard, lonely lives. They worked from early light to total darkness, raising their crops and tending their animals. The pilgrimages were also social occasions: a time for them to celebrate, a relief from the arduous daily regimen.

The Sukkot Pilgrimage

The three pilgrimage festivals, Sukkot, Pesach, and Shavuot, have both agricultural and historical themes. Sukkot, occurring in the month of Tishrei, has two biblical names: *Chag Ha-Asif* (Festival of Ingathering) and *Chag Ha-Sukkot* (Festival of Tabernacles). In its *Chag Ha-Asif* aspect it is a harvest thanksgiving festival. In its *Chag Ha-Sukkot* aspect it is a historical festival, commemorating God's protection of the Israelites during the forty years in the wilderness after the Exodus from Egypt.

While these two aspects have separate identities, and may once have been separate festivals, they are linked to each other in time and in basic ideas. Sukkot always occurs in the harvest season. God's pre-Exodus message to the children of Israel held out a double promise: freedom from slavery and a land flowing with milk and honey. The fulfillment of both promises is stressed in the rituals of Sukkot.

The link between the Exodus and the harvest accounts for the timing of the festival of Sukkot. According to tradition, the Jews, after leaving Egypt, arrived at the oasis of Sukkot on the fifteenth of Nisan. It was in Sukkot that God provided them with *sukkot* ("huts") for protection from the sun.

The Passover Pilgrimage

The pilgrimage of Passover, which starts on the fifteenth day of the month of Nisan, is also identified by two biblical names: *Chag Ha-Matzot* (Festival of Matzot) and *Chag Ha-Pesach* (Festival of the Paschal Lamb). Both names have historical significance. *Chag Ha-Pesach* reminds us of the events leading up the Exodus, and *Chag Ha-Matzot* commemorates the events following the Exodus.

35

PILGRIMAGE FESTIVAL STAMPS

Israeli Passover stamp, illustrating matzah baking. The quote is from Exodus and reads "Seven days you shall eat unleavened bread."

Shavuot stamp with biblical quotation, "the first of the first fruits of your ground you shall bring."

Sukkot stamp with biblical quotation, "you shall dwell in booths for seven days."

Stalks of wheat heavy with kernels ready for the reaping.

In addition, Passover is also called *Chag Ha–Aviv* (Spring Holiday) because it marked the season of the new cereal crops in ancient Israel. This agricultural theme is continued with the beginning of the *Omer*, or *Sefirah* ("counting"), which starts on the night of the second Seder and ends forty–nine days later on Shavuot.

The Season of Freedom

The Torah tells us that Passover is *Zeman Cheruteinu* (Season of Our Freedom). The Roman conquerors of Israel were very much aware of the Jewish thirst for freedom and were especially alert during the Passover pilgrimage. At Pesach time, when the city was crowded with pilgrims, Jerusalem became a hotbed of revolt. Roman spies searched the crowds for rebels. Agitators who were caught preaching rebellion, were condemned to death by crucifixion.

The Passover Haggadah

The Passover Haggadah contains the story of five rabbis, Eliezer, Yehoshua, Elazar, Akiva, and Tarfon, who were at a Seder and spent the whole night discussing the story of the Exodus. The commentators believe that in reality the rabbis were engaged in planning a revolt against the Roman oppressors. Sometime later, Rabbi Akiva and Bar Kochba led such a revolt, and both lost their lives in the fight for freedom.

The Pilgrimage of Shavuot

The third of the annual pilgrimages occurs on the sixth and seventh days of the month of Sivan. Shavuot also has two biblical names, *Chag Ha-Katzir* (Harvest Festival) and *Chag Ha-Shavuot* (Feast of Weeks). In English it is sometimes called Pentecost from its Greek name.

Shavuot ends the seven-week *Omer* period, which runs "from the time the sickle is put to the corn" until seven weeks later when the grain is ready for harvest. The historical theme is also echoed in its caution, "You shall remember that you were slaves in Egypt." The primary ancient ritual of Shavuot was an offering of new meal consisting of two loaves of bread baked from the flour made from the newly harvested crop of wheat. The loaves were called *lechem tenufah* ("wave loaves").

חטה

ירכבהו עַל בֳּמוֹתֵי אֶרֶץ וַיֹּאכַל
תְּנוּבת שָׂדָי וַיֵּנִקֵהוּ דְבַשׁ מִסֶּלַע
וְשֶׁמֶן מֵחַלְמִישׁ צוּר חֶמְאַת בָּקָר
וַחֲלֵב צֹאן עִם חֵלֶב כָּרִים וְאֵילִים
בְּנֵי בָשָׁן וְעַתּוּדִים עִם חֵלֶב כִּלְיוֹת
חִטָּה.

(דברים לב)

Chitah is the Hebrew word for wheat. It is one of the seven kinds. The quotation reads "He carried them over the world's highest places, to feast on the crops of the fields. He let them taste honey from the bedrocks, oil from the rocky cliff. They ate the cheese of cattle, the milk of sheep, the fat of lambs, lambs of Bashan, and luscious fat wheat."

36

The Talmud tells us that the wave offering was a prayerful act asking God to restrain storms and bad weather and to bless the fruit of the new harvest.

Symbolic reaping of the *Omer* at an Israeli kibbutz.

A Shavuot Custom

The offering of *bikkurim* was another Shavuot custom. Fruit began to ripen in the Shavuot season and was available as a *bikkurim* offering. Shavuot was celebrated at the height of the farming season, so there were fewer pilgrims than on Sukkot and Pesach.

The Counting of the *Omer*

The time between Passover and Shavuot became a time of seriousness and prayer. The farmer prayed to God for a successful harvest and a year of plenty and gladness. Passover was the season of the wheat harvest, and Shavuot was the season of the barley harvest. On the day after Passover, the Temple priests would make a special sacrificial offering of a measure of grain, called an *omer*. The priest would mix the *omer* of grain with oil and frankincense and wave it up and down and from side to side. This ceremony was interpreted as a prayer for God to protect the harvest from strong winds and harsh weather.

The grain was often stored in rough stone jugs like this one, unearthed in a cave in Galilee. It holds an *Omer* of grain.

Starting from this day, the people would count the days between the waving of the *omer* and Shavuot. We still call these seven weeks (or forty-nine days) the time of *Sefirat Ha-Omer,* which means "The counting of the *Omer.*" Jews the world over consider these weeks a time of solemnity. Some people do not go to parties, and most weddings are not held. Special daily prayers are said.

Both of these rituals, the wave offering and the *bikkurim,* were suspended after the destruction of the Temple and a new historical motif, the giving of the Torah on Mount Sinai, was introduced as the focus of the Shavuot Festival.

A nineteenth–century European *Omer* calendar. The numbers, top to bottom, indicate that this is the thirty-third day of the *Omer* (Lag Ba- Omer), or four weeks and five days since the beginning of the seven-week period between Passover and Shavuot.

Sukkot and Simchat Torah

TISHRE						תשרי
Sun.	Mon.	Tues.	Wed.	Thur.	Fri.	Sat.
	1	2	3	4	5	6
7	8	9	10	11	12	13
14	15	16	17	18	19	20
21	22	23	24	25	26	27
28	29	30				

Yom Kippur ends on the 10th day of Tishrei. The holiday of Sukkot comes five days later on the 15th day of Tishrei.

Five days after Yom Kippur, the holiest day of the Jewish year, comes one of the happiest of all festivals. It is called Sukkot. One of the nicest things about Sukkot is that it lasts for seven days and includes a variety of celebrations. (In Orthodox Judaism Sukkot is nine days long, but Reform Jews observe only one of the first two days, and combine the last two days.)

The holiday of Sukkot begins on the fifteenth day of the month of Tishrei. In the Bible, Sukkot is called *Chag Ha-Sukkot*, the Festival of Booths (or Tabernacles) and *Chag Ha-Asif*, the Festival of Ingathering.

The Origin of Sukkot

In the history of every people there are great moments which it likes to recall in order to be reminded of the past and to learn from a lesson for the future.

In Jewish history there is one event that we can never forget. Nor do we wish to. Every Shabbat, when we recite the blessing over the wine, we repeat the words *zecher litziat mitzrayim*, "in remembrance of the departure from Egypt." And on several of our holidays, we commemorate events connected with our emancipation from slavery. Sukkot is one of these holidays.

Years of Wandering

After our ancestors left Egypt, the Bible tells us, they wandered for forty years in the desert before they reached the Promised Land. During that time they lived in *sukkot*, booths made of dry palms and branches. The Bible tells us to dwell in booths seven days each year in remembrance of those years of wandering and hardship.

Israelites built huts of brush and leaves such as these during their 40 years of wandering.

38

Gathering the Crops

After our ancestors settled in Canaan, they discovered that the autumn, when Sukkot was celebrated, was also the time when they gathered in the crops. So Sukkot became a double celebration. We were thankful that we were no longer wanderers in the desert; and we offered thanks to God for the crops we were harvesting. Thus Sukkot became the Jewish Thanksgiving.

Sukkot is the third of the *Shalosh Regalim*, the three pilgrimage feasts, when Jews from all parts of Palestine and surrounding countries used to make pilgrimages to the Holy Temple in Jerusalem.

The grape harvest at a kibbutz vineyard. The Hebrew word for grapes is *gefen*. Israeli wines because of the quality of the grapes, have won many worldwide competitions.

Happy Harvest

Sukkot is also known as *Chag Ha-Asif*, the Harvest Festival. The fruit harvest was finished in ancient Palestine at this time. The grapes were ready to be made into wine, the olives pressed into oil. Today in Israel, this old meaning of the holiday has taken on fresh importance, and Israelis celebrate Sukkot with great thanksgiving.

The First Thanksgiving

In the summer of 1621 the settlers in Plymouth colony gathered to give thanks to God for a bountiful harvest after their first hard year in the New World. That was America's first Thanksgiving. In 1789, after Congress had adopted the Constitution, President George Washington proclaimed November 26 as a day of Thanksgiving for the new nation. From then on, some states observed it on one day, some on another. In 1863, President Abraham Lincoln proclaimed the last Thursday in November as a national Thanksgiving Day.

The Carmel Winery is famous for its excellent wines. This sign invites visitors to tour the facilities and taste the wines.

Pilgrims and the Bible

Where did the Pilgrims get the idea for a Thanksgiving Day? They were religious men and women. The book they loved most dearly was the Bible. Many of their laws and customs were based on the Bible, and they gave their children biblical names like Ezekiel, Moses, Solomon, and Hannah.

The Pilgrims called America the new Canaan. Cotton Mather, a Puritan minister and historian, spoke of the Pilgrims as "our happy Israel in America," and of William Bradford, the second governor of Plymouth, as a new Moses. Mather called

The Pilgrims and their Indian friends celebrating Thanksgiving.

A religious neighborhood in Israel. Each house has its own private *sukkah*.

This *sukkah* plaque is called an *Ushpizen* meaning "guests," in Aramaic. The seven traditionally invited guests are Abraham, Isaac, Jacob, Joseph, Moses, Aaron and David, who according to tradition visit every *sukkah* and participate in the festivities and the meal. A prayer is recited before the meal, officially inviting the guests to participate in the meal. Some *Ushpizen* add the names of the matriarchs to the lists of guests.

Israeli stamp featuring Jacob, one of the visiting patriarchs.

the early magistrates *ba'alei nefesh*, which is a Hebrew term meaning "people of spirit." The ministers were referred to as *chasidim ha-rishonim*, "first pious people," while John Winthrop, who was governor of the Massachusetts colony, was called Nehemias Americanus, the American Nehemiah, after the Nehemiah who was the Jewish governor of Palestine when the Jews returned from the exile in Babylon.

The Bible's Command

The pilgrims also knew of the festival of Sukkot, and the biblical command in Leviticus 23:39:

When you have gathered in the fruits of the land, you shall keep the feast of the Lord.

The spirit of the Bible, as well as Jewish history and custom, were all expressed in the first Thanksgiving celebrated by the Pilgrims in the summer of 1621.

Sukkot Observances In Israel Today

Many present-day Israelis go on a pilgrimage to Jerusalem on Sukkot. Just as the ancient Israelites streamed toward Jerusalem, modern Israelis crowd the intercity. Egged buses, laden with satchels of fruits and flowers, make their way to their beloved capital. They visit a big community *sukkah* on the top of Mount Zion and march in a special procession led by rabbis who carry Torahs. On the way, the marchers stop for a ceremony and a memorial prayer for the six million Jewish victims of the Nazi Holocaust.

Building the Sukkah

To show that Sukkot was close at hand, it became a custom to drive in the first nail or stake for the erection of the *sukkah* at the end of Yom Kippur.

In the days that follow, the whole family participates in building the *sukkah*. It is placed in the yard or on the roof, in the garden if the family has a garden, or on a porch which has an open roof. The *sukkah* is loosely covered with twigs and branches so that the stars may shine through. Everybody helps decorate the *sukkah* with apples, pomegranates, clusters of grapes, corn, and all kinds of flowers.

During Sukkot some people eat all their meals in the *sukkah*. Candlesticks are brought into the *sukkah* and traditionally mother lights them while pronouncing a prayer over them and reciting a special prayer for the occasion.

Citron and Palm

In the *sukkah*, too, except when they are being used in synagogue services, are the *etrog* and the *lulav*. The *etrog* is a citron, yellow and fragrant; it nestles in a box filled with flax to protect its delicate contents. The *lulav* is a sheaf of long palm fronds, fastened with myrtle and willow twigs.

The "Four Kinds"

The Bible commands us to take four things–the *etrog*, the *lulav*, myrtle branches, and willows of the brook–and rejoice before God for seven days when celebrating the harvest festival. In this way our ancestors showed their appreciation for God's goodness.

Every morning during the first seven days of Sukkot (except on the Sabbath), we take these "four kinds" and recite a blessing. The prayer is recited while standing and holding the *lulav* in the right hand and the *etrog* in the left, with the top pointing down. As soon as the blessing is ended, the *etrog* is turned over. Then, with the *etrog* held close to the *lulav*, so that they are as one unit, they are waved together slightly so that the *lulav* rustles.

What the *Arba Minim* Mean

Why do we use the *Arba Minim*, these "four kinds"? Our rabbis of old thought of several reasons. One explanation is that the *etrog* is like the heart, without which a person cannot live. The *lulav* is the spine, the myrtle is the eye, and the willow leaves are lips. Together, they declare that human beings ought to serve God with their whole soul and body.

Hakafot

On each of the first seven days of the Sukkot festival, the Ark in the synagogue is opened after the *Musaf* or additional service, and a procession called *Hakafot* takes place. First in line is

ARBA MINIM

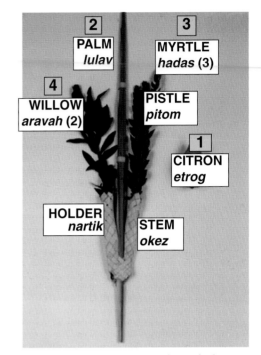

The "four kinds" consist of the *etrog*, *lulav*, myrtle branches and willows of the brook. Every morning during the Sukkot holiday, we take these "four kinds" and recite a blessing in appreciation for God's goodness.

SUKKOT BLESSINGS
You hold the *lulav* in your right hand and the *etrog* in your left, with both hands together. You recite the blessing holding the *etrog* with the tip downward. When the blessings are finished you turn the *etrog* and its tip upwards. Now you wave the *lulav* in all directions: east, south, west, north, up and down. All this time the *lulav* and *etrog* are held together.

Inside the *sukkah*

A panel of the mosaic pavement from the fourth-century C.E. synagogue of Hammat Tiberias. The panel shows a menorah, a *shofar*, a *lulav* and an *etrog*. At the time of the synagogue's existence Tiberias was the seat of the Sanhedrin.

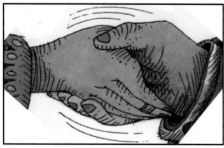

SUKKOT GREETINGS
On the holiday of Sukkot you greet people by saying "*Chag Sameach*" which means "Happy Holiday." You can use the same type of greeting for all happy holidays.

the cantor, followed by the rabbi, after whom come all the congregants holding *etrogim* and *lulavim*. They march around the bimah, or down the aisles, while the cantor chants the *Hoshanah* prayer.

In the Days of the Temple

Sukkot has been celebrated in the very same way for thousands of years. In the days when our Temple stood in Jerusalem, however, there was an additional and very colorful ceremony. This was known as *Simchat Bet Ha-Sho'evah*, the Feast of Water-Drawing.

At the morning service on each day of Sukkot, an offering of water was made together with the pouring of wine. The water was drawn from the famous Pool of Siloam, the remains of which have been found in our own time, and it was drawn in a golden pitcher.

In solemn procession, while all the spectators stood silent, the pitcher was borne to the water-gate of the Temple. Then everyone halted while the shofar was blown.

On the night of the first day of Sukkot, the outer court of the Temple was brilliantly lit with four golden lamps. The lamps were placed on high columns, the tops of which could only be reached with tall ladders. Crowds filled the court. Special galleries were built for women. Their shining eyes reflected the torches held aloft by the men below, who were dancing and singing psalms of praise to God. The Levites chanted the fifteen Songs of Ascents (*Shir Ha-Ma'alot*) of the Book of Psalms accompanied by flutes and other instruments.

The festivities lasted all night long, and the gaiety and light penetrated every corner of Jerusalem.

Chol Ha-Mo'ed

The four days following the first two days of *Sukkot* are called *Chol Ha-Mo'ed*, or semi-holidays. The *Hallel* prayers are recited at the morning service and the procession with *etrog* and *lulav* takes place. When one of the days of *Chol Ha-Mo'ed* falls on the Sabbath, the book of Ecclesiastes is read before the reading of the Torah portion.

Hoshanah Rabbah

The name Hoshanah Rabbah means the "great help." It designates the seventh day of Sukkot.

During the seven days of Sukkot, special prayers called *Hoshanot* are recited. On Hoshanah Rabbah, the *Hoshanot* are much longer. Seven times around the synagogue we march, carrying our *lulav* and *etrog*. Each person holds a little bundle of willows called *hoshanot*, and at the close of the service, these are beaten on the benches until all or most of the leaves have fallen off. Thus do we rid ourselves of all our sins. This, too, is an old, old custom, harking back to Temple days when our ancestors circled the altar bearing willow branches.

Shemini Atzeret

On the eighth day of Sukkot, the *etrog* and *lulav* are laid aside, for this is an entirely new festival, called *Shemini Atzeret*, the Eight Day of Solemn Assembly.

Several special features mark the morning service. Memorial prayers (*Yizkor*) are said for the dead. A prayer called *Geshem* ("Rain") is recited. In it, we ask God to provide rain in this season. In the Holy Land, the summer is the dry season, when there is no rain at all. It rains only during the winter. And in Israel the crops of the spring depend on the rains of October.

As a mark of devotion to our ancient homeland, we pray for the rain that is so necessary to be used during the dry season.

Simchat Torah

And then, at last, comes one of the gayest days in the Jewish year: Simchat Torah, the Rejoicing in the Law.

It is a holiday dedicated to a book–the greatest book of all–the Torah. On this day we end the reading of the Five Books of Moses in the synagogue and begin all over again with the wonderful story of creation. The last chapter of Deuteronomy is chanted, and then the first chapter of Genesis. Thus the cycle of Torah reading continues and the circle of the Torah is eternal, without beginning or end.

In the temple, Simchat Torah is celebrated with great merriment. Everybody comes–young and old, tall and small.

Sukkot prayers at the Western Wall

In 1960, Yigal Yadin, professor of archaeology at the Hebrew University in Jerusalem, launched an expedition to explore the caves in the mountains near the Dead Sea. A member of the expedition, exploring one of the narrow tunnels of a cave, discovered a basket filled with objects. Further inspection of the crevice revealed a treasure trove of artifacts which included sandals, knives, mirrors, jugs, bowls, and the greatest treasure of all–papyrus rolls containing about 40 letters from Bar Kochba.

In the letter shown here, Bar Kochba requests *etrogim*, *lulavim*, myrtles and willows-the "four kinds" needed for Sukkot.

***Simchat Torah* in the *Shtetl*, 1925, Marc Chagall.**

Simchat Torah in the Synagogue of Leghorn, Italy. This oil painting is by the English artist Solomon Hart, 1850.

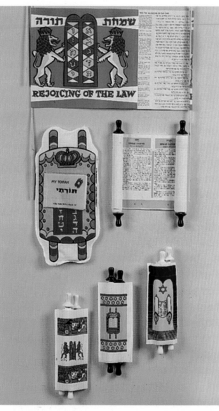

Simchat Torah is a time for flag waving and proudly marching around with Torot.

A *Kol Ha–Ne'arim* ceremony.

Torah Procession

On this festive occasion, all the Torah scrolls are taken out of the Ark and carried lovingly around the synagogue in a procession known as *Hakafot.* Children follow the grown-ups, gaily waving colorful flags. Seven times the procession makes its rounds.

The *Hakafot* are introduced by reading a collection of biblical verses called *Attah Horeyta.* As each word is read by the cantor or a member of the congregation, it is repeated by the participants. All the members of the congregation are given the opportunity of carrying a Torah scroll during the *Hakafot.* In many Reform and Conservative Temples a beautiful ceremony called Consecration is held. The children who will be starting religious school that year are called to the *bimah* and each is presented with a miniature Torah. The rabbi blesses the group and wishes all the children a happy and meaningful Jewish experience in the years of study in the religious school.

The Morning Service

At the morning service on Simchat Torah, everyone over thirteen years of age is called to the Torah to recite the blessing over the reading of the last *sidrah,* or portion, of the book of Deuteronomy. The last person to be called up is the *Chatan Torah* (bridegroom of the Torah), because he has the great honor of reciting the blessing over the conclusion of the Five Books of Moses. Then another person is called for the reading of the first chapter in Genesis; he is called the *Chatan Bereshit* (bridegroom of Genesis).

Kol Ha-Ne'arim

Just before these two are called, all the children under the age of thirteen come up to the Torah. A large tallit is spread like a canopy over their heads. All together, in one voice, they recite the blessing over the Torah. This is called *Kol Ha-Ne'arim* ("all the children") and it marks the one time during the Jewish year when even the smallest girls and boys are given the honor of being called to the Torah. Thus, in happiness and festivity, Simchat Torah slowly draws to a close, ending the High Holy Day season. The *sukkah* will be dismantled, to be used again after twelve months has taken its course.

Chanukah

Sukkot and Simchat Torah are now far behind us. Autumn leaves have been raked away; trees are bare and branches empty.

Just when it seems that holidays are so few and far between, the calendar announces that another festival is on its way. And as if to make up for lost time this holiday will be *eight* days long. Its name is Chanukah.

Stories of heroism and bravery never die. They are told and retold from generation to generation, and from father to son. Then, when they have become part of a people's culture they are written down by a talented scribe. They enter the world of literature to be judged and appreciated by every one who can read.

When it comes to tales of dauntless courage and spirit in the face of overwhelming odds, Chanukah is one of the world's greatest sagas.

Setting the Scene

To see the picture clearly, to know just what Chanukah means to every Jew and indeed to every free person, no matter what his race, religion, or creed, it is important to set the scene for this stirring episode of history. And to do that, you have to turn the time machine back well over two thousand years.

In the year 336 B.C.E., Alexander the Great, mighty king of Macedonia, assembled a huge army and crossed from his native Greece into Asia. He crushed the troops of Darius, king of Persia, and thus became ruler of the entire Persian Empire, which included Syria, Palestine, and Egypt.

KISLEV						כסלו
Sun.	Mon.	Tues.	Wed.	Thur.	Fri.	Sat.
				1	2	3
4	5	6	7	8	9	10
11	12	13	14	15	16	17
18	19	20	21	22	23	24
25	26	27	28	29		

TEVET						טבת
Sun.	Mon.	Tues.	Wed.	Thur.	Fri.	Sat.
					1	2
3	4	5	6	7	8	9
10	11	12	13	14	15	16
17	18	19	20	21	22	23
24	25	26	27	28	29	

The holiday of Chanukah is eight days long, one day for each lighted candle. The holiday starts on the evening of the 25th day of Kislev and ends on the third day of Tevet.

Mosaic found at Pompeii records the battle between the Macedonians and the Persians. Alexander the Great charges the bodyguard surrounding the Persian king Darius III.

Alexander the Great being greeted by the high priest Jaddua. From a 14th–century French picture.

Bronze bust of Seleucus I which was found near Pompeii, Italy.

A Greek relief of wrestlers at a gymnasium. The gymnasium was a sport stadium where games and concerts were held. Before an exhibition, there was a special opening ceremony in which the athletes paraded naked and offered sacrifices to the pagan gods. To the Greeks, it was a way of life. To the Jews, it was a road to idol worship and assimilation.

In the Name of the King

The rabbis tell many interesting stories about Alexander. One of them explains why "Alexander" is a name common among Jews to this very day. When Alexander the Great marched in triumph through Jerusalem he asked the High Priest that a statue in his image be erected in the Temple to commemorate his visit to the Holy City.

"O Alexander," said the High Priest, "it is forbidden by Jewish law to place statues or images of any kind in the Temple of God."

Alexander was displeased. At that moment, the High Priest had a brilliant inspiration.

"I shall build a living memorial to remind the Jewish people of Alexander's kindness to them," he said. "Every male child born during the year of the king's visit to Jerusalem shall bear the king's name, Alexander."

And the king was pleased. It was decreed, and thus it came to pass that the name of Alexander the Great has remained alive among our people to our own day.

War over Palestine

In time, Alexander the Great died. His great empire was broken into three kingdoms. There was war between two of these kingdoms, Syria and Egypt, for almost a hundred years. Little Israel was forced to serve as a land bridge between these two kingdoms and it was torn by the invading armies.

Finally the war ended, leaving Syria in possession of Israel. Once more, peace came to the little Jewish state. But it was a peace that depended on the whims of the Syrian kings. And it was the whim of such a king that destroyed the peace once and for all and provided us with the wonderful festival of Chanukah.

The Seleucids Rule of Israel / ca 198 B.C.E.

The Seleucid kings of Syria sought to win Palestine from the Ptolemies of Egypt. After many battles the Syrian king Antiochus III defeated Ptolemy V of Egypt in 198 B.C.E. Antiochus III reduced taxes and guaranteed that Jewish religious law would be respected. When his son, Antiochus IV,

46

ascended the throne in 175 B.C.E. conditions worsened, for he doubled the tax burden on Judea and abused the Jewish religion.

The Seleucid kings were Greeks, and like the Ptolemies of Egypt, they promoted and spread Greek culture. Antiochus took steps to induce the Jews to adopt Greek customs. All the important government posts went to those who complied. Before long, Greek ideas and the Greek way of life had become very fashionable among many of Judea's wealthy nobles and merchants.

A bust of Antiochus III (223–187 B.C.E.)

Hellenism and Judaism

Gradually, the people of Judea divided into two factions. Those who adopted the Greek way of life and Greek religious practices were called Hellenists. The majority who continued to adhere to the laws of the Torah were called Hasidim ("pious ones"). Whereas the Hellenists were willing to abandon Judaism in order to be accepted by their pagan rulers, the Hasidim adhered to the traditional Jewish ideal of living as servants of the one invisible God acting justly, showing mercy and obeying the commandments of the Torah.

Judaism Threatened

The Greek way of life opened the doors to a new world for affluent pleasureseekers who adopted it. Many Judeans were willing to cast aside their ancient traditions and lose themselves in the new life. The conflict between the Hellenists who advocated assimilation to Greek paganism, and the Hasidim, who upheld the ways of Judaism, was a bitter one.

Judaism was threatened abroad as well as at home. Because Judea was a small country that could not support a large population, many of its people had left their homeland and settled in other countries. Known collectively as the Jews of the Diaspora (Dispersion), they were exposed to strong Greek cultural influences in the cities in which they lived. In Alexandria and other places, many of them adopted Greek as their primary language. Knowledge of Hebrew began to die out. Although the majority remained committed to Judaism, they were unable to study the Torah, a serious problem that was finally solved by the Septuagint translation of the Bible.

Jewish ritual objects, including two seven-branched candlesticks, are shown on the base of a gold goblet of the 2nd century C.E. found in a Jewish catacomb in Rome, where it was hidden from the Romans. The objects shown on the goblet are believed to have been taken from the Temple in Jerusalem when it was desecrated by Antiochus IV of Syria in about 170 B.C.E.

A road sign in the village of Modin, directs visitors to the graves of the Hasmoneans.

47

Marble bust of Antiochus IV (175-163 B.C.E.)

Sacrificial pig near the altar at a pagan ceremony, as depicted on a Greek bowl (ca. 500 B.C.E.)

Statue of Zeus (Jupiter) found at Caesarea. Throughout Judea, Syrian overlords forced the Jews to worship before such idols at public altars.

The Hasidim

The Hasidim believed that Greek paganism and social practices would lead to immorality. Greek idol worship, love of conflict, and tolerance of drunkenness would weaken the Jewish way of life. At times there were violent confrontations between Hasidim and Hellenists.

The most extreme Hellenists urged their fellow Jews to use the Greek language and worship Greek gods.

Antiochus IV ca 175-163 B.C.E

The situation came to a head during the reign of Antiochus IV. He hoped to build his kingdom into a great power, but his dreams were threatened by a new empire rising in the West. The Romans had conquered Greece and Macedonia and marched on to Asia Minor. The Seleucid army was unable to stop them. As a result, Antiochus lost some of his western territories to Rome.

In order to raise funds to defend his kingdom against the growing Roman threat, Antiochus imposed high taxes on Judea to help defray the expense of hiring mercenary soldiers, equipping his vast army, and maintaining his splendid court in Antioch, the Syrian capital. In addition, Antiochus humiliated the Jews by placing a statue of himself in the Temple and forcing the Jews to bow down to it.

Antiochus and the Jewish Religon/ca 168 B.C.E.

Eventually, Antiochus outlawed Judaism. It became a serious offense to observe Jewish laws. The Torah was a forbidden book; the Sabbath, festivals, and holy days could no longer be celebrated in public. Antiochus added the Greek word *Epiphanes* ("God made manifest") to his name. Many Judeans, however, referred to him as Antiochus *Epimanes*, "Antiochus the Madman."

Although Antiochus had proclaimed himself a god and decreed that those who opposed him would die, brave men and women in Judea refused to pay homage at the Greek shrines.

Mattathias the Hasmonean

The first stirrings of revolt came in the village of Modin, near Jerusalem. Syrian officials and soldiers had come to Modin to collect taxes and force the people to worship the Greek gods. There was an old priest in the village, a man named Mattathias, of the Hasmonean family. Mattathias, surrounded by his five sons, walked up to the heathen altar. A Jew who collaborated with the Syrians had just bowed to the idols. Mattathias raised his sword high and his voice came out loud and clear:

"He who is with God, let him come to me!" he cried, and slew the traitorous idol worshipper. The old priest's bold act inspired his sons and followers. They fell upon the Syrian soldiers and officials and killed them. Only a few escaped.

The Revolt Begins

The long-awaited revolt had begun! News of the incident at Modin spread like wildfire until all Judea was inflamed. Mattathias, his sons, and their followers fled to the mountains and joined forces with the Hasidim.

Mattathias died soon after the beginning of the revolt, but his five sons-Judah, Yohanan, Simon, Eliezer, and Jonathan took over. The commander was Judah, who was called *HaMakkabi*, "the Hammerer." The letters of his name are said to have stood for the rebels' password and battle-cry: *Mikamokah ba'elim, Adonai!* ("Who is like you among the gods, O Almighty!"). The people of Judea rallied to the cause of the sons of Mattathias, now known as the Maccabees.

Although the revolutionary movement in Judea was growing day by day, Antiochus refused to take it seriously. He felt sure that his highly trained, well-equipped army could handle any threat.

Judah Maccabee, an able general and a fine strategist, avoided an open battle with the main Syrian forces. Biding his time, he conducted a classic guerilla campaign, striking here and there, attacking whenever feasible. He defeated a Syrian unit based in Samaria and later ambushed a sizable Syrian column passing through the narrow pass of Beth-Horon. The Syrians, taken by surprise, were routed. They fled in wild disorder, leaving their weapons and equipment behind.

A Syrian war–elephant. These huge beasts with sharp-shooting bowmen were the armored tanks of the ancient world.

An enameled picture of Judah Maccabee. It was painted in the 15th century by a French artist.

This old drawing shows Judah Maccabee and his soldiers fighting for the freedom of Jerusalem.

49

A Greek soldier under attack. He wears a metal helmet and breast-plate. This painting was found on an ancient stone coffin.

Judah Maccabee's Army

Judah Maccabee's army consisted of 6,000 untrained men armed only with equipment taken from the enemy and a few weapons made in Judea's crude forges. But the rebels had two advantages over the Syrians. First they knew the terrain, since it was their homeland. Second, they were fighting for a prize of untold value—their religion. They were determined to make a firm stand against the enemy no matter what the cost.

Still avoiding open battle, Judah and 3,000 men made a surprise attack at night on the Syrian encampment at Emmaus. Unable to rally in time, the Syrians again took flight. Their losses were heavy and their camp went up in flames. The Jews had won another great victory against overwhelming odds.

The Temple is Restored

Now the triumphant Jews marched on Jerusalem. A dismaying sight greeted them: the Temple was defiled by dirt and refuse and desecrated by idolatrous images.

Together, the victorious Jews set about cleaning their house of worship. Judah Maccabee and his men were assisted in this task by the priests and the people of Jerusalem. Joyfully the army of cleaners and polishers worked, erecting a new altar to the one God in order to rededicate themselves to their faith.

The Miracle of Chanukah / 165 B.C.E.

On the 25th day of Kislev, 165 B.C.E., three years after its desecration, the Temple was rededicated. The golden Menorah was lit once more. The Temple Menorah had only seven branches. It can still be seen today, in a relief on the Arch of Titus in Rome and on the official emblem of the State of Israel.

Tradition tells us that the victors found only enough oil in the Temple to keep the Eternal Light burning for one day. Yet miraculously the golden Menorah burned for eight full days. The eight-branched menorah of today and the annual eight-day celebration of Chanukah, the Festival of Lights, commemorate the victory won for freedom by Judah Maccabee and his courageous followers.

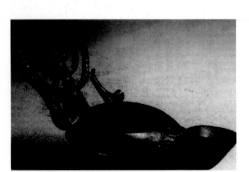

This bronze 4th century menorah was found in Egypt.

Chanukah Lights

Chanukah is a happy festival. It is marked by the lighting of candles in the home, beginning with one candle on the first night and adding one additional on each successive night of the holiday.

Many of us buy Chanukah candles made in Israel. Candles come forty-four to the box—enough for all eight nights of Chanukah, for we light one candle each night that acts as the *shammash* (which means "one who serves") with which we light the other candles.

The oldest historical sources that deal with the festival of Chanukah are ancient works known as the Books of the Maccabees. They tell us how Judah and his brothers came to the desolate Temple, how they cleansed it and re-dedicated it on the twenty-fifth day of the month of Kislev. Slowly, the custom of lighting Chanukah lights in every Jewish home was developed until Chanukah became the widespread festival that it is today.

For All to See

So that everyone may know that Chanukah is here, we place the candles near a window which faces the street. The lighting ceremony is accompanied by blessings and followed by song. The most popular Chanukah song is *Ma-oz Tzur,* or Rock of Ages.

There are no special Chanukah services in the synagogue. At the regular evening service, however, the candles are lit just as they are at home. Services during Chanukah also contain a number of additional prayers. One is *Hallel,* which consists of selections from the Book of Psalms. Another is *Al Ha-Nissim* ("for the miracles") which is repeated during the *Shmoneh Esreh* (the Eighteen Blessings) and in *Birkhat Ha-Mazon,* the grace after meals.

Chanukah Foods

A favorite Chanukah food is *latkes,* or potato pancakes. Originally, the pancakes were made of cheese. From the custom of eating cheese delicacies grew the custom of eating pancakes of all kinds. During the Middle Ages, Jews explained this custom by connecting it with the story of Judith which they linked with the story of Chanukah. Judith, according to

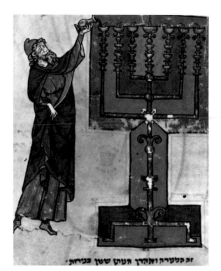

A 13th century French manuscript, written by Benjamin the Scribe, pictures Aaron, the High Priest pouring olive oil into the Temple Menorah.

The word *menorah* refers specifically to the huge seven-branched golden candle-holder that stood in the Temple of Jerusalem. It was removed by the Romans when they destroyed Jerusalem in 70 C.E. This bronze 4th century menorah was found in Egypt.

The Torah (Exodus 25:31–40) provides the details of the Temple Menorah. It was made by Bezalel and hammered out of a solid slab of gold. According to the Torah, it stood seven feet tall, weighed 100 pounds, and had seven branches.

For all to see.

Delicious Chanukah latkes

THE *DREIDEL* GAME

Now you play the *dreidel* game.
Watch it twirl and spin...
Round n' round the *dreidel* goes
NUN, GIMMEL, HAY, or *SHIN.*
Spin a *HAY,* you win but half,
NUN ...you take none.
Spin a *SHIN,* you must add,
GIMMEL...you have won!

This is a lead *dreidel* casting machine. It was designed by Asher Scharfstein in 1924 and was in use for more than 30 years and produced more than one million *dreidels.*
The mold is a scissor–action die with two moveable pieces. When the mold is closed the operator pours molten lead into the die. Within 10 seconds, the lead hardens, the mold is opened and the *dreidel* is removed. The casting of lead *dreidels* was discontinued due to labor costs and the toxicity of lead.

legend, was a daughter of the Hasmoneans. She fed cheese to the leader of the enemies of the Jews. He was made thirsty by the cheese and began to drink much wine. When he grew quite drunk, she cut off his head. For this reason, it was said, Jews ate cheese delicacies on Chanukah.

The Chanukah *Dreidel*

A favorite custom is the giving of gifts. Chanukah is also a time for "Chanukah gelt."

When the Maccabees returned to Jerusalem, they re-lit the Menorah and struck coins to show they were a free people. Ancient coins of Israel still exist, but we have our own version for Chanukah.

Chanukah Gelt

You can expect "Chanukah gelt" on this holiday and you may try to increase your share by playing a game of *dreidel.* For this game you need a *dreidel* or four-sided top whose four Hebrew letters stand for *Nes Gadol Hayah Sham*—"a great miracle happened there."

According to an old legend, the Chanukkah top was invented during the time of the Maccabees. Antiochus forbade the study of Torah. Nevertheless, people gathered in small groups and studied the Torah secretly, and by heart. If soldiers approached, the group scattered. Another means they used to escape detection was the *dreidel* game. The *dreidel* lay on the table. At the lookout's warning, the students spun the top. When the enemy arrived all he would see was Jews playing an innocent game. Thus the *dreidel* saved many a life.

Since the Middle Ages, the popular little *dreidel* has been part of Chanukah fun everywhere. In Eastern Europe, the tops were made of lead. Pouring the lead into molds was begun weeks earlier. They were cast in wooden forms. Made of wood, tin, lead, plastic, or what-have-you, the *dreidel* always bears the letters *Nun, Gimel, Hay, Shin.* These are initials for *Nes Gadol Hayah Sham:* a great miracle happened there. Spin it, and the dreidel tells you how you've done. *Nun,* and you take nothing from the pot. *Gimel,* and you take all. *Hay* means you get half. *Shin* tells you to put in.

The Chanukah Menorah

When Judah Maccabee triumphantly regained Jerusalem, the lamps of the Temple Menorah were relit and the rededication of the Temple was celebrated for eight days with feasting and with song.

Long before anyone thought of Chanukah, even while the Children of Israel were in the wilderness, the sacred Tabernacle had a beautiful seven-branched Menorah. When the Israelites entered the Promised Land, they set up the Tabernacle at Shiloh, and graced the Inner Sanctuary with the Menorah. The Sanctuary of Shiloh was destroyed by the Philistines and no one knows what happened to the Menorah, though some believe that it later stood in the Temple of Solomon.

But there it was not the only lamp, for no fewer than ten candlesticks shed their brilliant light in Solomon's Temple. After its destruction in 586 B.C.E., the candlesticks, with other precious Temple vessels, were brought to Babylon. From there, they were restored by the great Persian conqueror Cyrus, who allowed our people to return to Palestine and rebuild the Temple.

However, from that moment on, we hear no more about the other candlesticks. Henceforth only the large, magnificent golden Menorah, which was perhaps the same one made by Moses in the wilderness, drew the attention of friend and foe alike. Antiochus had the Menorah removed and broken, but the Maccabees repaired it and lit it again with the oil which miraculously burned for eight days.

Since then the Menorah has been used by our people in every place where we have lived. In Africa—in great Alexandria, down the Nile at the cataracts, and in busy Carthage; in Asia—in Yemen, Babylon, Persia, Palmyra, and on the border of the desert in the Decapolis and Pentapolis, in the Greek colonies in Syria and Asia Minor; in Europe—in Athens and Rome, in the Islands of the Mediterranean. In all these places the Menorah became a symbol of the Jewish people.

The *Chanukiah* grew to be a symbol of light and truth. We place it near a window so that all may see it and remember what it stands for. By the light of the *Chanukiah,* Jewish children were told the tale of Judah Maccabee, the hero who died for freedom.

A *Chanukiah* with a *klezmer* motif. *Klezmer* is a form of Jewish music that has been rediscovered. *Klezmer* is a Yiddish word that comes from the Hebrew words *klay zemer*, "musical instruments." *Klezmer* was the Jewish folk music of Eastern Europe and was played at weddings and other joyous occasions. *Klezmer* musicians played the violin, clarinet, and other easily transportable instruments. There are now *klezmer* groups throughout the United States.

An electric menorah

Israeli stamp featuring an 18th century brass oil Chanukah lamp.

LIGHTING THE *CHANUKIAH*
You place the first candle on the right side of the *Chanukiah*. The second candle is placed next to it, and so on, always moving towards your left. On each night you light first the *Shammos* candle and recite the *Chanukah* blessings. You light the candles always starting from the left and moving towards the right. As you light the candles you sing the hymn *Hanerot Hallalu*.

The torch is lit and the relay race begins.

The torch is passed from hand to hand and given to the President of Israel. With the torch he lights the giant Menorah at the Western Wall.

The Chanukah Menorah also became recognized as a symbol of our people's love for liberty. It shone in the synagogue, it glowed in the home, it guided the Jew through his life and often even accompanied him when he died, as an emblem on his tombstone.

When our ancestors made the first *Chanukiah*, they knew that it was forbidden to imitate the seven-branched candelabrum of the Temple. Besides, they wished to commemorate the little jar of oil that had lasted for eight days when the Temple was rededicated. For that reason, a special Chanukah lamp was designed for the festival of light, with an individual shaft for the *shammash* (servant) by which all the wicks were lit.

Many artists have produced wonderful *Chanukiot*, though none could equal the magnificence of the Temple candelabrum, which was taken by Titus to Rome, after the destruction of the Second Temple, where it was carried in his triumphal procession. On the famous Arch of Titus, which can still be seen in Rome, the Menorah is prominently portrayed.

Thus the Menorah, and especially the *Chanukiah*, awakens in every generation memories of a heroic past and rekindles a hope and faith in the future.

Chanukah in Israel

Chanukah is celebrated as a national holiday in Israel. There is a *Chanukiah* on top of almost every public building and synagogue in the country. People take trips to Modin, the city where Mattathias, and Judah and his brothers lived. There they honor the memory of the Maccabees and the great victory that they won.

Torah Relay

A special ceremony is held that begins in Modin. First the Israeli flag is raised above the field. Then a large bonfire is lit. A number of torches are lit from the bonfire. These torches are carried by runners for a distance. When they come to certain agreed–upon places they meet other runners who are there waiting for them. The runners who are waiting have unlit torches in their hands. The runners who have come from Modin with their blazing torches light the unlit torches of the second group of runners.

The second group of runners run with their torches until they meet up with a third group of runners, who continue to a fourth group, and so on. The last group of runners bring their torches to all the cities of the country.

The first torch is brought to Jerusalem, where it is given to the President of Israel. He uses the torch to light Chanukah candles. Then the torch is brought to Mount Zion, where a special memorial service is held for those who died in the Holocaust. The torches are also used to light Chanukah candles at the Western Wall and in all the towns and cities in the country. In this way all the cities and towns in the country are united with Modin where the story of Chanukah first began.

A family Chanukah celebration

The Lesson of Chanukah

All people owe much to the ancient Maccabees. Had their spirit been extinguished, not only would Judaism have disappeared, but its two daughter religions, Christianity and Islam, would never have been born.

Chanukah, then, tells us to be ever watchful against those who would harm us. It tells us to grow closer to our faith and our people and to drink deep from our ancient heritage.

Above all, it tells us that we are heirs to a great tradition. Chanukah teaches us that we do our part only if we keep this noble tradition alive and transmit it to each succeeding generation.

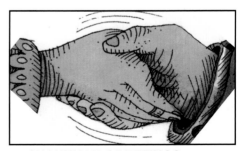

CHANUKAH GREETINGS
On Chanukah you greet people by saying *Chag Chanukah Sameach* meaning "A happy Chanukah."

Tu Bi-Shevat

SHEVAT						שבט
Sun.	Mon.	Tues.	Wed.	Thur.	Fri.	Sat.
						1
2	3	4	5	6	7	8
9	10	11	12	13	14	15
16	17	18	19	20	21	22
23	24	25	26	27	28	29/30

The holiday of Tu Bi-Shevat is celebrated on the 15th day of the month of Shevat.

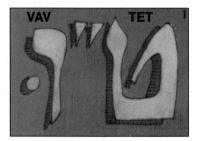

The word *Tu* is made up of two Hebrew letters, *Tet* and *Vav*. *Tet* has the numeral value of 9, and *Vav* has the value of 6. Added together they equal 15. The holiday of Tu Bi-Shevat is celebrated on the 15th day of the month of Shevat.

The Importance of Trees

Towards winter's close we celebrate the New Year of the Trees. The Bible commands the Jewish people not to destroy trees even when attacking an enemy city. "You may eat of them, but you must not cut them down."

The rabbis said that when one chops down a fruit-bearing tree, the wanton destruction makes the tree's cry go forth from one end of the world to the other.

Said Rabbi Yochanan ben Zakkai in the Talmud, explaining the great importance of tree planting in Israel, "If you hold a sapling in your hand, ready to plant it, and you are told," 'The Messiah is here!'; first plant the sapling, and then go forth to welcome him."

Flowers and trees and all growing things mean so much to every human being. Our ancestors knew this. They realized that trees are among our best friends. Trees help feed and clothe us. They give us wood for our houses, paper for books, fruit to eat, and shade from the hot sun. Trees keep the soil rich and fertile, and give beauty to the world.

Tu Equals Fifteen

Our ancestors were aware of the importance of trees, and they set aside the fifteenth day of the month of Shevat (*Chamishah Asar Bi-Shevat*) as Jewish Arbor Day. It is usually called Tu Bi-Shevat, because the abbreviation *tu* represents the two Hebrew letters which numerically equal fifteen.

In Israel, the rainy season lasts till February; then the first buds on the trees appear and lo, it's Tu Bi-Shevat!

It was in the Mishnah that the New Year of the Trees received its name. But long before that, the Torah showed the way. The Bible, for example, says that fruit trees may not be cut down even in time of war (Deuteronomy 20). The Torah itself is called a "tree of life." And King David, in the book of Psalms, says that a righteous person is "like a tree planted by the streams of water."

Tu Bi-Shevat has two other names which describe its origin: *Chag ha-Perot*, the Holiday of Fruits and *Rosh Hashanah la-Ilanot*, New Year of the Trees.

There are many references to trees in the Bible. They show our love for trees and how they were used in religiously important ways. Here are a few passages:

Harvesting dates on a moshav with a mobile picking machine.

Cedar
And Solomon built the Temple, and finished
it . . . and he built the walls with boards of cedar
. . . all was cedar; there was no stone seen. *I Kings 6:14—18*

Willow
By the rivers of Babylon we sat down and wept,
when we remembered Zion. We hanged our
harps upon the willows . . . *Psalms 137:1—2*

Palm
Take on the first day [of Sukkot] the branches
of palm trees . . . and dwell in booths seven days.
Leviticus 23:40—41

Citron
On Sukkot . . . take the fruit of the beautiful trees . . . this is
the fragrant citron, or etrog. *Leviticus 23:40*

Cypress
And King David and all the house of Israel
played before the Lord on all kinds of instruments made of
cypress or fir wood, on harps and on drums. *II Samuel 6:5*

Gopher
And God said to Noah: Make an ark of gopher-wood . . . and
come into the ark with your sons, your wife, and your sons'
wives . . . and of every living thing bring two of
each sort into the ark. *Genesis 6:14—19*

Fig
Adam and Eve sewed fig leaves together and
made themselves aprons. *Genesis 3:7*

The patriarchs and matriarchs of Israel traveled to and around the ancient city of Beersheba. The Bible mentions a treaty that Abraham made with Abimelech, a Philistine king. The treaty involved settling a dispute about a well that Abimelech's servants had seized from Abraham. Abraham sealed the treaty by giving the king seven sheep. Some say that Beersheba means "well of the seven," referring to the seven sheep and the well. As a sign of the treaty, Abraham planted a tamarisk tree at the "well of the seven."
Today in Beersheba there is an ancient well near a tamarisk tree, which some say dates from the time of Abraham.
This photo shows a tamarisk tree with Beersheba in the background.

The Jewish National Fund's best known task is planting trees. Through the JNF, Jews around the world help plant trees in the land of Israel. These young forests are used for recreational purposes. At certain times of the year, such as Tu Bi–Shevat, Israeli students help with the planting of young saplings, some of which were purchased through donations by other students around the world. Trees are planted to commemorate various occasions: births, anniversaries, a Bar or Bat Mitzvah, or graduation. Sad occasions are remembered as well as happy ones.

In ancient Israel, parents would plant a tree when a child was born. When two young people married branches were cut from their trees. These branches were used to support their *chuppah*—the canopy under which the wedding ceremony took place.

Olive

The Lord spoke to Moses, saying: Command the Children of Israel to bring pure olive oil, beaten for the Menorah, to cause a light to burn always in the tabernacle of your congregation.

Exodus 27:20—21

Strength and Fragrance

Many customs grew up around Tu Bi-Shevat. In ancient Palestine, it was customary to plant a tree when a child was born: a cedar for a boy, and a cypress for a girl. The cedar stood for height and strength, the cypress for tenderness and fragrance. When the children grew up and were married, branches from their trees were cut and used to support the bridal canopy, for good luck. Between birth and marriage they cared for their own trees. Through this custom everyone learned to love trees.

In the *Cheder*

When our people were forced to leave the Holy Land, they did not forget Tu Bi-Shevat. In the cities and townlets of Russia and Poland Tu Bi-Shevat came in the winter. In the *cheder*, or Jewish school, after Hebrew lessons, the children opened the little bags they had brought from home, bags filled with tropical fruits that reminded them of Zion: dates, figs, raisins, and *bokser*, the dried fruit of the carob tree.

Faraway Customs

In Kurdistan, raisins and other sweet fruits used to be placed in a ring around trees on Tu Bi-Shevat. Then the people prayed for an abundant fruit season and for the birth of many children.

In sixteenth–century Palestine, the people of some Jewish communities drank four cups of wine on Tu Bi-Shevat. The first cup was white wine, to symbolize winter. The second was rose, for spring. The third: deep red, for summer. The fourth: red mixed with white, to symbolize fall.

Another unusual custom was observed in the town of Safed in Israel, long ago. On Tu Bi-Shevat the inhabitants would do their best to sample at least fifteen (for *chamishah asar*, which equals 15) different kinds of fruit!

And, finally, a touching custom was that followed by Sephardic Jews in the sixteenth century. They had a *Ma'ot Perot* fund: money was collected to provide fruit for the poor on Tu Bi-Shevat.

In Israel Today

In modern Israel, Tu Bi-Shevat marks the end of the rainy season and is celebrated in all its ancient glory. In 1949, on the first Tu Bi-Shevat after the Jewish state gained its independence, thousands of people gathered to plant life-giving trees in a forest which will one day contain six million trees–the number of Jews killed in the Holocaust by Hitler's wrath. It is known as the Forest of the Martyrs.

Tu Bi-Shevat also reminds us of the way Israel has bloomed under the tender care of the *chalutzim* (pioneers). Jewish settlers have worked wonders of reclamation in the cool northern regions of Galilee, in the hot waterless plains of the Negev, and in the tropical coastal areas.

Imaginative Jewish farmers introduced the grapefruit and varieties of oranges into Israel. They developed crop rotation so that the soil would not become weary and barren from growing the same plants over and over.

At the beginning of the twentieth century, there were very few vegetables in Israel. The soil was too dry. Jewish pioneers sank wells to tap underground sources. Today there are thousands of acres of truck farms. Only thirty or forty years ago, potatoes were a big farm problem in Israel: no one knew how to store them. Then it was discovered that if enough ventilation was provided, the potatoes would keep from sprouting little shoots before the market was ready for them.

Land of Promise

Modern Israel grows a great variety of fruits, vegetables, and flowers. You will find many different kinds of growing things. In the north, where it is cooler, there are apples and pears. Galilean villages produce peaches and apricots. The tropical Jordan valley has banana, persimmon, avocado, and papaya groves.

The maritime plain along the shores of the Mediterranean boasts the large citrus belt: oranges, grapefruits, and lemons.

Tu Bi–Shevat is tree–planting time in Israel. These Israeli schoolchildren are planting saplings which will grow into trees for shade and for beauty.

THE IMPORTANCE OF TREES
The Bible commands the Jewish people not to destroy trees even when battling a city. "You may eat of them, but you must not cut them down." The rabbis said that when one chops down a fruit-bearing tree, the wanton destruction makes the tree's cry go forth from one end of the world to the other. Said Rabbi Yochanan ben Zakkai in the Talmud, explaining the great importance of tree planting in Israel, "If you hold a sapling in your hand, ready to plant it, and you are told, 'The Messiah is here!'—first plant the sapling, and then go forth to welcome him."

The Kennedy Forest is dedicated to the memory of John F. Kennedy, a President of the United States who was a staunch supporter of Israel.

Israeli stamp commemorating the establishment of the Keren Kayemet Le'Yisrael (Jewish National Fund).

A Keren Kayemet poster in Hebrew, Polish, and Yiddish inviting settlers to settle in the valley of Jezreel, in Palestine.

The land for the first settlements in Palestine was purchased by Keren Kayemet le'Yisrael (Jewish National Fund), established in 1901 as the land-purchasing agency of the Zionist movement.
The Jewish National Fund depended on small sums of money collected from Jews throughout the world. The blue-and-white JNF box found a place in millions of Jewish homes.

Lots of other crops, including tobacco, grapes, melons, almonds, pistachio nuts, and pomegranates, to name but a few, show that Israel has truly earned its description as a land of promise.

We Help the JNF

One way we in the United States observe Tu Bi-Shevat is by contributing to the Jewish National Fund, which plants young trees in Israel. These trees help reclaim for cultivation the earth which has been worn out by centuries of erosion and shifting sand dunes. In less than a century of existence, the JNF has planted millions of trees and built hundreds of agricultural settlements.

The JNF has dedicated itself to the following tasks:

1. To use contributions to acquire land in Israel.
2. To lease this land to farmers and home builders.
3. To drain swamps, plant and conserve forests, develop water resources and irrigation.
4. To lease land for housing new immigrants.

Much of the credit for making Israel bloom, as in days of old, belongs to the JNF. When, for example, the famous Valley of Jezreel was bought by the JNF, it was a wasteland, a mass of swamps. Today the Emek is a beautiful valley, studded with orchards and little farms. All this was achieved by the *chalutzim* with the help given by Jews everywhere through the Keren Kayemet le-Yisrael, the Jewish National Fund.

Eating Fruits from Israel

We also show our love for Tu Bi-Shevat and the ideals for which it stands by eating fruits from Israel on this day. And there's something else which many children enjoy doing: growing plants and little trees indoors.

Tu Bi-Shevat Flower Legend

Not only customs, but legends as well, have clustered about Tu Bi-Shevat. One legend describes the history of the shy, graceful cyclamen, a flower also called *keser shelomoh*, "Crown of Solomon." It is said that when Solomon became king, he chose the lovely cyclamen as the model for his crown. Centuries later, when Jerusalem was conquered by the Babylonians the royal crown was stolen from the royal treasury. The cyclamen bowed its head in sorrow, saying: "Only when a son of David again ascends the throne and the crown is returned to Jerusalem shall I once more stand erect." To this day, the cyclamen droops its head.

Rip van Winkle

Another beautiful legend is that of Choni and the carob tree.

Said Rabbi Yochanan: All his life Choni, the righteous one, was troubled about this verse: *"When the Almighty brought back those that returned to Zion, we were like unto them that dream" (Psalms 126:1)*. Since seventy years elapsed between the destruction of Jerusalem and the return to Zion, Choni wondered whether it was possible for anyone to sleep for so long a time without interruption.

One day, while walking in the countryside, Choni noticed a man planting a date tree. Said Choni to the man: "You know that it takes seventy years before a date tree bears fruit; are you sure that you will live seventy years and eat therefrom?"

"I found this world provided with date trees," the man replied. "As my ancestors planted them for me, so I plant them for my children."

Thereupon Choni sat down to eat and was overcome by sleep. As he slept, a grotto was formed around him, which screened him from the human eye. There he slept for seventy years. When he awoke, he saw a man gathering carobs from the carob tree and eating them.

"Do you know who planted this carob tree?" Choni asked.

"My grandfather," the man replied.

"I too must have slept seventy years!" Choni exclaimed. This, then, is the story of Tu Bi-Shevat, which is celebrated by Jews the world over. It is a festival that symbolizes our love for the Holy Land and shows our feeling for trees and plants as living, fruitful things. Tu Bi-Shevat also reminds us that God, when creating the world, planted the Garden of Eden and placed Adam and Eve in it.

The ibex is a protected species on several of Israel's nature preserves.

Soldier opening the valve of an irrigation pipe at a new Nahal (army) settlement in the Aravah.

In Judaism, there is a *mitzvah* that defines how we can use nature. This is the *mitzvah* of *bal tashchit*, a Hebrew term meaning "do not destroy." It is based on a commandment that tells us, that when there is a war, and a city is under siege, the soldiers may eat from the trees around the city but they are not allowed to chop them down. In this way, the trees will be there to provide food for years to come.

Purim

ADAR						אדר
Sun.	Mon.	Tues.	Wed.	Thur.	Fri.	Sat.
	1	2	3	4	5	6
7	8	9	10	11	12	13
14	15	16	17	18	19	20
21	22	23	24	25	26	27
28	29	30				

The cheerful holiday of Purim is celebrated on the 14th day of Adar.

Purim is time for masquerades, puppet shows, reading the Megillah, making noise with large *graggers* and eating lots of *hamantashen*.

Purim, the Feast of Lots, is a holiday of gift-giving and great fun. No other holiday makes us feel so gay and cheerful; on no other holiday are so many goodies eaten. Because Purim celebrates the downfall of a tyrant who wished to wipe out the Jewish people and because the Megillah (Scroll of Esther) which is read on Purim tells us to keep the fourteenth of Adar as a day of joy and happiness, the Feast of Lots has always been a time for merry-making.

In days gone by, bands of musicians roamed the streets on Purim, going from home to home to play and then to receive Purim gifts. In every Jewish school and center, Purim plays and carnivals are the order of the day. In fact, just as the robin is a messenger of spring, so a rehearsal with wigs and make-up and poppyseed cakes is a sign that Purim's just around the corner.

The Jews of Persia

The rulers of Persia were usually thoughtful and generous. Although Judea, as the Land of Israel was known in those days, was a province of the Persian Empire, it was allowed to govern itself in accordance with its own laws. Similarly, the Jews of Babylonia, which was also under Persian control, fared well and had much freedom.

A dramatic glimpse of Jewish life under Persian rule is provided by the biblical story of Esther, which took place in Shushan (Susa), the capital of Persia, in 486—485 B.C.E The Persian king in the story is named Ahasuerus; the ancient Greeks called him Xerxes. According to the Bible, his kingdom extended from Ethiopia to India, and he ruled over 127 provinces.

Beauty on Parade

Ahasuerus asked his wife, Vashti, to dance nude for the drunken guests at a palace party. When she refused he decided to punish her disobedience by finding a new queen.

Young women from the entire Persian Empire were invited to compete for the king's hand in marriage. Hundreds upon hundreds of contestants arrived and paraded before Ahasuerus.

Among the inhabitants of Shushan was a Jew named Mordecai, who had been carried away from Jerusalem with the captives when Nebuchadnezzar, the king of Babylon, destroyed the Temple. He had an adopted child named Esther, his uncle's daughter. Esther was very beautiful, and after her father and mother died, Mordecai took her as his own daughter.

Esther was one of the many maidens brought to the royal palace at Shushan. Ahasuerus immediately selected her and she became the new queen of Persia.

Sometime after this, Mordecai refused to bow down to Haman, the king's grand vizier. Haman was very angry; he went to Ahasuerus and accused the Jews of plotting against the government. "Their laws are different," he said, "and they do not obey the king's rulings. If it pleases the king, let them be destroyed."

Just as the Nazis tried to destroy all the Jews in Europe, Haman wanted to wipe out all the Jews in the Persian Empire. Ahasuerus agreed to his proposal.

Esther Saves the Jews

When Mordecai found out about the impending pogrom against the Jews of Persia he urged Esther to save her people. Bravely violating a law that prohibited anyone from approaching the king without an invitation, Esther went to Ahasuerus. She revealed that she was Jewish and that Haman's bloodthirsty plot would destroy her people.

The king ordered Haman hanged on the very gallows he had built for Mordecai. Ahasuerus appointed Mordecai one of his advisors and as a token of trust gave him Haman's signet ring. The Jews of Persia were given permission to defend themselves against their enemies.

Archaeologists at Persepolis have uncovered stone palaces from the time of Darius and Exerxes. This is the Hall of Pillars with its 72 giant pillars. It was large enough to accommodate 10,000 celebrants.

This gold cup with a lion base is from the 5th and 6th century. Such cups were in use during the reign of Xerxes.

A fresco found at the 3rd century Dura–Europos Synagogue shows Ahasuerus and Esther. The king is being given a letter by one of his attendants. Esther, the queen, is seated on the throne to the king's left. Esther's head is covered with a full crown.

Purim Ball, New York, 1865 Frank Leslie's *Illustrated Newspaper*.

An ingenious wooden *gragger*, made in Poland 1935, depicts Haman and his 20th-century counterpart, Hitler.

A wooden Purim *gragger* engraved with the Hebrew words, *arur Haman* meaning, "cursed is Haman."

The holiday of Purim was instituted to commemorate this series of events.

The Holiday of Purim

On the fourteenth day of the month of Adar, the Jews of Persia rested and made it a day of feasting and rejoicing. Ever since the fourteenth of Adar has been observed as a day of rejoicing and feasting and a holiday, and as a day on which Jews send gifts to one another. But the Jews in Shushan rested on the fifteenth day of the same month and made it a day of feasting and rejoicing.

Purim Means "Lots"

The name origin of the name Purim is quite interesting. It comes from the word *pur*, meaning "lot." When Haman plotted to wipe out the Jews of Persia, he cast *purim* ("lots") to select the day of the pogrom. The name of the holiday commemorates the defeat of his evil plan.

Reading the Megillah

The Megillah, or Scroll of Esther, is read in the temple on the evening of Purim. Although it is a religious service, it is a time of fun and hilarity. The behavior that is permitted in the temple on Purim at the reading of the Megillah is not allowed at any other time.

Many worshipers come to the temple in costumes and masks. All the children (and many adults) bring *graggers*, special Purim noisemakers. As the reader chants the Megillah in the traditional trope, everyone listens carefully for the mention of the name of Haman. Whenever they hear it, they make as much noise as they can with their *graggers*. They are trying to blot out the name of Haman. And just as Haman's name is blotted out, Jews hope that all their enemies will be eliminated.

The Purim Party

After the service there is usually a party. All sorts of good things are served. But no Purim party would be complete without *hamantaschen*. These are small three-cornered pastries filled with poppyseeds, prune jam, or other fillings.

The history of the *hamantasch* is very interesting. The Jews of Germany used to eat a cake filled with poppyseeds on Purim. It was called a *mantasch*, which means "poppyseed packet." Since it was served on Purim, it soon came to be called a *hamantash* in memory of Haman. The three-cornered shape, it was said, was because Haman wore a three-cornered hat. In Israel, these cakes are called *oznay Haman*, which means "Haman's ears." But whatever you call them, or whatever filling is used, they are delicious.

All dressed up for Purim.

Shalach Manot

One of the most delightful customs of Purim is that of *shalach manot*, or exchanging gifts. In the shtetl, the small Jewish town of Eastern Europe, *shalach manot* was a very important custom. For days before the holiday arrived each home would be filled with the delicious aromas of all sorts of good things being baked.

Then, on the morning of Purim, plates of goodies would be prepared. Each plate would be covered with a white napkin. The children, usually dressed in costumes, would deliver the plates to the homes of neighbors and friends. In each home they would receive a few small coins. What fun the children had. For them it was the best day of the year.

A Purim masquerade parade.

The Carnival

In religious schools across the country, Purim is a very busy time. It is the time of the yearly carnival. All the classes have been busy for weeks preparing games of chance and skill. On the Sunday before or after Purim, the games are set up and the children of the school are invited to play. There are games like Pin the Hat on Haman's Head, Hit Haman in the Nose, Find Your Way to Shushan, and many, many others. Usually children come in costume and prizes are given for the best costume, the funniest costume, the most original costume, and so on.

Many children (and their parents) consider Purim the best Jewish holiday of the year. "It's too bad," they say, "that it doesn't come at least every other week."

Three Israeli stamps with Purim scenes and three quotations from the Megillah.

Purim Carnivals in Israel

Purim is the one day of the year when the rabbis encouraged

A page from the 15th–century Italian "Rothschild" manuscript recording the tradition of the deliverance of Persian Jewry from the evil designs of Haman. Haman ordered the death of all Jews in his Empire, but Queen Esther interceded and Haman and his ten sons were hanged. This illustration shows Haman and his ten sons hanging from a tree.

A Purim *Shalach Manot* plate. France, 18th century.

An 18th century, illustrated Scroll of Esther (Megillah) from Alsace, France.

people to get drunk. We are told to get so drunk on this day that we do not know the difference between the words "Blessed be Mordecai" and "Cursed be Haman." In Hebrew the rabbis used the phrase *ad lo yada*, "until one didn't know." Modern Israelis have adopted these three words as the name for the jolly carnival that has become an Israeli Purim custom. Thus it is called the *Adloyada*.

In Tel Aviv every Purim, an elaborate *Adloyada* parade proceeds with great fanfare through the city streets. Headed by mounted police to the music of bands, colorful floats tell the story of Esther. There stands the beautiful young queen in her shining golden crown and royal robes. There goes Mordecai, riding in triumph on a white horse. Oh! There's the villain Haman with his ten sons! Everyone is dressed in costumes and full of fun. People dance and sing in the streets.

The Meaning of Purim

Purim started out as a holiday celebrating the deliverance of the Jews from Haman during the time of the Persian Empire, but it is now much more. It is a festival on which Jews rejoice in God's protection of the Jewish people from any threatened evil. The name Haman has come to stand for any enemy of Israel. Mordecai is a name for every wise Jewish leader, and Esther for every brave Jewish woman.

The Megillah and Art

Beginning in the Middle Ages the Scroll of Esther was often ornamented with beautiful illustrations. Cases of graceful and unusual design, delicately carved in silver and gold, were made to house the Megillah.

The earliest known Purim scroll dates back to 1637; it may be seen in the Jewish Museum of London. Handsomely designed Megillot also appeared in other countries, including Holland, Italy, Germany, Poland, and Russia.

The illustrations in Purim scrolls include scenes from the story, such as Haman on the gallows, and Mordecai being led on the king's horse. Many scrolls were intended for the use of youngsters and are illustrated in a fairy-tale style. The borders of Megillot were usually decorated with flowers, birds and animals, and graceful designs.

The following words belong to the Purim vocabulary that has developed over the centuries. These words will enrich the meaning of Purim for you.

Gragger

Noisemaking at the mention of Haman's name during the reading of the Scroll of Esther is an old, old custom. The *gragger* has been in use since the 13th century in France and Germany. In some countries, people wrote Haman's name on the soles of their shoes and stamped them on the floor during the Megillah reading.

Mishloach Manot

Often called *shalach manot*, *mishloach manot* means "sending of gifts." The custom is mentioned in the book of Esther: "make them days of feasting and joy, of sending portions to one another." That's where we get the oh-so-wonderful custom of giving and receiving presents on Purim!

Zachor

The word *zachor* means "remember," and *Shabbat Zachor* is the Sabbath before Purim. An extra portion from the Torah is read. It tells about the evil that Amalek did to our ancestors. The *Haftarah*, or portion from the prophets, read on *Shabbat Zachor*, describes King Saul's meeting with Agag, ruler of the Amalekites. The point is that Haman is portrayed as an Agagite, a direct descendant of Amalek, and therefore a deadly enemy of Israel.

Fast of Esther

The day before Purim (the thirteenth of Adar) is the Fast of Esther. We remember on this day the fast decreed by Esther, and the gathering of the Jews for public fasting and prayer on the day before the date set by Haman for the massacre of the Jewish people.

Hamantaschen

These are the special pastries without which no Purim celebration would be complete. They are three-cornered little cakes filled with poppyseeds or fruit jam. Some say that the name comes from *mohntaschen*, or "poppyseed pockets"; others,

The Washington Megillah was illustrated by Joel ben Simeon the most profilic Hebrew artist-scribe of the 15th century. He illustrated more than 11 manuscripts which are now in the posession of libraries in Europe, Israel and America.
The Megillah states that " the work was completed on the 25th of Shevat 5238" (January 29, 1478).

A poster at the Western Wall reminds the visitors that Purim is a time to give charity to the poor.

67

A form for baking *hamantaschen*; Poland, 19th century.

A 19th century Purim feast with lots to drink, Safed, Palestine. The background inscription reads *"Adloyada"*.

Chinese Megillah, early 19th century. Specially written and illustrated for the Chinese Ki-Fend-Fu community.

that the cakes resemble Haman's hat. An interesting sidelight is that in modern Hebrew a *hamantasch* is called "Haman's ear."

Adloyada

There's a talmudic saying that one should drink merrily on Purim, until one is so tipsy that one knows not *(ad lo yada)* the difference between "blessed be Mordecai" *(baruch Mordecai)* and "cursed be Haman" *(arur Haman)*. This expression has given the name to the annual *Adloyada* Purim carnival in Tel Aviv, a gala affair, complete with floats, streamers, costumes, and balloons.

Purim Katan

Purim Katan, or Little Purim, occurs during a Jewish leap year. As we explained in the first chapter, an extra month of Adar is sometimes added to the Jewish lunar calendar in order to coordinate it with the solar calendar. When this happens, the festival of Purim is celebrated in Adar Sheni, the second month of Adar, and the fourteenth of the first month of Adar is observed as Purim Katan.

Shushan Purim

The day after Purim is called Shushan Purim. According to the book of Esther, the Jews of Shushan (Susa), the Persian capital, celebrated the victory over Haman a day later than did Jews in other parts of the Persian Empire because they were engaged in battle with their enemies for an additional day.

Megillat Esther

The book of Esther is one of the *Ketuvim* ("Writings") that comprise the third section of the Holy Scripture. It is the last of the five *Megillot*, or Scrolls. The Megillah is read in the synagogue after the evening service on the eve of Purim, and again on the morning of Purim.

Machatzit ha-Shekel

Before the Scroll is read, every adult contributes to charity, in remembrance of the biblical tax of a half-shekel per person which was used to keep up the Holy Sanctuary.

Special Purims

One of our ancient sources of wisdom, the Midrash, says that anyone who experiences a miraculous deliverance from danger, and especially the inhabitants of a city that is saved from danger, may make that day Purim. There have been at least thirty instances in Jewish history of communities setting aside a special day as a Purim to commemorate deliverance from great evil.

One example is the Purim of the Baker Woman. In 1820 the city of Chios in Greece was attacked by Greek rebels, and a baker woman accidentally shot off a cannon. This warned the Turkish forces and the city was saved.

Another Purim took place two centuries earlier in Germany. It became known as Vincent Purim (or Purim Fettmilch) after Vincenz Fettmilch, a baker who called himself a new Haman and blamed the Jews for Germany's hard times. He spurred a mob attack on the ghetto of Worms and then on the ghetto of Frankfurt. Luckily, the governor looked upon these pogroms as acts of civil disobedience. He quickly quelled the riots and the "new Haman" was hanged. The governor ordered damages paid to the Jews. The Jews of Frankfurt established a special Purim in 1614.

Throughout the ages Purim was a very happy and often tipsy holiday. These clowns blowing horns are parading through the streets of a European ghetto. This drawing is from the *Book of Customs*, Amsterdam, 1773.

Passover

NISAN						ניסן
Sun.	Mon.	Tues.	Wed.	Thur.	Fri.	Sat.
				1	2	3
4	5	6	7	8	9	10
11	12	13	14	15	16	17
18	19	20	21	22	23	24
25	26	27	28	29	30	

The holiday of Passover starts with the Seder on the 14th day of Nisan and ends eight days later on the 22nd of Nisan. Reform and Israeli Jews celebrate Passover for seven days and have one Seder.

A decorative and instructive Passover Seder plate. The center contains the names of the six symbols of Passover. The outside edge contains the names of the 15 steps of the Seder ceremony.

How does this night differ from all other nights? On all other nights we eat bread and matzah; why on this night do we eat only matzah?

We were slaves to Pharaoh in Egypt; and Moses was sent down to free our people from bondage . . .

The question is the same every year, and so is the answer. For both are part of a ceremony that has remained unchanged for centuries upon centuries. This ceremony is called the *Seder*, and it marks the beginning of Passover.

What Passover Is

Passover, or Pesach, is many things. It is a festival of freedom, when we recall how the Almighty released our ancestors from slavery in Egypt and helped a free people come into existence.

Passover is an agricultural festival, reminding us of the Land of Israel in ancient times. Our ancestors were farmers, and Passover marked the beginning of the grain harvest.

Passover is also a pilgrimage festival. Three times a year, the Israelites went in joyous procession to Jerusalem, there to celebrate the festivals of Passover, Shavuot, and Sukkot.

Passover is all of these things but it is especially a holiday for children. Our ancestors were instructed: "You shall tell it to your child." The Seder service, the reading of the Haggadah, the Four Questions, the stealing of the *afikomen*—all these are meant for boys and girls, to teach them the importance of this great holiday in the history of the Jewish people.

Turn Back the Clock

To learn the story of Pesach we must wend our way across the sands of time to a distant age and a strange land. There, in ancient Egypt, lived Joseph, the favorite and gifted son of Jacob. Joseph had been sold by his brothers to Midianite merchants, who in turn had brought him to Egypt.

One day Joseph was thrown into prison on false charges. Soon afterwards, Pharaoh, the ruler of Egypt, had a strange dream in which seven lean cows devoured seven fat ones. Not a single wise man or wizard in all the land could tell the meaning of the dream. Then Joseph, who had interpreted dreams for the royal cupbearer and the royal baker, was called before the Pharaoh.

"I have dreamed a dream and none can interpret it," said the Pharaoh. Joseph answered, "God is the interpreter of dreams. Perhaps through me He shall grant the Pharaoh peace of mind."

Joseph listened and then told the Pharaoh that his dreams meant that seven years of famine would follow seven years of plenty in the land of Egypt.

Joseph Becomes Governor

The Pharaoh rewarded Joseph by making him governor over all the land. The new governor built huge granaries to be filled during the years of plenty. When the years of famine came, the full granaries saved Egypt from starvation.

Hyksos in Egypt

A time of famine came to Canaan, and the thoughts of the patriarch Jacob turned longingly to the fertile land of the Nile, where food was plentiful even when other countries experienced famine. Joseph, one of Jacob's sons, was now living in

A group of wooden Nubian soldiers excavated from the tomb of an Egyptian prince. They placed such models in tombs in the belief that they would serve the owner in the afterworld.

A wall painting from about 1900 B.C.E. in an Egyptian tomb. This beautiful painting shows a group of Semites bringing gifts to the Egyptians.

The Israelite slaves made bricks out of clay, mud, and straw. The straw which the taskmasters supplied held the bricks together. The Torah says that Pharaoh wanted to punish the Israelites and ordered them to find their own straw.

In some poor Middle Eastern countries, peasants still build their houses out of sunbaked bricks, just as the Israelites did thousands of years ago. This peasant is setting his mud bricks out to dry in the hot sun. Note the straw strewn around the pile of bricks.

Rameses II was most probably the Pharaoh who enslaved the Hebrews.

Egypt, where he had risen from servitude to a position of great power, second in command only to the Pharaoh. At Joseph's invitation, Jacob brought his family and flocks to Egypt.

The Pharaoh assigned the territory of Goshen to the Israelites. It was good grazing land and for many years the Israelites lived there in peace.

Modern historians believe that these events occurred about 1700 B.C.E., during the time when the Hyksos, a warlike tribe from Syria, swept into Egypt. The Hyksos ruled Egypt for about 120 years. Joseph was probably a high-ranking official under one of these powerful foreign rulers.

Slaves of the Pharaoh

Eventually the Hyksos were defeated, and Egyptian kings once more ruled over the land. The new Pharaohs, as the Bible tells us, "did not know Joseph." No longer were the Israelites respected as the privileged descendants of a noble ancestor. Instead they were enslaved. Some historians believe that this took place during the reign of Rameses II (ca. 1290—1224 B.C.E.). Egypt was a growing empire at this time, and the Pharaohs had great need for slaves to build new cities and magnificent palaces.

Rameses feared an uprising among the slaves and took cruel precautions to prevent it. He issued a decree that all male children born to the Israelites must be killed. In this merciless way, Rameses hoped to keep the Israelites from growing in numbers.

Baby Moses

Soon after this decree was issued, a male child was born to Jochebed, an Israelite woman, and her husband, Amram, of the tribe of Levi. Desperate to save the infant, they put him in a basket and set him afloat among the bulrushes of the Nile. The baby was found by an Egyptian princess while she and her handmaidens were bathing in the river.

The princess called the baby, Moses, a name, which means "drawn out of the water."

As a boy, Moses was given all the advantages enjoyed by members of Egypt's royal family.

Fighting for Freedom

One day Moses, now a prince, was outraged to see an overseer beating an Israelite slave. Moses killed the overseer and fled to the land of Midian in the Sinai desert. There he became a shepherd, living with a Kenite priest named Jethro. Moses married Jethro's daughter, Zipporah, who bore him two sons.

The Burning Bush

In the rugged mountains of Sinai, Moses had an inspiring experience. Through a vision of a burning bush that was not consumed, God told him to go down to Egypt, confront Pharaoh, and lead the slaves to freedom. At first Moses refused, but eventually accepted the responsibility. From that time forward, Moses was a man dedicated to the great task of leading his people to freedom.

Many obstacles were placed in his path by the Pharaoh. Again and again Moses, accompanied by his brother Aaron, stood before Pharaoh and pleaded for the Israelites. Pharaoh, full of power, turned a deaf ear to his pleas.

Ten Plagues

Egypt had to be stricken by ten disastrous plagues before Pharaoh, fearing the wrath of the God whom Moses and his people worshipped, finally consented to release the Israelites and allow them to leave the land. A multitude of about 600,000 men, women and children left Egypt on that memorable night of the Exodus. There was barely time to prepare the food they would need.

The Israelites left so hurriedly that they had no time to bake their bread. They spread the raw unleavened dough on pieces of wood and tied them onto their shoulders. The hot desert sun baked the dough into matzot. This was the origin of

Bust of Merneptah (1235-1227 B.C.E.), son of Rameses II. Some historians believe that he was the Pharaoh of the Exodus.

God sent 10 plagues into the land of Egypt. The first plague turned the waters of the Nile into blood and all the fish in the river died. This drawing from a Hebrew manuscript produced at Barcelona, Spain, in 1320, shows Aaron, brother of Moses, turning the waters of the Nile into blood.

This scene of an overseer beating a slave was found in an Egyptian tomb.

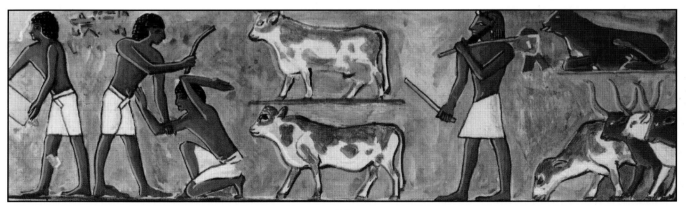

73

This picture of Pharaoh Tutankhamen in his chariot was found in his tomb. The chariot reins are tied around the Pharaoh's waist, freeing his arms and enabling him to shoot his arrows. The Torah describes the pursuit of the Israelites by "the chariot of the king of Egypt."

Miriam and the Israelite women dancing with joy after their liberation from Egypt. This painting is from the Sarajevo Haggadah.

The opening words of the psalm in the *Hallel* prayer which begins, "When Israel left Egypt ..."
This illustrated *Hallel* prayer shows the Children of Israel leaving Egypt. They are led by Moses and are passing through the gate of a medieval town from which the Egyptians are looking down.

the custom of eating unleavened bread (matzot) on Passover, the festival that commemorates the victory won for freedom so many centuries ago.

The Exodus: A March to Freedom
So the great march out of Egypt began, with families gathered together, each with its own tribe, twelve tribes in all. However, Pharaoh suddenly changed his mind and sent charioteers to bring the slaves back. According to the Bible, Moses did not dare lead them by the established route which was dangerously near Egypt's border–forts, where soldiers might have attempted to prevent their escape. Instead, the great throng of people, young and old, carrying their meager belongings, marched slowly eastward to avoid the border posts.

The Sea of Reeds
The march was halted suddenly by an obstacle that seemed to be insurmountable. Silent and disheartened the Israelites stood, the light of hope slowly fading from their eyes as they gazed at the vast expanse of water before them. They had come to the end of dry land, to the shores of the Sea of Reeds (*Yam Suf*), the Suez arm of the Red Sea.

Those who looked back in the direction of their former homes were greeted by a sight that chilled their already sinking hearts.

Bearing down upon them was a column of Egyptian soldiers. With the sea before them and the army of Pharaoh closing in from behind, the Israelites were trapped.

The Miracle
Then, miraculously, a strong east wind arose. It drove back the waters of the sea, making a path of dry land. With joyful hearts, the throng followed Moses to the opposite shore. In fierce pursuit, Pharaoh's soldiers also took the dry path through the Sea of Reeds, but the wind turned and the tide rolled in. Back rushed the waters, engulfing the chariots and drowning the soldiers.

Free at Last
The Bible tells of how the Israelites rejoiced when they found themselves safely across the sea. Moses composed a poem of

74

praise to God. The women danced joyously to the music of their timbrels and sang a song composed by Miriam, Moses' sister.

Ahead of them lay untold dangers, but on this great day there was but one song in the hearts of the Israelites—a song of gratitude for their newly won freedom.

The Long Trek

The Israelites wandered for forty years until they reached Canaan, the Promised Land beyond the river Jordan. In Canaan they began a new life. They built homes and planted vineyards and celebrated their harvest festivals.

Since those days, we begin the celebration of Pesach on the eve of the fifteenth day of Nisan. During the week of the festival (observed for seven days by Reform Jews and Israelis, for eight by others) we eat unleavened bread to remind us of the bread our ancestors baked in haste when they left the land of Pharaoh.

The Exodus from Egypt

Archaeologists, historians, and Bible scholars have always been interested in learning more about the Exodus. They have been concerned with such questions as: Who was the Pharaoh of the Exodus? When did the Exodus take place? What route did the Israelites follow? And so on. They have found the answers to some of these questions.

On the basis of historical and archaeological evidence, most scholars believe that the Exodus took place about 1290 B.C.E. (about 3,300 years ago), and that Rameses II was the Pharaoh of the Exodus. Here are some of the reasons they give:

1. The Bible tells us that the Hebrews lived in Goshen, near the Pharaoh's palace. This is in the Nile Delta in Egypt. Historians have learned that Rameses II built his capital in the Nile Delta.

2. The Bible tells us that the Hebrews built the store-cities of Pithom and Rameses for the Pharaoh. Archaeologists have found these cities. The city of Rameses was originally called Avaris, but in 1300 B.C.E. it was rebuilt by Rameses II and renamed after him.

God punished the Egyptians with a series of plagues. The plagues were not sent to inconvenience or afflict the Egyptians. They were an attack against the religious system of Egypt. Many of the creatures, such as frogs, were sacred and no one was permitted to kill even one.
The Torah in the Book of Exodus says: "The Nile River will swarm with frogs, and they will come into your houses and into your beds! Every home in Egypt will be filled with them...You and your people will be immersed in them."

A page from the Barcelona Haggadah, written in the last half of the 14th century. The text features the Exodus procession, "He brought us out of Egypt with a strong hand and a outstretched arm, and with great terror, and with signs and wonders."

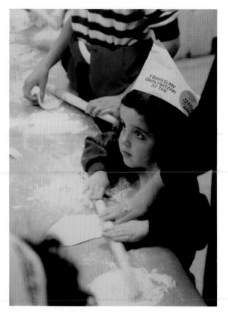

A young matzah baker.

Old European tools for matzah making.

A roller used to put holes in matzot, Bohemia, 19th century.

3. Archaeologists have excavated some of the ancient cities of Canaan. These excavations have shown that in the period several decades after 1290 B.C.E., many of the cities underwent much destruction, apparently from a war. This date is in keeping with the biblical account of the conquest of Canaan by the Children of Israel, which began under the leadership of Joshua after their forty years of wandering in the desert.

A few other scholars, however, think that Merneptah, the son of Rameses II, was the Pharaoh of the Exodus.

Preparing for Passover

Preparations for the holiday begin in every home many weeks before Pesach. Everything in the house is scrubbed and polished. Carpets are cleaned, floors are scrubbed, fresh curtains are hung. Just before Passover, year-round kitchen utensils are put away, to be replaced by those specially reserved for the holiday.

Then comes the matzah, enough to last for the entire festival period. Matzah is the only kind of bread permitted in a Jewish home on Passover.

Matzah Designs

In the time of the Talmud, the perforated matzot were quite artistic. In the house of Rabbi Gamaliel, the little holes in the matzot shaped figures: animals, flowers, and such. The perforating was done with a tool that looked like a comb. In later years, the perforating tool was a wheel; it had sharp teeth and a handle. The perforator would run the wheel through the matzot at right angles in rows about one inch apart.

In olden times, matzot were made in the home as well as by professional bakers. During the Middle Ages, there were community ovens. The matzot were usually made in a round shape, but sometimes they were triangular.

Ma'ot Chittim

A fund known as *Ma'ot Chittim* ("wheat money") was set up in every community. This was to provide Passover provisions for the poor and the needy. In our day, we can participate in the mitzvah of *tzedakah* by contributing to the *Ma'ot Chittim* fund.

A Special Matzah

A special kind of matzah is called *shemurah matzah* ("guarded matzah"). Many Orthodox Jews use it, particularly on the two Seder nights. *Shemurah matzah* is made from wheat that is watched during harvesting, milling, and baking. The wheat is carefully protected against leavening, either by rain swelling the grain or dampening the flour, or by too much kneading and slow baking.

All set for the Seder.

Around 1875, matzah-baking machinery was invented in England. Soon after, it was introduced in America. Although some matzot are still made by hand, most Passover matzot today are made by machine. Actually, matzot are used all year round. On Passover, however, only matzot which are prepared for the holiday may be eaten. The only day one may not eat matzot is the day before Pesach; this is to ensure that they are eaten with greater enjoyment during the Seder.

Selling the *Chametz*

Since traditionally there must not be any *chametz* or leavened bread in Jewish homes on Passover, Orthodox Jews perform a ceremony known as *mechirat chametz* several days before the holiday. A bill of sale is written out, and all the *chametz* is "sold" to a non-Jew for the duration of Passover. This transaction is usually handled as a collective sale by the rabbi of the congregation, but in order for it to be valid, the members must personally ask the rabbi to be their agent. The bill of sale is prepared with the understanding that the *chametz* will be returned immediately after the holiday.

Baking *shemurah* matzot

The Search for *Chametz*

The last cleansing ceremony, *bedikat chametz*, takes place on the night before the first Seder night arrives. To symbolize the change from the old to the new, from leavened to the unleavened bread, a family member has taken bits of bread and put them on window sills and shelves.

Now, someone else, takes a quill and a wooden spoon, and with the help of children, looks for *chametz*.

Naturally, someone finds the bits of bread, for this is a symbolic search. The bread is brushed onto the wooden spoon. When all the bread crumbs are found, they are wrapped,

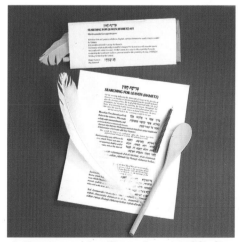

A Passover *bedikat chametz* kit. It contains the prayers, a spoon, a feather, a candle, and a paper bag, in which to burn the *chametz*.

A matzah cover with three matzot.

The Seder leader gets ready to break the middle matzah and prepare the afikomen.

A very popular complete Passover Haggadah.

together with the spoon, in a piece of cloth and put away until morning. Then they are burned, together with any bread left at breakfast.

After ten in the morning on the day before Passover (*erev* Pesach) no *chametz* may be eaten. Neither are matzot eaten that day, so that the real Pesach matzot will taste fresh and new when they are eaten at the Seder.

Everything has been taken care of. The holiday is about to be ushered in. For eight days, beginning at sundown on the fourteenth day of the month of Nisan, the family celebrates the festival of Pesach. The first two and the last two days are traditionally observed as full holidays by Orthodox and Conservative Jews; the intervening four days (*Chol Ha-Mo'ed*) are semi–holidays.

The *Seder*

On the first *Seder* night the table is decked in gleaming white, the candles cast a warm, flickering glow, and the proud wine cups stand ready to play their part in the annual drama of the Pesach *Seder*. The *Seder* table helps to celebrate Passover properly.

The Hebrew word *Seder* means "order" or "arrangement"; and the arrangement of foods at the *Seder* tells of the many-sided meaning of Passover, the great festival that marks the birth of a free people thousands of years ago and still has an important message for every one of us.

What items can be found on the *Seder* table?

Candles

As on every Sabbath and festival, candles grace the table. The blessing over the candles gives warmth to their light as they cast a holiday glow over the *Seder* and those who have come to celebrate Passover.

The Haggadah

"You shall tell it to your child," says the Torah. The Haggadah (from the Hebrew *hagged*, "to tell") recounts the Passover story and adds thanksgiving prayers and children's songs. It makes Pesach a holiday the whole family looks forward to.

Four Cups of Wine

Everyone at the Seder table drinks four cups of wine, in the order mentioned in the Haggadah. There are four cups because in the Torah, God's promise to free the Israelites from slavery is repeated four times.

The Cup of Elijah

At the Seder, each person drinks four cups of wine. But a fifth cup of wine is also poured. Known as the *Kos Eliyahu*, it honors the prophet Elijah. The Bible tells us that Elijah did many wonderful and miraculous deeds. There are many legends about Elijah and the wonderful things he could do. According to one of the legends, Elijah will come back to earth. When he does, it will be the beginning of a golden age. The whole world will be at peace and we will all love one another and be good to one another.

The fifth cup of wine at the Seder is for Elijah. It symbolizes our hope that Elijah will soon come and that everyone in the world will soon learn to live in peace.

The Matzah Cover

In the center of the table is a decorated cloth with three pockets in which we place three whole matzot. Each of the matzot represents one of the three classes of ancient Israelites: priests (*kohanim*), levites (*levi'im*), and lay people (*yisraelim*).

Half of the middle matzah will be used as the *afikomen*, or dessert. The child who hides the *afikomen* will receive a gift for returning it. The *Seder* cannot be completed until the *afikomen* is returned.

Many families now add a fourth matzah which is called the Matzah of Hope. This fourth matzah helps us to remember that there are still Jews who live in countries where they cannot celebrate Passover in freedom.

Karah

Next to the matzah cover is the *Karah*, or *Seder*plate. On it are *maror* (bitter herbs), a shankbone, *charoset* (a mixture of apples, nuts, and wine), a roasted egg, and *karpas* (a green vegetable, such as parsley or celery). Each of these stands for something important.

The blessing over the wine from the Barcelona Haggadah. This illuminated Haggadah was written in the 14th century and is one of the most beautiful illuminated Haggadot. It is a valuable source of information on Jewish life in medieval Spain.

A specially engraved silver Cup of Elijah.

This silver Passover plate (Austria, 1807), has three compartments for the three matzot. Decorations: figures of Moses, Aaron, and Miriam, and three groups of men, carrying small dishes for symbolic Seder foods.

Roasted Egg

The egg symbolizes the festival offering sacrificed on Pesach in the Temple of Jerusalem. The egg is used in the Seder because it is a Jewish symbol of mourning, in this case for the destruction of our ancient Temple where the sacrifices were brought.

Maror

The bitter herbs (usually horseradish) is for the bitterness of slavery. It was bitter in Egypt in those days; it is no less bitter for people wherever there is tyranny.

Karpas

Greens (lettuce, parsley, or celery) symbolize the poor nourishment the Israelites had while in Egyptian slavery. The dipping of *karpas* into saltwater is to remind us of the salty tears they wept under Egypt's cruel yoke.

Matzah

After the ten plagues, the Israelites, pressed by the Egyptians to leave, snatched up their bread dough even though it was unleavened and had not yet risen. This is memorialized by the unleavened matzah. There are three special matzot at the *Seder*. Half of the middle matzah will be used as the *afikomen*, or dessert. For children who find the *afikomen*, there usually is a present for returning it upon request.

Shankbone

This roasted bone is a symbol of the Pesach lamb sacrificed at the Temple of our ancestors.

Charoset

Although this mixture of apples, nuts, cinnamon, and wine symbolizes the mortar made by our ancestors under the lash of Egyptian taskmasters, it tastes delicious. Why? Because its sweetness, it is said, is a symbol of God's kindness which made even slavery bearable.

The Haggadah

The Haggadah has already been mentioned, but it deserves closer attention, for it plays a central role at the Seder.

The frontispiece to the van Geldern Haggadah, showing a family Seder in an 18th–century Jewish home in Bavaria. Notice the open door for the entrance of Elijah the prophet. This painting was by a Moravian artist, 1717.

Why is this night different?

A ceramic Seder dish, Hungary, 19th century. The center shows a family at the Seder table. Around the border are two blessings which are recited during the Seder. The bottom of the plate has the inscription *Ha Lachma Anya,* "let all who are hungry come and eat."

The Haggadah is a kind of guidebook for the celebration of Pesach. It has directions on how to conduct the Seder, explanations of the Pesach symbols, selections from Psalms (113–118), interesting stories, children's folk songs, riddles, and prayers. Most important of all it tells the story of why we celebrate Passover.

Ancient Haggadah manuscript. Found in the Cairo Genizah.

The Haggadah has a long history. It is more than 2,000 years old. Even before it was written down, the leader of the family would tell the story of Pesach at the Seder table. He was following the commandment in the Bible, "You shall tell your child in that day, saying: 'It is because of that which the Lord did for me when I came forth out of Egypt.' The very term Haggadah, as we have seen, comes from the Hebrew word *hagged*, which means "to tell."

As time went by, more parts were added to the Haggadah, even though it was still not written down: prayers, hymns, selections from the Mishnah. By the Middle Ages so much had been added that it was necessary to put the Haggadah in writing. But even then the Haggadah was not a separate book, but a part of the prayerbook. Soon after the Middle Ages the Haggadah became a book in its own right.

This beautifully illuminated Haggadah has numerous enriched commentaries. It is published by the Rabbinical Assembly (Conservative).

What the Haggadah Tells

It is in the Haggadah that we learn how the sacrificial lamb (*pesach*), unleavened bread (*matzah*), and bitter herbs (*maror*) were used in ancient times. It includes the beautiful thanksgiving psalms of *Hallel*, and ends with the songs of *Adir Hu* and *Chad Gadya*.

One of the most stirring parts of the Haggadah is recited at the beginning of the Seder, beginning with *Ha-Lachma Anya*, "This is the bread of affliction." The leader of the Seder rises, lifts the plate of matzah in his hands, and recites, *This is the bread of affliction which our ancestors ate in the land of Egypt. Let all who are hungry come and eat. Let all who are in need come and celebrate Pesach with us. Now we are here. Next year may we be in the Land of Israel. Now we are slaves. Next year may we be free people.*

Ha-Lachma Anya is one of the oldest parts of the Haggadah. It is written in Aramaic, a language spoken by our ancestors in Israel almost 2,000 years ago. It was once customary for the head of the house to step out into the street and

This artistically illustrated Haggadah is published by the Central Conference of American Rabbis (Reform).

The Four Questions by the artist Arthur Szyk. It took seven years of hard work to complete his illuminated Haggadah. It was published in an edition of 250 signed and numbered copies. The Haggadah was edited by the historian Cecil Roth.

Israeli stamp picturing the Exodus from Egypt. Notice the Children of Israel and the pursuing Egyptians. The caption from Exodus reads: "Israel walked on dry land through the sea."

recite *Ha Lachma Anya*, so as to invite any poor people to the Seder. Today the invitation to the poor is recited inside the home, but the spirit of hospitality remains the same.

The Four Questions

Following Ha-Lachma Anya, the youngest child recites the Four Questions:

Why is this night different from all other nights?
1. On all other nights, we eat either leavened or unleavened bread. Why on this night do we eat only unleavened bread?
2. On all other nights, we eat all kinds of vegetables and herbs. Why on this night do we eat only bitter herbs?
3. On all other nights, we do not dip even once. Why on this night do we dip twice?
4. On all other nights, we eat sitting upright or reclining. Why on this night do we all recline?

The Four Children

Then comes the long story of the Exodus from Egypt, followed by descriptions of the four different kinds of children a family might have: wise, wicked, simple, and one who asks no questions.

The wise child eagerly asks about Pesach and why it is celebrated, and is given a full explanation.

The wicked child scoffs at Pesach, and would have been unworthy of being saved in the time of the Exodus from Egypt.

The simple child asks a simple question and gets a simple answer.

The fourth child asks nothing but the parents volunteer the information. This child, too, is told why we celebrate Pesach.

The Haggadah and Art

The Haggadah has played an important part in the development of Jewish art. In Haggadot, artists found many subjects they could illustrate: the four sons, the ten plagues, Jacob's ladder, the crossing of the Red Sea, the matriarchs and patriarchs, the baking of matzah, and many other things. The artists of the Haggadah all expressed themselves in their own way.

The Amsterdam Haggadah

In the seventeenth century, Amsterdam became a center of Jewish printing. In 1695, the famous Amsterdam Haggadah appeared "in the house and to the order" of Moses Wesel. This Haggadah was illustrated with copper engravings. On the title page are the words: "Formerly the pictures used to be cut in wood. That was not so beautiful. Now that they are engraved in copper, everyone will realize the difference, which is like that between light and dark." In a later Amsterdam Haggadah more pictures were added, borrowed from a woodcut Haggadah which had once appeared in Venice.

The sages of Bene–Berak discussing the Passover Seder. This Haggadah was illuminated by Joseph Leipnik in Moravia, 1712.

The Darmstadt Haggadah

Even rarer than the few surviving early printed Haggadot are the manuscript Haggadot from a still earlier era before the invention of printing. These handwritten and painstakingly illustrated Seder guides, each of them a work of art, are one-of-a-kind items. Outstanding among them is the world-famous Darmstadt Haggadah.

The Darmstadt Haggadah was written on parchment in the fourteenth century by Israel ben Meir of Heidelberg. Israel only did the lettering. One artist then painted in large gold-and-blue initials and decorated the borders; a second artist drew scenes of Jewish life, especially Seder scenes. Mingled among the Seder scenes are illustrations of wildlife. Birds, bears, lions, and other animals abound on the pages.

Many Heidelberg Jews had come from France. In the Haggadah, they wear the lavish holiday dress of prosperous French citizens. The beautiful Darmstadt Haggadah belonged for centuries to German Jewish families. In 1780, a Baron Hopsch bought it for his collection. It then made its way into the library of Darmstadt, Germany where it has remained to this day.

The *Seder* Is Ended

The *Seder* is ended, the Haggadot are closed. The questions have been answered and the story has been told.

A page from the Darmstadt Haggadah. It reads *Ha Lachma Anya,* "this is the bread of affliction."

The Samaritan Passover

The Samaritans were once a fairly sizable religious community. Today only about 600 people still accept the Samaritan

The Torah of the Samaritans is housed in the synagogue in Nablus. It is written in ancient Hebrew and is extremely old.

Samaritans, dressed in white robes, celebrate Passover atop Mount Gerezim, the site of their ancient capital.

An page from the Rylands Spanish Haggadah. The illuminations are for the poem Dayenu.

faith. Half of them live in the town of Nablus, near Mount Gerizim. The other half live in Holon, near Tel Aviv.

In ancient times the Samaritans were often in conflict with the Jews. They acknowledge Moses as a prophet and claim to be descended from Ephraim and Manasseh, the two sons of Joseph. They accept the Torah and the book of Joshua as holy, but not the rest of the Bible.

Passover is the Samaritans' most important holiday. It is celebrated on top of Mount Gerizim. The Passover feast is celebrated just as it was thousands of years ago. A lamb is sacrificed and matzot are baked the ancient way.

Faraway Customs

Customs vary, but the Seder is observed wherever there are Jews, and the Haggadah is the guidebook.

The Caucasian Jews of southern Russia have an interesting ritual. They greet the Passover seated on the earth, dressed in their best clothes, with a spear close at hand. This is their way of portraying the dangers that beset the Israelites in the hurried Exodus from Egypt.

And in the eastern provinces of Portugal, near the Spanish border, in several communities descended from the Marranos, there is a custom that shows what life was like in the days of the Inquisition. Since the entire family would have been killed if the Inquisition's police had found a single matzah in their homes, these people do not have a Seder at home. Instead they go to the countryside for a festive outing. It may look like a picnic to outsiders, but the Marrano participants make sure to say a special prayer in memory of the Seder service their ancestors enjoyed. After the festive meal, which has been eaten very slowly, to symbolize that we are now a free people and no longer slaves who can be forced to hurry, traditional songs are sung by the whole family.

The family sings: *"Who knows one? I know one! One is our God in heaven and on earth. . . . Who knows two? I know two,"* and so on, up to thirteen, which is the number of the qualities of God.

The Little Kid

Then comes the final song for which the children have been waiting all evening. It is about a little goat that father bought for two coins. The song seems to have an endless number of verses, but at last it comes to a stop with:

Then came God
Who smote the Angel of Death,
Who slew the slaughterer,
Who killed the ox,
Who drank the water,
That quenched the fire,
That burned the stick,
That beat the cat,
That ate the little goat
That father bought with two coins.

Ani Ma'amin

In some homes a new ceremony has been introduced before the door is opened for the prophet Elijah. During the ceremony we remember the six million Jews who were murdered by the Nazis and the heroes of the ghetto revolts.

We sing the song *Ani Ma'amin*. This song of hope was sung by the martyrs in the concentration camps.

The words were written in accordance with the teachings of the famous Jewish philosopher Moses Maimonides.

I believe
I believe, I believe
with all my faith, with all my faith
that the Messiah will come,
that the Messiah will come
I believe.

That is the story of Pesach, a heroic revolt against oppression and glorious freedom from slavery. Throughout the ages, Passover has symbolized freedom: whether escape from Egypt, rescue from the Crusaders of the Middle Ages, or liberation from the Nazis.

A page from a Passover Haggadah written and illuminated in Hamburg, Germany in 1740. It illustrates the labors of the Israelites in Egypt. The Israelites are pictured as contemporary Jews working in a German town.

A Yemenite family at the Seder. Adults and children are dressed in costume and the table is set for the Seder.

THE TEN PLAGUES

Pharaoh refused to let the Israelites leave Egypt, so God punished Egypt with ten plagues. After the tenth plague Pharaoh permitted the Israelites to leave.

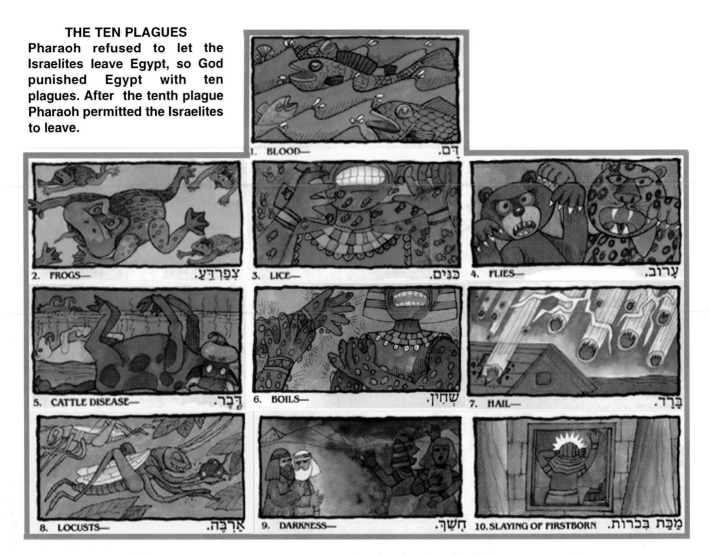

1. BLOOD— דָּם.
2. FROGS— צְפַרְדֵּעַ.
3. LICE— כִּנִּים.
4. FLIES— עָרוֹב.
5. CATTLE DISEASE— דֶּבֶר.
6. BOILS— שְׁחִין.
7. HAIL— בָּרָד.
8. LOCUSTS— אַרְבֶּה.
9. DARKNESS— חֹשֶׁךְ.
10. SLAYING OF FIRSTBORN— מַכַּת בְּכֹרוֹת.

Just as we overcame our enemies in the land of Egypt, so will the Jewish people ever vanquish its oppressors. That is the message of Passover which must forever be kept alive in our hearts.

Yom Ha-Shoah

Blessed is the match that is consumed
in kindling flame. Blessed is the flame that burns
in the secret fastness of the heart.
Blessed is the heart with strength to stop
its beating for honor's sake.
Blessed is the match that is consumed
in kindling flame.

NISAN						ניסן
Sun.	Mon.	Tues.	Wed.	Thur.	Fri.	Sat.
				1	2	3
4	5	6	7	8	9	10
11	12	13	14	15	16	17
18	19	20	21	22	23	24
25	26	27	28	29	30	

The tragedy of Yom Ha-Shoah is commemorated on the 27th day of Nisan.

These words are a farewell message to the world. They were written by a young woman named Hannah Senesh, who parachuted into Hungary to help rescue Jews from the death camps. Caught by the Nazis, Hannah Senesh was killed in 1944 at the age of twenty-three.

Her poem symbolizes the meaning and significance of Yom Ha-Shoah, the Day of Remembrance of the Six Million, which we commemorate each year on the twenty-seventh day of the month of Nisan.

On Yom Ha-Shoah we think of the bravery of six million men, women, and children—-the flower of European Jewry—-whose lives were viciously snuffed out by the cruelty of the Nazis while an unfeeling world looked on in silence. As we ponder what might have been, we think, too, of a statement made over 700 years ago by Moses Maimonides, great Jewish philosopher of the Middle Ages, who said:

If a Jew is murdered for no other reason except that he is a Jew, and, had he not been a Jew, he would have remained alive; then it may truly be said that he sacrificed his life al kiddush ha-Shem, for the holiness of God.

Adolf Hitler

Racist attitudes in Germany developed from the idea that the Aryan-Nordic race was superior. The Nazis turned it into a reality which was applied to society.

The Nazi death camp of Auschwitz. Thousands of Jews were gassed, shot, and burned to death there.

The Yad Vashem Memorial: Ohel Yizkor–Hall of Remembrance. The walls are built of large, unhewn black lava rocks. On the mosaic floor are inscribed the names of the 21 largest concentration camps, and near the wall in the west burns a light.

SS Colonel Adolf Otto Eichmann was chief of operations in the scheme to exterminate all of European Jewry. At the end of the war, he escaped to Argentina, but in 1960 was kidnapped by the Israelis. Eichmann was tried before the Jerusalem District Court and was sentenced to death by hanging. Eichmann was the only criminal ever put to death in Israel. His body was cremated and his ashes were scattered over the Mediterranean.

Maimonides spoke with a prophet's vision, as if he were foreseeing and lamenting the terrible Holocaust of mass murder that will forever be a blot on the record of human history no matter how many centuries go by.

How can one tell the story of the Holocaust? Only by remembering incidents, recalling heroism, and building memorials, in stone, in wood, in concrete, and in words.

It is fitting that the State of Israel, itself born out of the fire of the Holocaust, should be the home of the most important memorial of all–Yad Vashem.

The Shrine in Jerusalem

On the crown of Mount Herzl lies buried the man who dreamed of a Jewish state and founded modern Zionism, Theodor Herzl. Nearby is the Hill of Remembrance, *Har Ha-Zikaron*, dedicated to the six million Jews killed by the Nazis. Here are the buildings put up by Yad Vashem (literally, "hand and name"; figuratively, "monument and memorial").

The memorial is a stark, low-slung building of rough concrete. The heavy iron doors, designed by David Palombo and suggesting barbed wire and iron splinters, lead into a bare chamber in which a *ner tamid* casts its flickering light on the names of Nazi death camps set in the mosaic floor.

Nearby is a small exhibit building and lecture hall, and a synagogue dedicated to the memory of the thousands of European synagogues destroyed during the Holocaust. In the exhibit area, photos of the faces of Jewish victims form part of the permanent display. Concentration camp clothing and photos of bunks behind barbed wire are chilling reminders of the Germans' cruelty. On the walls are a variety of "Jew-badges" created by the Nazis.

The well-stocked research library is unlike any other in the world. In it are gathered letters, books, and documents relating to the Holocaust, as well as individual records of the dead who have been given "memorial citizenship" in Israel. This library provided much of the detailed evidence for the trial of Adolf Eichmann, the Nazi war criminal captured in Argentina by Israeli agents.

Each year, as Yom Ha-Shoah (Remembrance Day) draws near, it is fitting to think of Yad Vashem and all that it stands for, and to draw such comfort as we can from the knowledge that this is a place of pilgrimage which Jews from all over the world will visit for generations to come.

The Warsaw Ghetto Uprising

No single event more perfectly captures the meaning of Yom Ha-Shoah, however, than the uprising in the Warsaw Ghetto. By early 1943 all but some 40,000 Jews in the Warsaw Ghetto had been swallowed by the Nazi death camps. On April 19, the final Nazi attack began. Men and women, old and young, fought with fantastic heroism despite impossible odds. The ghetto was destroyed, but the memory of the Jewish heroes endures.

The story of the Warsaw Ghetto can be briefly told, but it needs a slower, more detailed description, for human lives deserve a thoughtful memorial.

The Memorial

There is a memorial. In the form of a lonely monument standing in Warsaw, Poland, and it marks the spot where the heroes of the Warsaw Ghetto fought and died.

This memorial in granite by sculptor Nathan Rappaport portrays the wall of a secret hideout where a group of ghetto fighters fulfilled the vow of the underground movement in its last appeal to the outside world:

We may all perish, but we will not surrender. This is a fight for your dignity as well as ours. . . . We will avenge ourselves for the crimes of Treblinka, Maidanek, and the other death camps.

The Nazis in Warsaw

When the Nazis marched into Warsaw in October, 1939, they took a count and found 360,000 Jews in the city. They then erected an eight-foot wall around the Jewish section and began to issue decrees:

Jews coming into Warsaw must live within the walled area.

All Jews in Warsaw must move into the ghetto.

All Jews in Warsaw are to be resettled in the East, beginning on July 2, 1942, 11 A.M.

Mordecai Anielewicz helped organize the revolt against the Nazis in the Warsaw Ghetto. He died fighting the Germans. This statue in memory of Mordecai Anielewicz is at Kibbutz Yad Mordecai in Israel. The water tower was destroyed by Egyptian shells during the War of Independence, in 1948.

The Warsaw Ghetto aflame. Thousands of Jews burned to death rather than surrender to the Nazis.

This famous photograph, taken from German archives, shows Nazi soldiers rounding up "the enemy" in the Warsaw Ghetto. The last survivors, almost unarmed, held off an armored Nazi division for many days in the heroic Battle of the Warsaw Ghetto.

Fifty Jewish combat groups—a thousand men and women armed with 80 rifles, three light machine guns, a few hundred revolvers, and 1,000 hand grenades - put up a desperate fight against 2,000 members of the occupying forces under SS General Stroop, who had been ordered to destroy the Warsaw Ghetto.

Jewish inmates in a concentration camp barracks.

Each day hundreds of people in the Warsaw Ghetto died of hunger and disease. Death was so common that people hardly paid any attention to the dead bodies.

Memorial to the Warsaw Ghetto Uprising at Yad Vashem.

Within two years only 40,000 Jews were left in Warsaw. The survivors formed the Jewish Fighters Organization, led by twenty-three-year-old Mordecai Anielewicz. Arms were smuggled in and training sessions were held at night.

The first real test came on January 18, 1943. Nazi troops marched into the ghetto to round up a batch of Jews for deportation. They were met by a hail of bullets and by bombs hurled by Jewish fighters disguised in German uniforms. The Nazis retreated.

The Final Attack

On April 19, the final attack began. Nazi units marched in. The ghetto was strangely silent. Suddenly a bomb fell on the leading tank. It had been thrown by a girl from a high balcony and it signaled the counterattack. Blue-and-white flags appeared on roofs. Posters on shattered walls declared: "We will fight to the last drop of blood!"

The Nazis returned in greater numbers. They threw fire-bombs, turning whole blocks into smoking ruins. They shut off the water supply. Observation planes directed the heavy artillery.

The Jews had only one possible goal left—to make the German victory as shameful as possible. The enemy was awaited in every doorway. Each defender took several Nazis with him when he died.

On May 31, the Polish Underground Headquarters received a message from Warsaw. The Battle of the Warsaw Ghetto was over.

The Heroes of the Ghetto

The 500,000 Jews who had originally been jammed into the Warsaw Ghetto had dwindled to 40,000 when the uprising began. When the ghetto was finally reduced to smoking rubble, only 80 Jewish fighters managed to flee via the sewers.

The night of April 19 was also the beginning of Passover. So the heroism of the Warsaw Ghetto has become forever bound with the historic meaning of the festival of freedom. And, in the words of the Passover Haggadah, even though enemies "arise in every generation to destroy us, the Lord rescues us from their hands."

The Heroine

The heroism that spells Yom Ha-Shoah is made up of the deeds of individuals. None was a brighter spirit and a more selfless soul than Hannah Senesh, whose deathless message graces the opening of this chapter. Listen to her story.

In the winter of 1945, an empty vessel was found drifting off the coast of Palestine. The passengers had vanished. "Illegal" immigrants, they had been smuggled under cover of night into the Holy Land. A few days later, a flag fluttered in the sand near the beached vessel. On the flag were these words: "The name of this ship is *Hannah Senesh*."

The name was fresh in the minds of all who had known her, for Hannah had been gone but a short time.

She was born on July 7, 1921, to a wealthy, cultured, and assimilated Jewish family in Hungary. At the age of nineteen she went to Palestine to start life anew. In the agricultural school at Nahalal she trained herself for a life on the soil. But within her there burned an impatience, a sense of duty to do more important work.

Hannah Volunteers

Hannah confided to her diary: "I feel that I have a mission. I don't know what my mission is, but I know that I have a responsibility to others."

Then Hannah heard that volunteers were being sought to parachute behind enemy lines in Europe. She knew at once that this was what she had been waiting for. On March 10, 1944, she left Palestine.

Having parachuted into Yugoslavia, Hannah Senesh was assigned by the underground to live with the guerrilla partisans and to perform sabotage for the British as well as rescue work for the Jews. Hannah did her job well, but she was anxious to cross into Hungary to rescue prisoners and organize Jewish resistance. Besides, her mother still lived in the city of Budapest. On June 9, 1944, with the aid of Yugoslav partisans, she became the first to cross the border into Hungary.

Captured by the Nazis

There she fought with the partisans until she was captured by the Nazis. She was thrown into prison, where her mother came to see her. By bribing the guards, Hannah managed to carry on

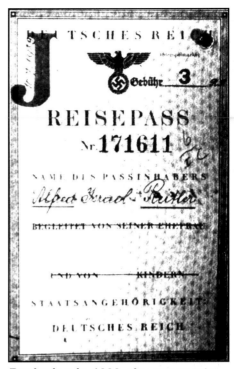

Beginning in 1939, the passports of all German Jews were marked with the letter "J." Also, the name "Israel" was added to the names of all Jewish males, and "Sarah" to all Jewish females.

The passport of Hannah Senesh.

Hannah Senesh wrote this short letter before she parachuted into Yugoslavia.

Dr. Janusz Korczak, a physician, writer, and educator, headed a children's orphanage in the Warsaw Ghetto. On August 12, 1942, he accompanied the children to the gas chambers, although he could have escaped and saved his life.

her rescue work even while behind bars. She made contact with friends on the outside and relayed information to fellow prisoners.

On July 11, 1944, Hannah was taken from her prison cell. No one was at her side to ease her pain. She refused to have her eyes bound, but stood straight and unmoving. A pistol barked. The young girl, who had left freedom to fight for it, was dead.

In March, 1950, her body was brought to Israel on the S.S. *Hannah Senesh* of the Israeli navy and returned to Jerusalem.

The Children of the Camp

And what of the children? They too have left us a heritage to bear in mind on Yom Ha-Shoah. They studied in classrooms in the Warsaw Ghetto, they sold homemade cigarettes for scraps of food, they pleaded for a life that was not destined to be theirs, and they wrote poetry and drew pictures.

They left us a whole collection of verses and sketches in the Theresienstadt concentration camp. The drawings and the words are all that remain of the youngsters who passed through Theresienstadt between 1942 and 1944, and whose ashes have mingled with the dust of ages.

There were 15,000, and 100 came back. But their drawings and poems ended up in the State Jewish Museum in Prague, Czech Republic. They were collected in a book entitled (after one of the poems) *I Never Saw Another Butterfly*.

Here is a sample, written by a boy who was born on January 7, 1931, in Prague who was deported to Theresienstadt and died in Auschwitz. The poem is called "A Butterfly."

The last, the very last,
So richly, brightly, dazzlingly yellow.
Perhaps if the sun's tears would sing
against a white stone . . .
Such, such a yellow
Is carried lightly 'way up high.
It went away, I'm sure, because it wished
to kiss the world goodbye.
For seven weeks I've lived in here,

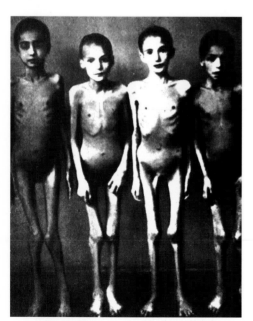

Josef Mengele was physician of the Auschwitz camp, where he conducted cruel medical experiments on Jewish inmates. After the war, Mengele was traced to Argentina, but he escaped. These are some of Mengele's victims.

Penned up inside this ghetto
But I have found my people here.
The dandelions call to me
And the white chestnut candles in the court.
Only I never saw another butterfly.
The butterfly was the last one.
Butterflies don't live in here,
in the ghetto.

Pavel Friedmann, June 4, 1942

Despite the horrors of the extermination camp, actors, artists, poets, and writer tried to create an imaginary normal life. The talented artist Carol Deutsch, painted colorful, happy scenes for the children. The above is one of his mystical paintings. His life and those of the other six million make clear that each shortened life was a tiny world filled with great human potential.

Let the World Remember

And then there are the monuments aside from Yad Vashem in Jerusalem and the Warsaw Ghetto memorial. They remind us of an old Jewish custom: when building a home, one leaves a tiny part unfinished. Another tradition is to have a black square on the white wall of the living room. These customs are said to be *zecher le-churban*, "in memory of the destruction," dramatic reminders of destruction of the First and Second Temples in Jerusalem (586 B.C.E. and 70 C.E.) and of other sad events in Jewish history.

The great tragedy that befell our people in the twentieth century, the Holocaust, is memorialized differently and in public places. Throughout the world there is a growing number of memorials to the Jewish martyrs who fell during the Nazi era. There are already several hundred of these, many in remote corners of Eastern Europe where no Jews live anymore, off the beaten track of tourists in small towns and villages of Poland, Lithuania, Latvia, Russia, Czechoslovakia, the former Yugoslavia, Germany, and Austria.

A *Ner Tamid* in Paris

First and foremost is the Memorial to the Unknown Jewish Martyr in Paris. This impressive and moving memorial is located in the city's old Jewish quarter, known as the Pletzel. The memorial is a four-story building in a large paved court, with granite walls along two sides. The front of the building is a black stone wall, bearing inscriptions in Hebrew and French.

A huge bronze cylinder in the center of the courtyard is shaped to resemble an urn. It bears the names of the death camps and the Warsaw Ghetto. Two flights down lead to the Hall of Remembrance, where six chests built into the walls,

A survivor mourns her family. Her yellow star, which Jews were forced to wear, lists her years of concentration camp life.

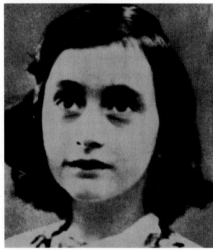

Remonstrantsche Gemeente
te 's-Gravenhage

In het doopregister is ingeschreven:

Moritz Frankenhuis, geb. 24 Februari 1894 te

Burgsteinfurt i/Westph.

zoon
dochter van: Karel Frankenhuis, geb. 12 Maart 1862

te Oldenzaal   en

Julia Frankenhuis-Frankenhuis, geb. 11 October 1865
                              te Haaksbergen

Gedoopt: 17 September 1939.

's-Gravenhage, 17 September 1939.

Het Bestuur
der Remonstrantsche Gemeente.

The Dutch Church issued baptismal certificates to Jews. Many Jews were saved because of these certificates.

Anne Frank, the author of the single most compelling personal account of the Holocaust.

contain books in which are inscribed the names of thousands of martyrs. The Unknown Martyr's tomb, shaped like a *Magen David*, with an Eternal Light above it, bears a text from the Bible:

See if there is any pain like my pain . . .
the youth and the old man, my maidens and young men,
are fallen by the sword.
Lamentations 1:12, 2:21

An Immortal Diary

The Anne Frank House is a modest building alongside a canal on a spotless street in spotless Amsterdam.

Anne's story must be told again and again, so that every generation may learn about this teenage heroine who hid with family and friends in Amsterdam. In 1942, Anne received a diary for her thirteenth birthday and began to record entries faithfully. In August, 1944, the Gestapo raided the hideaway. All the occupants were sent to concentration camps; only Anne's father returned. In March, 1945, Anne died in Bergen-Belsen of malnutrition.

The Anne Frank House

Anne Frank left a priceless legacy, her diary. But there is another memorial which reminds people daily of the valor of this child and what she symbolizes. That is the Anne Frank House, the very building where the Franks hid in the attic where Anne wrote her immortal diary.

Rebuilt with gifts from people in many countries, the Anne Frank House, at 263 Prinsengracht, is kept up by royalties from the diary and the play based on it. The two adjoining houses have been converted into the International Youth Center of the Anne Frank Foundation.

Visitors to the Anne Frank House can see the swinging bookcase that covered the entrance to the Annex where the Franks took refuge, and the bulletin board on which Anne pinned photos of movie stars. Here, too, is the original diary which Anne left to the world. The diary was found on the floor amid a pile of old books, magazines, and newspapers when Anne's father returned to Amsterdam after the war.

The Anne Frank house in Amsterdam is now a museum.

The dream of this young martyr is expressed in her classic diary: "I want to go on living," she wrote, "after my death."

Some other places where memorials may be seen are:

Philadelphia, with a five-ton bronze sculpture at Benjamin Franklin Parkway and 16th Street.

Rotterdam, with its famous Dock Worker statue.

Belgrade, with huge symbolic stone wings in the Jewish cemetery on Cardak Hill.

Prague, with walls around the Torah Ark in the Pinkas Synagogue engraved with names of 77,297 Jewish victims of the Nazis, their dates of birth and death.

Bergen-Belsen, with a marker indicating the site where 30,000 Jews died.

New Jersey's, Temple Beth Shalom in Livingston has created a garden and study center. The garden contains a railroad track, a sculpture of a child, and a Wall of Remembrance, enshrining victims of the Holocaust related to congregational members.

Much time has passed since the last Nazi murder. The Holocaust still challenges us. How can we understand it without getting lost in a quicksand of facts without falling victim to hatred and disillusion?

Perhaps we can pluck the answer out of the law by which the Knesset (Parliament) of Israel established Yom Ha-Shoah:

The twenty–seventh day of Nisan shall be the Day of Remembrance of the Holocaust and of Heroism. This day shall be dedicated annually to recall the catastrophe inflicted by the Nazis upon the Jewish people, and to remember the deeds of resistance and heroism of those days.

Resistance and heroism, and a sense of belonging to the long chain of history that links the generations of our people. On the twenty-seventh day of Nisan, our martyrs and brave spirits–from the Maccabees to Hannah Senesh–come to tell us that they belong to us and we to them, and that *am Yisrael chai*, "the Jewish people is eternal."

The Righteous Gentiles

The Egyptian princess found a child floating in a watertight basket. She knew that it was one of the Hebrew babies that her

In an effort at conciliation between Catholics and Jews, Pope Paul II paid a historic visit to the extermination camp at Auschwitz. He prayed for forgiveness for the deeds of the past.

Wedding rings confiscated by the Nazis. Each ring represents a martyred Jewish soul.

Avenue of the Righteous in the Yad Vashem Memorial is lined with trees planted in honor of individual Gentiles who helped Jews during the Nazi regime.

Raoul Wallenberg distributed Swedish passes, with which he is believed to have saved at least 30,000 Jews.

Joop Westerweel, a non-Jewish school principal in Holland, helped Jewish children escape over the Pyrenees into Spain. He was caught and executed by the Gestapo.

Abraham Zuckerman was saved by Oskar Schindler. Mr. Zuckerman has devoted himself to memorializing this noble act. Thanks to his efforts several streets in New Jersey towns have been named in Schindler's honor. This is a photo of Oskar Schindler on one of the many streets named in his honor.

father, Pharaoh, had decreed to be killed. The princess was also aware that anyone hiding a Hebrew baby would immediately be put to death.

Despite the danger, her feelings of love and respect for human life forced her to save the child. The princess acted out of a spirit of pity and righteousness. During the Holocaust there were many non-Jews (gentiles) who risked their lives to save Jews from the Nazis. These non–Jews are called Righteous Gentiles.

The Righteous Gentiles of Le Chambon

In France, the 2,500 people who lived in the village of Le Chambon saved about 2,000 Jews. The villagers worked with an underground organization to smuggle Jews into Switzerland and safety. The Jewish refugees found shelter among the villagers and farmers. Le Chambon became known as "the nest of the Jews." Although the people of Le Chambon lived in fear, not one person among the 2,500 villagers informed the Nazis. The Danish people also courageously resisted and saved many Jews from the death camps.

Raoul Wallenberg

Raoul Wallenberg, a Swedish diplomat in Hungary, issued false passports and saved thousands of Jews. Wallenberg was captured by the Russians and disappeared. To this day nobody is certain what happened to him.

Joop Westerwill

Joop Westerwill was a teacher in Rotterdam. When the Nazis conquered Holland, Westerwill assisted in the escape of Jewish children. For twenty months he managed to evade the Nazis and save many Jews. On March 11, 1944, he was caught trying to smuggle two Jewish girls into Spain. He was condemned to death and shot.

Oskar Schindler

Oskar Schindler was ethnic German born in Czechoslovakia, in the Sudetenland which was annexed by the Third Reich in October 1938. Towards the end of 1939 he arrived in Cracow, Poland, and took over an enamelware factory that had belonged to Jews.

Under Schindler's management, the enamelware firm manufactured pots and pans for the German army. Before long it had 900 employees, most of them Jews.

As the Russian army advanced into Poland, the Germans began moving vital industries to safer areas. Schindler persuaded the Nazis to transform his enamel plant into a munitions plant, producing shells for the German army. This made it a vital industry that had to be moved. As a result, he was allowed to move the plant and its workers, saving his entire Jewish labor force.

In his new plant, Schindler did everything to treat his 1,100 Jews well and managed to obtain food and medicine for them. Thanks to Schindler's humane efforts, most of the workers at his factory survived. Schindler himself said, "I hated the Nazis and could not see people destroyed. I did what my conscience told me I must do." More that 1,200 Jews were saved by this brave man.

Oscar Schindler's grave lies in the Roman Catholic cemetery on Jerusalem's Mount Zion. Schindler visited Israel annually as a guest of his former workers whom he called "children." After his death in 1974, Schindler was buried in Jerusalem at his own request.

The Museum of the Jewish Heritage

The Museum of the Jewish Heritage in New York City is a living memorial to the Holocaust. Its three floors trace the history of the Jews in three stages. The first floor houses pre-Holocaust exhibits which sketch a portrait of Jewish people dispersed throughout the world. The second floor contains Holocaust exhibits. The third floor is devoted to life and renewal–those who survived the horrors to recreate Jewish vitality and civilization.

The Shoah Visual History Foundation

The Shoah Visual History Foundation in Los Angeles has videotaped testimonies from Nazi survivors. In four years it has recorded the recollections of 45,000 men and women in more than fifty countries.

In essence, these tapes are preserving the memories and testimonies of survivors so that future generations can listen and learn.

The Simon Wiesenthal Center

Simon Wiesenthal was known as the Nazi hunter. He spent four years in Nazi concentration camps during World War II. Ninety family members and relatives were exterminated, and he himself ended the war as a living skeleton.

Simon Wiesenthal in his office with a map of the Third Reich. The stars on the map indentify the death camps.

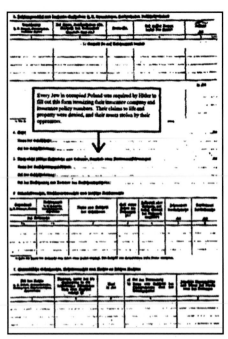

Every Jew in occupied Poland was required by Hitler to complete this form itemizing their insurance company and insurer's policy numbers. All claims to life and property were denied, and their assets were stolen by their oppressors.

German and Swiss insurance companies all over Europe, especially in Jewish population areas refused to cooperate and compensate the families of the victims. The Swiss insurance industry was one of the major forces encouraging Swiss authorities to accept Nazi gold.

After much political pressure, Swiss banks have agreed to repay more than a $1.5 billion to the Holocaust survivors. An Italian insurance company has also agreed to pay $100 million to its insureds.

United States Holocaust Memorial Council Chairman Emeritus Harvey M. Meyerhoff, President Clinton, and Elie Wiesel light the eternal flame at Museum Dedication Ceremony.

Wiesenthal devoted his life to the pursuit of war criminals and brought more than 1,100 Nazis to trial. The Center is located in Los Angeles, where it continues the work begun by Simon Wiesenthal.

The Museum of Tolerance

The Simon Wiesenthal Center has a Museum of Tolerance which stages exhibits and sponsors conferences dealing with national and international topics related to the Nazi regimes.

The goal of the Center is to help establish a paper trail to historical truth and give the victims a voice. It has investigated Switzerland's handling of Jewish refugees, the insurance policies of the victims, stolen art treasures, and restitution of assets. In addition, the Center is involved in investigating German industrial complexes which benefited from Jewish slave labor.

The Weisenthal Center was in the lead on behalf of more than 100,00 claimants against the Swiss banks that hid more than $7 billion of Jewish assets.

The banks laundered Jewish monies and held on to funds deposited by Holocaust victims. Swiss financial institutions helped Nazi Germany convert the gold it stole from individuals and conquered countries into foreign exchange for purchasing war supplies. These supplies helped to prolong the war and were responsible for killing thousands of Allied soldiers. Swiss commercial banks betrayed the trust of Europe's doomed Jews, keeping for themselves the money left behind by depositors who died in the Holocaust.

The U.S. Holocaust Memorial Museum

The Holocaust Memorial Museum in Washington, D.C., officially sponsored by the government of the United States as a memorial to the six million, was opened on April 23, 1993. It uses permanent and temporary displays, interactive videos, and special lectures to document the entire history of the Holocaust, beginning with the origins of anti-Semitism and dealing with events from the time the Nazis gained control of Germany until the end of World War II. It is open every day of the year except Yom Kippur and December 25. Visited by great numbers every year, it has become one of the capital's most popular tourist attractions.

Yom Ha-Zikaron

Yom Ha-Zikaron, the Day of Remembrance, is a day of great sorrow. On this day, the fourth of Iyar, we remember all the soldiers who were killed defending Israel and fighting to create a strong, independent homeland for the Jewish people.

Israel's Memorial Day commemoration begins at sunset with a siren blast. A parent whose child died in the defense of Israel presents a torch to the President of the country, who uses it to light a flame in memory of all Israel's fallen martyrs.

Special prayers are said in the synagogue on Yom Ha-Zikaron and on the Shabbat preceding it. At mid-morning on the fourth of Iyar, sirens are sounded throughout Israel. Everything comes to an absolute standstill. Tailors put down their needles and thread. Bakers stop kneading dough. Teachers stop their classes, and children put down their pencils and close their books. Cars pull over to the side of the road.

Everyone stands silently at attention for a moment, sadly thinking of the brave men and women who gave their lives for Israel. A special ceremony is held on Mount Herzl, where torches are lit, symbolizing the eternal memory of the dead. All day long, mournful music is played on the radio.

At seven in the evening another siren goes off. This signals the end of Memorial Day and the beginning of *Yom ha-Atzma'ut* (Israel Independence Day). The two days are joined together in recognition of the fact that without the courage and self-sacrifice of the fallen soldiers, there could be no *Yom ha-Atzma'ut.* Israel would not have been able to preserve its independence.

IYAR						אייר
Sun.	Mon.	Tues.	Wed.	Thur.	Fri.	Sat.
						1
2	3	4	5	6	7	8
9	10	11	12	13	14	15
16	17	18	19	20	21	22
23	24	25	26	27	28	29

Yom Ha-Zikaron **is commemorated on the 4th day of Iyar.**

Parents mourn their son Hayim, who was killed in defense of his homeland, Israel. More than 20,000 young men and women have died in the Arab Israeli wars.

Yom Ha–Atzma'ut

Yom Ha-Atzma'ut is celebrated on the 5th day of Iyar.

An Israeli stamp showing part of the Declaration of Independence.

The scene is Israel, and the date is the fifth of Iyar on the Hebrew calendar. This is Independence Day in the Jewish state and the excitement, pride, and national spirit have to be seen to be believed.

The day before this red-letter date is set aside throughout the country as *Yom Ha-Zikaron*, a day of remembrance for the many heroes and heroines who have fallen in defense of Israel. The kindling of memorial candles in homes and synagogues marks the observance. Places of entertainment are closed. Memorial meetings and ceremonies are held at monuments throughout the land.

Getting Ready

And then, as sirens sound all over the country at 7:00 p.m. the national blue-and-white flag, which has flown at half-mast for the last twenty-four hours in honor of the nation's sacred dead, is hoisted by the Knesset guards. The speaker of the Knesset declares the mourning over and the celebrations under way.

A fire of remembrance is then lit at the tomb of Theodor Herzl, the founder of Zionism, atop Mount Herzl, and a group of young men and women kindle beacons commemorating the military units that fought in defense of the new State of Israel in its War of Independence in 1948.

Let Joy Reign

Now Jerusalem begins to rejoice. There is dancing in the streets, and the night is turned to brilliant day by fireworks.

In the Hebrew University Stadium, the President of Israel, accompanied by the nation's political leaders and by foreign dignitaries, watches more than a thousand Gadna boys and girls carrying red-, green-, and yellow-beamed flashlights into the stadium in formation. On a platform stage, the stars of Habimah, the national theater, read stirring tributes to the country's youth who died so that Israel might live.

And the next day there are parades, with tanks and other military hardware. Helicopters and jet fighters streak by in the sky.

All of it, the joy and the national sense of triumph, and, yes, the sobering knowledge that peace is as yet more hope than reality, adds up to the glory that is *Yom Ha-Atzma'ut*, Independence Day.

And the nation is still young enough to remember the first Independence Day, when a small group of thirty-seven leaders gathered in a small museum in Tel Aviv, headed by David Ben-Gurion, to issue its Proclamation of Independence.

A Condensed Timetable

The fateful drama that was acted out that day was performed against a backdrop of history. A condensed timetable of events offers a capsule review:

November 5, 1914: Turkey, of which Palestine is a part, becomes an ally of Germany in World War I. Palestine has a Jewish community of 80,000 souls.

November 2, 1917: Britain announced the Balfour Declaration promising to establish a national home for the Jews in Palestine; later it is endorsed by the French and Italian governments and by President Woodrow Wilson of the United States.

December 11, 1917: General Allenby enters Jerusalem at the head of the victorious British army; 400 years of Turkish rule come to an end.

Theodor Herzl

The Balfour Declaration

A banner headline announces the birth of the new state. Although the State of Israel was proclaimed on Friday afternoon, May 14, 1948, the paper is dated Sunday, May 16, because The *Palestine Post* of Israel was not printed on the Jewish Sabbath.

101

A Haganah member stands guard at a defense perimeter.

Vladimir Jabotinsky (1880-1940) in the uniform of the Jewish Legion, which he founded during World War I. Jabotinsky was imprisoned by the British for organizing the Haganah. Later, he founded the Zionist Revisionist movement and the Irgun Zvai Le'umi.

July 24, 1922: The British Mandate over Palestine is approved by the League of Nations; one of its conditions is the establishment of the National Home for the Jews, as stated in the Balfour Declaration.

May 17, 1939: Following Arab riots, the British White Paper is issued stating that the country is to become an Arab state within ten years, with a Jewish minority comprising thirty percent of the population.

April 30, 1946: Britain rejects a report recommending the admission into Palestine of 100,000 Jewish refugees—survivors of the Nazi Holocaust in Europe.

November 29, 1947: The United Nations General Assembly votes 33 to 13 to partition Palestine into two states, one Jewish, the other Arab.

On the same day that the Partition Resolution was approved in New York, the first Arab attack took place in Jerusalem.

Britain declared that the Mandate would end May 14, 1948. Its civil and military administration began to depart the country without handing the reins of power to anyone. The Arab populace started to stream out of Jewish-controlled areas. The armies of seven Arab states massed on the borders of Palestine, ready to move in as soon as the Mandate ended and to drive the Jews into the sea.

The Declaration of Statehood

This was the setting against which Jewish leaders gathered on Friday, May 14, in the Municipal Art Museum of Tel Aviv. Distinguished visitors were in attendance, with Haganah guards patrolling the area. At one minute after midnight, the Mandate would end. The Declaration of Statehood was to be made in the afternoon in order not to violate the Sabbath.

As the clock struck four, David Ben-Gurion called the meeting to order. The assembly rose and sang *Hatikvah*, the Jewish national anthem, the prophetic words which were about to be fulfilled. Then Ben–Gurion began to read:

"We, the members of the National Council, by virtue of the natural and historic right of the Jewish people and of the resolution of the United Nations General Assembly, hereby proclaim the establishment of a Jewish State in Eretz Yisrael, to be called Israel."

With these words, 1,878 years after the Roman legions destroyed the Second Temple in Jerusalem, the Third Jewish Commonwealth was created.

Since that great moment, Israel has lived through an epoch in which every Yom Ha-Atzma'ut has marked a year studded with events of towering significance.

The War of Independence

The Promised Land first became a Jewish kingdom 3,000 years ago. Over the centuries it was ravaged by Assyrians, Babylonians, Romans, Muslims, Crusaders, and Turks. But the biblical text "If I forget you, O Jerusalem" was engraved on every Jewish heart, and at Seder tables around the globe the concluding words of the Passover ritual were always, "Next year in Jerusalem."

It was only after six million people were murdered by the Nazis, however, that the 2,000-year-old dream became a reality. On November 29, 1947, the United Nations offered the pitiful remnant of European Jewry a plan under which Palestine would be partitioned into two states—one Jewish, one Arab.

The Arabs rejected the idea. On May 14, 1948, when David Ben-Gurion stood up in Tel Aviv and declared the birth of the State of Israel, they attacked in ugly fury.

When the War of Independence was over, the newborn Jewish state was victorious. It had gained 2,380 square miles of territory in addition to the 5,760 granted by the Partition Resolution and had lost 700,000 Arabs, who fled at their leaders' command. The neighboring state of Jordan, however, moved in and took over much of the area that the United Nations had intended for the Palestinian Arabs. And the seven Arab states that had attacked Israel, Egypt and Syria foremost among them, remained as hostile as ever.

With the war's end, Israelis turned to the enormous task of building a new country. But the Arab world refused to admit that Israel even existed. They sent terrorists called *fedayeen* to

Israeli soldiers shout in triumph as they reach their military objective.

A Haganah volunteer posts an appeal to the Arabs of Palestine, December, 1947. A section of the appeal is translated below.

The Jewish Haganah organization begs you to keep calm and at the same time presents you with a firm ultimatum. For the past two days the peace of this country has been disturbed by a group of incited Arabs who have engaged in shooting, arson, and murder. We have stressed that our aims are peace and good relations with our neighbors. . . . Now, we offer you peace, but we also extend a grave warning. If the bloodshed continues we shall be forced to resort to extreme measures . . . . We call on you to take our appeal for peace to heart. Heed our warning.

David "Mickey" Marcus was born in Brooklyn and attended the U.S. Military Academy at West Point. After World War II, Marcus left the army and returned to New York to open a law office. Sometime later he was approached by a member of the Haganah, who said, "You have studied military tactics at West Point and can help us build an army in Palestine." Marcus, given the code name of Michael Stone, was smuggled into Tel Aviv through the British blockade. Thanks to Marcus's military tactics, the Jewish forces successfully opened the road to Jerusalem, saving the city from starvation and capture. Before dawn on June 11, 1948, David Marcus was accidentally shot and killed by a Jewish sentry. David Marcus is buried in the cemetery of the U.S. Military Academy at West Point. He was posthumously awarded the Israeli Medal of Independence. A village in Israel, Mishmar David, is named after him.

conduct cowardly attacks on Israeli civilians. They blocked the Strait of Tiran to Israeli ships and forbade Israel to fly over the Gulf of Aqaba. Finally, they decided to close the Suez Canal.

The Suez Campaign

The Suez Canal, a waterway in Egypt connecting the Mediterranean Sea with the Red Sea, is one of the world's most important maritime trade routes. It was planned and built by the French in 1859, but in 1875 the British gained control of the canal. Under the terms of a treaty signed at that time, they were to turn the Canal over to Egypt in 1968.

President Gamal Abdel Nasser of Egypt, driven by hatred for Israel, was unable to wait. In 1956 he took over the Canal and closed it to Israeli shipping and to ships trading with Israel. With the connivance of Syria, he began to apply pressure against Israel on all sides, slowly choking the young nation's economy.

In addition to harming Israel, Egypt's seizure of the canal endangered the British and French economies and their political positions in the Middle East.

The Allies Attack

On October 29, 1956, Israel, France, and Britain launched a combined attack against Egypt. In an eight-day campaign, the Israeli forces, under the command of General Moshe Dayan, captured the Gaza Strip and the entire Sinai Peninsula. Israel's motorized troops barreled their way to the Suez Canal. Meanwhile, the combined British and French forces managed to capture parts of the Suez Canal.

At this point, however, the United States and Russia stepped in, forcing the British and French to withdraw. Israel refused to withdraw from its position on the Suez Canal, though, until a United Nations peace-keeping force was stationed along the Egypt-Israel border. As part of the settlement the United Nations guaranteed that Israeli shipping would have complete access to the Suez Canal.

A decade passed, during which the Arabs plotted revenge. In the spring of 1967, bolstered by a huge supply of Russian armaments, Nasser felt the time for action had come. He demanded that the 3,400–man UN force withdraw from its buffer position in the Sinai. Once again he closed the Suez Canal to Israeli shipping. This was an act of war.

The Six-Day War

The tension was terrific on Sunday, June 4, 1967. Tel Aviv and Cairo buzzed with rumors. Tiny Israel, hemmed in by foes, listened to bulletins coming over Kol Yisrael. Iraq had joined Egypt and Jordan in a military pact. Nasser had proclaimed that Israel would be driven into the sea. Ahmed Shukeiri, head of the Palestine Liberation Organization, went to Amman, the capital of Jordan, and announced: "When we take Israel, the surviving Jews will be helped to return to their native lands." Then he added: "But, I think that none will survive."

The cities of Israel were emptied; virtually every male between the ages of eighteen and forty-nine had left for the army. Yet spirits were high in this country the size of Massachusetts with 2.5 million people—about the number found in one American telephone directory. Surrounded by 110 million Arab enemies Israelis, from Kibbutz Ein Gev on the eastern shore of the Sea of Galilee, scarcely more than a mile from the Syrian border, down to Eilat, which looked out upon the Gulf of Aqaba now closed by Egypt in an effort to choke Israel to economic death, dug trenches and foxholes and waited.

And there was evening and there was morning . . . Monday, June 5th. As day broke and the rim of the blazing sun edged up over the distant Moab hills, the orange sky was filled with Israeli planes, while tanks and motorized infantry in three main columns, had plunged deep into enemy territory. The scales of history were trembling, and shadows of the past–of the brave Hasmoneans, of plucky David facing a giant Goliath, of countless heroes of Jewish history–stirred to life to strengthen the modern Maccabees of Israel, now engaged in a desperate struggle for survival.

Speed and Surprise

"Kill the Jews," cried Baghdad Radio in Iraq. "The battle will be total," said Egypt's Nasser. "Our basic aim is the destruction of Israel."

On the first day of the conflict, the gleaming Israeli jets rained tons of bombs on Arab airfields. Armored columns

Israeli tanks blast their way up the Golan Heights in Syria.

An Israeli commander briefs his officers for battle during the Six–Day War in 1967.

After the Six-Day War in 1967, France embargoed all arms shipments, including Mirage fighter planes, to Israel. At that point the leaders of Israel decided that they could not depend on foreign sources for armaments and had to build their own weapons.

One of the most important projects was the development of a made–in–Israel fighter plane. This supersonic, air–to–air fighter is called the *Kfir*. The Hebrew word *kfir* means "young lion."

A destroyed Syrian tank on the roadside in the Golan. The battle for the Golan Heights was fierce and many Israeli soldiers lost their lives.

After the battle, this Israeli paratrooper prays at the newly captured Western Wall.

Rabbi Shlomo Goren, Chief Chaplain of the Israel Defense Forces, prays at the liberated Western Wall.

plunged into the sands of the Sinai Desert. To the east tanks and half-tracks rolled toward the 329-mile-long border with Jordan.

By sundown Israel had destroyed 410 enemy planes and won total air superiority. The Gaza Strip had been cut off, El Arish taken. Meantime, President Lyndon Johnson and Premier Alexei Kosygin, using the famous "hot line," had assured each other that both superpowers wished only peace in the Middle East; and the UN Security Council had met in New York to hammer out a cease–fire resolution.

By Thursday, Egypt and Jordan had been defeated. The Old City of Jerusalem was in Jewish hands. Only Syria remained on the field of battle. Now the entire Israel Air Force, some 400 planes, began flying nonstop raids against deeply-dug Syrian gun emplacements on the heights above the Sea of Galilee. The morning sun on Shabbat revealed Syrians running toward Damascus on roads littered with equipment and clothing. Israel's ground forces then conducted a mopping-up operation. At 6:30 p.m. a cease-fire was put into effect. When three stars blinked in the sky at the time for *Havdalah*, a brilliant campaign, one of the most remarkable in military history, was over.

Soon afterward, on a sunlit day, three men stepped up to the Western Wall: Levi Eshkol, Prime Minister of Israel; Moshe Dayan, Defense Minister, and Yitzchak Rabin, the Chief of Staff. Each one had written a prayer to place in a crevice in the wall.

"What did you write?" curious reporters inquired. "*Shema Yisrael*," said Eshkol. "May peace be upon all Israel," said Dayan. "This is the Lord's doing: it is marvelous in our eyes," said Rabin, quoting *Tehillim*, the biblical book of Psalms.

With these symbolic utterances did the Six–Day War join the Exodus from Egypt, the Inquisition, the Martyrdom of the Six Million, and the Rebirth of Israel.

All of this, and much more than ever can be expressed in words or in song (remember the moving "*Yerushalayim shel Zahav*" and the haunting "*Sharm el-Sheikh*"), lies behind *Yom Ha-Atzma'ut*.

The Yom Kippur War

Almost daily between 1968 and 1970, marauding Arab terrorists sneaked across Israel's borders to attack innocent people. Tel Aviv was shelled. A school bus was blown up in Eilat, injuring 28 children. Russia encouraged the Arabs and sent them billions of dollars worth of arms.

On October 6, 1973, the holy day of Yom Kippur, the Arabs attacked Israel on two fronts simultaneously. Syria attacked Israel's northern Golan front and Egypt attacked across the Suez Canal into the Sinai.

Since Yom Kippur is the most sacred day of the Jewish year most of Israel's soldiers were in synagogues with their families. The Arab sneak attack succeeded and caught Israel off guard. Massive Egyptian and Syrian armies penetrated the Israeli defenses.

By the third day, Israel had recovered and began to take the offensive. Israeli soldiers had left the synagogues and went straight to the battlefield. In nine days the Israeli army pushed back all the invaders. The Egyptian army was surrounded in the Sinai and Israeli troops threatened Cairo, Egypt's capital.

The Syrians, too, were forced back. Israel was poised to attack Damascus, Syria's capital. Now that Israel was winning, the Arabs and Russians went to the United Nations and pleaded for help. And so Israel agreed to a cease-fire despite its position of strength. On October 24, just 18 days after the Arab invasion, the fighting stopped.

After the cease-fire, all of Israel mourned the nation's loss of its finest soldiers. Golda Meir, the Prime Minister, said: *"For the people of Israel, each human life is precious. Our dead soldiers are the sons of all of us. The pain we feel is felt by all of us."*

As a result of the surprise attack, Prime Minister Golda Meir was forced to resign because many voters had lost confidence in her. Yitzchak Rabin became the new Prime Minister.

The Israel-Egypt Peace Treaty

In May 1977, a new government was elected in Israel. The Likkud Party, headed by Menachem Begin, became the largest party in the Knesset. The new Prime Minister invited President Anwar Sadat of Egypt to come to Jerusalem. Menachem Begin wanted peace for Israel, and he hoped that through talks with the Arab leader a peace agreement with Egypt might be reached.

Golda Meir

Israeli tanks blast their way through enemy lines.

Peace Agreement with Egypt (Camp David Accords).
Left to right: **Begin, Carter, and Sadat after the peace treaty was signed in Washington on March 26, 1979.**

On September 13, 1993 Israel signed an agreement with the Palestinians in the United States in the presence of U.S. President Bill Clinton. The agreement was signed by Palestinian Authority Chairman Yassir Arafat, Israeli Prime Minister Yitzchak Rabin, and his Vice-Premier Shimon Peres.

ISRAEL'S PRIME MINISTERS
David Ben-Gurion (1948-53)
Moshe Sharett (1953-55)
David Ben-Gurion (1955-63)
Levi Eshkol (1963-69)
Golda Meir (1969-74)
Yitzchak Rabin (1974-77)
Menachem Begin (1977-83)
Yitzchak Shamir (1983-84)
Shimon Peres (1984-86)
Yitzchak Shamir (1986-92)
Yitzchak Rabin (1992-95)
Benjamin Netanyahu (1996-)

This huge bronze menorah is in the Knesset courtyard in Jerusalem. It was a gift to the people of Israel from the Jews of England.

Sadat Visits Israel

In November 1977, for the first time ever, an Arab leader, President Anwar Sadat of Egypt, visited Jerusalem. Sadat spoke in the Knesset of his wish for peace between Egypt and Israel. On March 26, 1979, a peace treaty was signed between Israel and Egypt in Washington, D.C. Prime Minister Menachem Begin of Israel, President Anwar Sadat of Egypt, and President Jimmy Carter of the United States worked hard to bring about this historic agreement.

The Camp David Agreement

The Israel-Egypt treaty is called the Camp David Agreement, from the name of the place where the three leaders met with one another. The other Arab states bitterly opposed Sadat's steps toward peace with Israel. In October 1981, Sadat was killed by an assassin's bullet.

The Oslo Peace Agreement

The Middle–East Peace Conference convened in Madrid, Spain, in 1991. While further meetings were taking place in Washington in 1992, a tiny group of delegates from Israel and the Palestine Liberation Organization met secretly in Oslo, Norway.

The secret discussions continued for 15 months, but they ended with an agreement. On September 13, 1993, Prime Minister Yitzchak Rabin of Israel and Yasir Arafat, head of the PLO signed a peace agreement in Washington. On September 3, 1993, the Israeli Knesset, which has 120 members, approved the agreement by a vote of 61 to 50. Although all Israelis yearn for peace, many did not trust Arafat and the PLO, and felt that Israel was giving up too much too soon.

The Assassination of Rabin

Saturday night, November 4, 1995, was one of the most fateful times in the history of modern Israel. On that darkest of nights, Yitzchak Rabin, Israel's Prime Minister and one of its great military heroes, was assassinated. That evening 100,000 Israelis had assembled in Tel Aviv to participate in a political rally. Rabin delivered a speech and joined in singing the "Song of Peace."

After the rally, Rabin and Foreign Minister Shimon Peres began to walk to their cars. Lurking in the dark shadows of the night a young assassin named Yigal Amir was waiting. As Rabin approached his limousine Amir quietly stepped out of the shadows and from about a yard away pumped three bullets, point-blank into, the Prime Minister.

The Election of 1996

On June 2, 1996, Benjamin Netanyahu of the Likkud Party defeated Shimon Peres and became Israel's new Prime Minister. His victory was in large part due to public disquiet about the way the peace agreement with the PLO was proceeding.

Symbols of Israel

Every country in the world is different. Each and every country has its own special language, its national anthem, and emblem, and its own colorful flag. Israel's population is made up of people from all over the world who speak a dizzying variety of languages, eat different foods, and sing and dance to their own special music. With these differences there are links which connect all of these people into one solid unified nation. These links are in language, anthem, flag and national symbol. Each of these links is rooted in Israel's historical experiences and religious ideals.

Hatikvah

Although the situation sometimes seems bleak, Israelis continue to hope for the best and strive to do as well as they can. This idea is embodied in their national anthem, *Hatikvah*, the title of which, in English, means "The Hope."

The anthem was composed in 1878 by the poet Napthali Herz Imber. Its title was based on the simple yet profound reality that throughout the thousands of years of exile, the Jews never lost hope. They always had *tikvah* that they would someday return to the restored nation of Israel. In 1948 their hope was finally realized when Israel was reborn.

Today, wherever Jews live and work, in Israel and in the Diaspora, they sing *Hatikvah* with pride. The State of Israel is a partial fulfillment of the hope Imber's poem expresses. The dream for peace is also part of the hope. Perhaps someday it too will be fulfilled.

Naphtali Herz Imber, the composer of the Israeli national anthem.

Eliezer Ben–Yehuda.

The blue-and-white flag of Israel.

The emblem of Israel.

A thorny sabra plant and its sweet and juicy fruit. Israelis are called sabras because they are thorny on the outside, but friendly when you get to know them.

The Hebrew Language

Israel's official language is Hebrew. The same 4,000–year old-language that our Jewish ancestors spoke in Israel long, long ago. Even when Jews were driven out of Israel, they continued to study the Torah and to pray in Hebrew. The ancient language was never forgotten. In 1811, Eliezer Ben Yehuda began to revive and modernize the Hebrew language. He compiled a large dictionary with thousands of new words that made it possible to discuss modern ideas and technology in Hebrew. Today, Hebrew is spoken in the beauty parlors of Tel Aviv, the soccer fields of Haifa, and the supermarkets of Israel. The 4,000–year–old language is alive on TV, newspapers, records and computer programs.

The Flag of Israel

The Torah describes the flags of the twelve tribes of Israel, but there is no mention of a flag for the nation of Israel. In 1889, David Wolffsohn designed the flag of Israel that is in use today. He used the blue–and–white stripes of the *tallit* and added a *Magen David* (six–pointed star) in the center. The six-pointed star is known in English as the Star of David. Some people believe that King David had a six pointed star on his battleshield.

The Emblem of Israel

The emblem of Israel consists of a Menorah and olive branches. It tells us much about the ideals and history of the Jewish people. The Temple Menorah reminds us of the ancient glory of the city of Jerusalem and its sad destruction. The olive branches are symbols of peace. They tell the world that Israel wishes to live in peace with its neighbors.

The People of Israel

Israel's population is over 5,000,000 and is still growing. It is a "coat of many colors" with Jews of varied races and back-grounds from every continent and climate. Israel's "coat of many colors" includes Ashkenazim, Sephardim, *Edut Ha-Mizrach* (Oriental Jews) Falashas, and more than 500,000 newly arrived Russians. This diverse population has combined the special skills, talents and energy of its members to build the most modern state in the Middle East. In Israel these groups are not separated by barriers of space and distance. They live side by side, their children attend the same schools, and their sons and daughters serve in the same army.

They all speak the same language Hebrew, and their children, born in Israel, have one common name: Sabra. The Sabra is the fruit of a cactus bush, prickly and tough on the outside, and juicy and soft on the inside. this word has become the nickname for native born Israelis.

Israel At 50

In 1998, the State of Israel celebrated its 50th anniversary on *Yom ha-Atzma'ut*. During this half-century, many extraordinary things happened. A people exiled and dispersed for 2,000 years in 140 countries, speaking a babel of 100 languages, miraculously managed to return to its homeland and begin speaking its ancient biblical tongue: *Ivrit*. From 600,000 embattled Jews, many the victims of the Holocaust, surrounded by more than 110 million hostile Arabs, Israel has managed to grow into a prosperous, high-tech country of almost 6 million. From a patchwork of small farms and kibbutzim, it has blossomed into a global power in science, technology, agriculture, computers, and the arts. Despite the overwhelming military powers of its sworn enemies, it has won victory after victory.

Israel and Its Neighbors

Through five wars, Israel has survived the assaults of its Arab neighbors. Its defenders have compiled a roll-call of heroism that lends nobility to the Jewish people. Unfortunately, the price has been paid in blood and tears, for 20,000 of Israel's finest have fallen in the defense of the besieged state.

Peace Is Still a Distant Goal

Hate and terror remain constant threats. For 50 years, 24 hours a day, the airwaves and the media have preached the annihilation of Israel. The despotic rulers and absolute monarchs of the surrounding Arab states continually accumulate and update their military arms and weapons of mass destruction. Israel is threatened by ballistic missiles, nuclear bombs, poison gas, and germ warfare.

Ethiopian immigrants on an Israeli Air Force plane from Addis Ababa to Israel during Operation Solomon.

Newly arrived Russian Jewish immigrants to Israel. More than 500,000 Russians have found new homes in Israel. As the political situation in Russia deteriorates many new families are welcomed.

The Knesset building in Jerusalem. The Knesset is the legislative body of the State of Israel. Its 120 members, called *chavrei knesset,* are elected by a secret ballot.

Israel, the Land of the Bible has many devoted friends all over the world. This group of Japanese supporters have come to Israel to show their solidarity with its political aims.

In 1996 Benjamin Netanyahu of the Likkud Party was elected Prime Minister of Israel.

On September 20, 1998, President Clinton met with Prime Minister Benjamin Netanyahu and the Palestinian leader Yasir Arafat. At the meeting, Israel agreed to withdraw from 13 percent of the West Bank if the Palestinians met the security concerns of Israel. Such an agreement, if the unresolved issues are settled, would leave the Palestinians with political control of 40 percent of the West Bank, including 98 percent of the Arab population.

Israeli stamp with the theme of "Life of Peace." Despite the problems with the Palestinians and their Arab neighors, the Israelis still yearn and hope that a peaceful solution will be coming in the near future, and both Arab and Jew can enjoy a Life of Peace.

Is Peace Possible?

With neighbors like these, can Israel sell its security by accepting vague promises? The battle for a just, secure, and lasting peace is still being waged in blood and tears. The prophet Isaiah prophesied that Israel would become "a light unto the nations." May the light continue to burn brightly and shed its radiance on all the nations.

Israel and its Dangerous Neighbors

Iraq, Iran, and Syria have acquired North Korean and Russian know-how and have missle capabilites which can target Israel. In addition, some Arab countries are experimenting with germ warfare. In August 1998, U.S. missles destroyed a germ warfare installation in the Sudan.

Lag Ba-Omer

Lag Ba-Omer, the youngest of the Jewish festivals, arrives well into spring, on the eighteenth day of the month of Iyar. Like many Jewish holidays, it tells of the Jewish people's fight for freedom against the dark forces of oppression.

Lag Ba-Omer is a happy day, a day for weddings and picnics, and outdoor sports. Bow-and-arrow games and other contests of skill are fitting for this holiday. And after the games are over, it is time to listen to the retelling of the story of Lag Ba-Omer, sometimes called the scholars' holiday.

Reign of Terror

Long ago, nearly 2,000 years ago, Israel was conquered by the Roman general Titus and the Temple was destroyed. For many years, the Land of Israel was ruled by governors appointed by the Roman emperors. The Roman governors did all they could to wipe out the Jewish love of independence. They taxed the people heavily and forbade them to study the Torah. The mighty Roman legions kept the Jews in constant terror.

The Second Jewish Revolt

During the reign of the emperor Trajan, revolts broke out in many parts of the Roman Empire. Trajan's successor, Hadrian, continued his cruel policies. He built a temple with Roman gods in Jerusalem, a circus, and an arena where gladiators fought each other to the death. Hadrian made it difficult to practice the Jewish religion. He decreed that any Jew studying the Torah would be killed. He outlawed circumcision and closed religious schools. All this the Jews refused to accept.

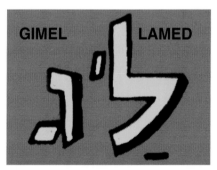

IYAR						אייר
Sun.	Mon.	Tues.	Wed.	Thur.	Fri.	Sat.
						1
2	3	4	5	6	7	8
9	10	11	12	13	14	15
16	17	18	19	20	21	22
23	24	25	26	27	28	29

The holiday of Lag Ba–Omer is celebrated on the 33rd day of the counting of the *Omer*, on the 18th day of Iyar. It is a time for singing, dancing, bonfires, picnics, hiking, and playing with bows and arrows.

The word *Lag* is made up of two Hebrew letters, *lamed* which has a numerical value of 30, and the letter *gimel*, which has a value of 3, making a total of 33.

Engraved stone with the name of Emperor Trajan, found in Caesarea.

Bust of Hadrian.

Rabbi Akiva instructing his pupils. From the Sarajevo Haggadah.

A silver coin issued by the revolutionary government of Bar Kochba. He and his followers set up a Jewish state in 132–135 B.C.E. which was soon crushed by the Romans.

Scholar and Soldier

Under the leadership of Bar Kochba, the Jews rose up in revolt. The great religious teacher Rabbi Akiva encouraged his students to join Bar Kochba's forces. To Rabbi Akiva, freedom was the dearest possession anyone could have.

In fact, it was Rabbi Akiva who gave Bar Kochba his name. Akiva had been searching for a leader to spearhead a rebellion against the Romans. One day there came to him a man, fierce of visage, sturdy as a mighty boulder.

"My name is Shimon Bar Kosiba," he said. "I am ready to strike the blow of vengeance. Will you bless me, great Akiva?"

And Akiva answered: "In the Book of Numbers of the Bible it is written: 'There shall step forth a star out of Jacob, and a scepter shall rise out of Israel and smite the corners of Moab and destroy the children of Seth.' You shall be the leader, and people will call you Bar Kochba–Son of a Star."

The Revolt

In 132 C.E., led by Shimon Bar Kochba and Rabbi Akiva, the Jews revolted against Rome. At first Bar Kochba's army won many victories. His troops captured Jerusalem and built an altar on the Temple Mount.

Under Bar Kochba's leadership Judea had several years of freedom. Special coins were struck to commemorate Judea's independence.

However, Hadrian wanted to use Judea as a lesson for the other captive nations that made up the Roman Empire. He sent an army to Judea under the command of Severus, his best general. One by one Severus destroyed the strongholds of the Jewish fighters. Bar Kochba and his warriors retreated to the mountain fortress of Betar, where they made their final stand. No water or food reached the Jewish soldiers and many died of thirst and starvation. Bar Kochba and all of his soldiers died in the last battle defending Betar.

Hundreds and thousands of Jews were captured and sold into slavery throughout the Roman Empire. Jerusalem was renamed Aelia Capitolina, and Judea was renamed Palestine, in order to blot out all memory of the connection between the Jewish people and the Holy Land.

The Thirty-third Day

On the holiday of Lag Ba-Omer we remember Bar Kochba and Rabbi Akiva who sacrificed their lives for freedom. The name of the holiday refers to the thirty-third day of the *omer*, which was a measure Israelite farmers used for measuring their grain. The days between Passover and Shavuot were known to our farmer ancestors as *omer* days, for this was the time when the Jews gathered their harvest. They are also known as *sefirot*, or counting days. The Jews counted the days from Passover to Shavuot to know when to celebrate the end of the harvest season.

The days between Passover and Shavuot are a solemn period on the Jewish calendar. They recall the suffering which the Jews endured under Roman persecution. No weddings, are held during the *sefirah* days by traditional Jews. But Lag Ba-Omer comes to break the series of solemn days.

Among traditional Jews, Lag Ba-Omer is the one joyous day of the *sefirah* days. It is a joyous day because tradition says that Bar Kochba won a great victory on the thirty-third day of the *omer*. Another story tells that a plague which was raging among Akiva's students suddenly stopped on the thirty-third day of the *omer*. For this reason, Lag Ba-Omer is also called the scholars' holiday.

Simeon Bar Yochai

In most countries, Jewish children celebrate Lag Ba-Omer by holding picnics in forests and fields and shooting bows and arrows. The bows and arrows are a reminder of the disguises worn by the students of Simeon Bar Yochai. He was a great scholar who went off to live in a cave when the Romans forbade him to teach Torah any longer. There he studied and taught in secret for many years, living on carobs and other wild fruit and drinking the waters of a spring that had appeared miraculously in the cave. When his students came to visit him, they pretended to be hunters so that the Romans would not realize where they were going. That is why they carried bows and arrows.

Before Simeon Bar Yochai died, he asked his followers to celebrate rather than mourn his death. That is why the day he died is celebrated as a joyful outing, and bows and arrows are brought to Lag Ba-Omer picnics.

In 1960, Yigal Yadin, professor of archaeology at the Hebrew University in Jerusalem, launched an expedition to explore the caves in the mountains near the Dead Sea. A member of the expedition, exploring one of the narrow tunnels of a cave, discovered a basket filled with objects. Further inspection revealed a treasure trove of artifacts which included sandals, knives, mirrors, jugs, bowls, and the greatest treasure of all—papyrus rolls containing about 40 letters from Bar Kochba.

The Romans developed a wooden catapult that could throw giant stones very far. Because of its kicking action it was called an onager. An onager is a wild donkey which defends itself by kicking wildly.

Israeli stamp by the artist Reuven shows the dancers at Meron.

Today in Israel many Jews travel to Meron on foot and by car to visit the grave of Shimon Bar Yochai. It is a tradition to sit around bonfires all night, telling stories and singing songs about Shimon Bar Yochai, Rabbi Akiva, and the hero Shimon Bar Kochba.

The holiday of Lag Ba–Omer is celebrated on the 33rd day of the counting of the *omer*. It is a time for singing, dancing, bonfires, picnics, hiking, and playing with bows and arrows.

On the holiday of Lag Ba–Omer Jews remember the heroes who fought the Romans. On Lag Ba–Omer Jews especially remember Rabbi Akiva's student Shimon Bar Yochai. Under Roman rule he and his students continued studying Torah in a cave high on Mount Meron. The students disguised themselves by carrying bows and arrows and pretending they were hunting so the Romans would not arrest them.

For 13 years Rabbi Shimon Bar Yochai kept the knowledge of Torah alive. This brave rabbi died on Lag Ba–Omer .

Festival at Meron

Israel has its own way of celebrating Lag Ba-Omer. On that day, many Israelis visit the grave of Rabbi Simeon Bar Yochai, which is in Meron, near the town of Safed. It is night when the celebration at Meron begins. From every direction, hundreds of men and women come streaming toward the grave of the scholar. There are so many people that it is difficult to edge your way into the building which is built over the tomb. This building is a *bet ha-midrash*. Thousands of candles and lamps are lit. People dance and sing.

No one seems to walk. Everyone dances. Some sing, "Rabbi Akiva said . . ." and others respond, "Bar Yochai, happy are you." Drums are beaten. Violins and flutes add their voices to the music coming from the throats of thousands of men and women. At last, at midnight, a huge bonfire is lit. Into it, men, women, and children throw fine embroidery work–lace handkerchiefs, silken scarves–as the flames shoot up. The singing grows louder. Only at dawn does the celebration end.

The idea of celebrating Lag Ba-Omer with a bonfire has spread to other parts of Israel. It is a field day for boys and girls. In the evening, in Haifa, Jerusalem, Tel Aviv, and many of the *kibbutzim*, bonfires are lit. Around the burning flames stories are once more told about Bar Kochba, Rabbi Akiva, Bar Yochai–and the heroes who defied tyranny and carried forward the torch of Israel's hopes.

Yom Yerushalayim

Yom Yerushalayim

The newest holiday on the Jewish calendar is *Yom Yerushalayim*. Jerusalem Day is celebrated each year on the twenty-eighth day of the month of Iyar. On this day in 1967 (Wednesday, June 7, on the civil calendar; the third day of the Six-Day War), after bloody fighting against the Jordanian army, Israeli forces broke through Jerusalem's dividing wall and reclaimed the Old City. Hardened soldiers wept as they neared the ancient Western Wall.

United Jerusalem once again became the nation's capital. Today, *Yom Yerushalayim* is celebrated with joy and festivity. Special study classes are scheduled to teach the history of Jerusalem, triumphant psalms and prayers are sung, and special meals are prepared.

But *Yom Yerushalayim* is also a day of commemoration. We remember the pain and struggle and sacrifice of Israel's soldiers. Eighteen torches are lit at the Western Wall honoring the memory of those who fell in the battle to reclaim Israel's capital.

IYAR						אייר
Sun.	Mon.	Tues.	Wed.	Thur.	Fri.	Sat.
						1
2	3	4	5	6	7	8
9	10	11	12	13	14	15
16	17	18	19	20	21	22
23	24	25	26	27	28	29

Yom Yerushalayim the youngest of the Jewish holidays is celebrated on the 28th day of Iyar.

The Romans conquered Jerusalem in 70 C.E. and burned the Temple to the ground. All that remained was the Western Wall, which became a sacred place where Jews prayed. All through the centuries of exile Jews have worshipped at the Western Wall. The Wall has become a place for Jews to write prayers and requests and place them in the cracks between the stones.

Shavuot

SIVAN						סיון
Sun.	Mon.	Tues.	Wed.	Thur.	Fri.	Sat.
1	2	3	4	5	6	7
8	9	10	11	12	13	14
15	16	17	18	19	20	21
22	23	24	25	26	27	28
29	30					

The holiday of Shavuot is celebrated on the 6th and 7th days of Sivan. Reform Jews celebrate only one day.

The holiday that follows hard on the heels of Lag Ba-Omer is Shavuot. The name Shavuot means "Weeks," and the holiday falls exactly seven weeks after the second day of Passover, on the sixth and seventh days of the month of Sivan. (Reform Jews observe only the first of the two days.) The Greek name for Shavuot is Pentecost, which in Greek means "fiftieth," because it takes place on the fiftieth day after the beginning of Passover.

Shavuot is a triple holiday; a threefold celebration which commemorates the giving of the Torah on Mount Sinai, the harvesting of wheat in Israel, and the ripening of the first fruits in the Holy Land.

The rabbis declared Shavuot to be the most pleasant of all Jewish holidays. In a way, it is the conclusion of the great festival of Passover. For on Passover the Jews were freed from slavery, and on Shavuot the freed slaves were made into free people by the Ten Commandments.

A Torah Festival

As a Torah Festival, Shavuot is also known as *Zeman Matan Torateinu*. This means "The Time of the Giving of Our Law." It was on Shavuot that God spoke to Moses atop Mount Sinai and gave the Israelites the Ten Commandments.

Mount Sinai

When the Israelites reached Mount Sinai, sometime around 1280 B.C.E., Moses ordered them to pitch their tents. Here occurred the most important moment in Jewish history.

Moses bringing down the Ten Commandments. From the Sarajevo Haggadah.

The Ten Commandments

The Bible (in chapters 19 and 20 of the book of Exodus) vividly tells the story of how God bestowed the Torah on the Jewish people.

In the third month after they left Egypt, the Children of Israel came to the wilderness of Sinai. There they camped in front of the mountain. While they waited, Moses went up to God. And the Eternal called to him from the mountain, saying, *You shall say to the Children of Israel: "You saw what I did to the Egyptians, and how I saved you and brought you to Me. Now, if you will listen to My voice and obey My laws, you will be My treasure from among all peoples."*

Moses told the people what God had said. And the people answered, "All that the Eternal has said, we will do."

All the people sanctified themselves and waited for the Torah. And there was thunder and lightning, and a thick cloud surrounded the mountain. Then the sound of a shofar blowing very loudly was heard and the people trembled. Soon the mountain was completely surrounded by smoke and flames; the shofar became louder and louder and the whole mountain shook.

Then God spoke these words, saying:

1. *I am the Almighty your God.*
2. *You shall have no other gods before Me.*
3. *You shall not take the name of the Almighty in vain.*
4. *Remember the Sabbath to keep it holy.*
5. *Honor your father and your mother.*
6. *You shall not kill.*
7. *You shall not be unfaithful to wife or husband.*
8. *You shall not steal.*
9. *You shall not bear false witness.*
10. *You shall not desire what is your neighbor's.*

The Ten Commandments sealed a covenant between the young nation of Israel and the one God. No other nation had a code of laws so just and humane. The Israelites now truly abandoned the ways of Egypt and dedicated themselves to live by this lofty code.

Some historians identify Mount Sinai with Jebel Musa, meaning "The Mountain of Moses." Here, according to tradition, the Israelites encamped while Moses went up "to see God." As part of the Israeli–Egyptian peace treaty, the Sinai peninsula and "The Mountain of Moses" was returned to Egypt.

An artistic rendition of the Ten Commandments.

Winnowing the wheat the old–fashioned way. The stalks of wheat are tossed into the air and the kernels of wheat which are heavy fall to the bottom of the pan. The straw which is lighter flies into the air and falls to the ground.

The Torah

According to tradition, the entire Torah was revealed to Moses on Mount Sinai. The Torah, also known as the Five Books of Moses, recounts the early history of the Jewish people and lays down the rules, laws, and ethical teachings of Judaism.

The Torah scroll used in the synagogue is written on parchment by a scribe in ancient Hebrew letters. As in days gone by, it is written with a feather pen and specially prepared ink.

Harvest Holiday, Too

Besides being a Torah festival, Shavuot is a harvest holiday. In ancient times, the grain harvest was begun on the second day of Passover with the ripening of barley. On this day, an *omer* of grain was brought to the Temple as thanksgiving to God.

The forty-nine days from Pesach to Shavuot were counted publicly, and this period is still called *Sefirat Ha-Omer* (counting the *omer*). A special prayer was, and is, recited each day at the end of the evening service. This prayer counts the days in a distinctive way, referring to them as the first day of the omer, the second day of the *omer*, and so on, so that an accurate count of the days elapsed can be kept.

After seven weeks of counting came the harvesting of wheat–the last cereal grain to ripen.

Thus Shavuot is also known as *Chag Ha-Katzir*, the Festival of the Harvest. A successful harvest meant prosperity for the coming year-one more reason why Shavuot was a happy festival in ancient Palestine.

And Ripe, Ripe Fruits

Just about the time the wheat was harvested, the first fruits began to ripen on tree and vine in Israel. The Torah commanded the farmers to bring their first fruits as an offering of thanks to God. In Jerusalem, at the Temple, our ancestors were grateful to God for a bountiful harvest.

The Bible says, in Deuteronomy 8:7:

For the Lord your God brings you into a good land, a land of brooks of water, of fountains in valleys and hills; a land of wheat and barley, and vines and fig trees and pomegranates; a land of olive trees and honey.

Of these "seven kinds," every farmer was to bring his first fruits as a thank-offering to God. That is why one name for Shavuot is *Chag Ha-Bikkurim,* the Festival of First Fruits.

The rabbis tell how the first ripe fruits were selected. Upon visiting his field and seeing a fig, or a cluster of grapes, or a pomegranate that was ripe, the owner would tie a thread around the fruit, saying, "This shall be among the *bikkurim.*"

The Seven Kinds

Each of the seven kinds of fruits mentioned in the Bible played an important part in the Torah and in Jewish history.

Wheat and Barley

Israel's rainfall is heaviest during the winter months, so the best harvests come from the winter crops of wheat and barley. Barley ripens about Pesach time, and was brought to the Temple during Passover. Wheat needs more rainfall and ripens later. So important was the harvest that it was used to record events and dates. The arrival of Ruth and Naomi in Bethlehem, for instance, is not dated by the name of a month but by saying that they came at the beginning of the barley harvest.

Grapes

Grapes need plenty of rainfall for growth and lots of sunshine to allow the leaves and fruit clusters to develop. Israel has both. The first grapes ripen early in Sivan, in time for Shavuot. The spies sent by Moses to Canaan brought back a cluster of grapes so heavy that "they bore it between two on a staff" (Numbers 13:23). The Bible says: "And Judah and Israel dwelt safely, every man under his vine and under his fig tree" (1 Kings 5:5).

Figs

The Torah has been likened to a fig. All fruits have some waste material: seeds, pits, or rind; the entire fig, however, can be eaten, and so it is with every word in the Torah. The Talmud says: "When you see a fig tree, make a blessing: 'How pleasant is this fig tree; blessed is God Who created it!'

An embroidered tapestry with the names and pictures of the seven kinds. The Torah quotation, starting from the top, right reads: "Land of wheat, barley, grapes, dates, pomegranates, olive oil and honey."

At the *bikkurim* festival of the first fruits, all the age groups of the kibbutz take part. The children wear laurel wreaths and carry baskets of fruits and vegetables; the young men and women dance in the fields and the adults cut sheaves of grain and bring them to the platform. Around this central point, the entire kibbutz is gathered and nearby there is a display of the produce of the soil—the fruit of the kibbutz harvest from its orchards, vegetable garden and field crops.

The pomegranate had many uses in ancient Israel. It was used as a dye, and for writing ink. In addition, ancient doctors used the juice of the pomegranate for medical purposes. Pomegranate juice is also an excellent thirst quencher.

A display of fresh green olives. The Hebrew word for olive is *zayit*.

An oil press from talmudic times. Ripe olives were crushed and olive oil was extracted. Olive oil was a basic food in ancient Israel.

Pomegranates

The spies sent to Canaan brought back pomegranates. Because it ripens in late summer, its blossoms were used to adorn the sheaves of grain brought to the Temple on Shavuot and the fruit was brought after it had ripened. Farmers quenched their thirst with pomegranate juice and the rind was used to make dyes and ink. The clothes of the *kohanim* (priests) in the Temple were decorated with artistically carved pomegranates, and the silver ornaments used to crown the Torah scroll are called *rimonim* ("pomegranates").

Olives

The olive tree is very common in the Mediterranean. Its small leaves are covered with a thick, shiny coat and can well stand the scorching summer sun. The branch of the olive tree has become a symbol of peace. Noah's dove, sent from the ark to find out whether the flood had gone abated, brought back an olive branch. Olive oil lit the Temple Menorah, and was one of the most important exports of ancient Israel.

Dates

During the picking season dates are moist and juicy; later they are dried. The best area for dates in Israel is the Jordan Valley. The date-palm is not sown with seeds, but with shoots which sprout from its roots. The Midrash says:

A righteous person will flourish like a date-palm; its dates are eaten, its branches are used to thatch roofs, its fibers are made into ropes. The Children of Israel are the same; some study Torah, some the Mishnah, some the Talmud.

Then and Now

In ancient Israel, a long procession would wind its way through the streets of Jerusalem, made up of men, women, and children carrying baskets filled with the produce of the soil, the first fruits, to the Temple.

Today, in modern Israel, this custom has been revived. Long lines of children march with their baskets and guide beautifully decorated floats. The fruits are sold for the benefit of the Jewish National Fund.

What do we do on Shavuot? We decorate our homes and synagogues with plants and flowers. The greenery reminds us that it is a harvest festival and also that Mount Sinai was covered with green foliage when Moses ascended it to receive the Torah.

Jerusalem pre-kindergarten children with floral crowns and basket of first fruits at a Shavuot celebration in Independence Park.

In the Synagogue

In the synagogue, in addition to the regular holiday service, the Book of Ruth is read on Shavuot. The reason is that this beautiful story of faith and devotion took place during the harvest season. Moreover, King David was descended from Ruth, and it is believed that he was born and that he died on Shavuot.

The Book of Ruth

The Book of Ruth is one of the Five Megillot. It is recited in the synagogue on Shavuot because its story is set in the harvest field and its leading character embraces Judaism.

The story of Ruth took place in Judah around the twelfth century B.C.E. During a famine a Judean man named, Elimelech with his wife Naomi and their two sons Mahlon and Chilion fled to Moab. Soon afterwards, Elimelech died and his two sons married Moabite girls. Chilion married Orpah, and Mahlon was wed to Ruth.

The sons also died and Naomi, widowed and childless, decided to return to Judah. Her two daughters-in-law offered to accompany Naomi back to her homeland. Orpah, after much discussion, was persuaded to remain in Moab, but Ruth insisted on remaining with Naomi.

The gleaners.

Ruth said to Naomi: *"Wherever you go, I will go, wherever you stay, I will stay; your people shall be my people; and your god shall be my god; wherever you die, I will die, and there I will be buried."*

The Harvest Season

The two women arrived at Bethlehem during the spring grain harvest. The farmers were busy harvesting and cutting stalks of grain with sharp sickles. According to Jewish law, any grain that dropped was left for the poor, who were allowed to glean the stalks. Ruth and Naomi joined the gleaners. Boaz, a wealthy farmer, saw Ruth gleaning in the hot sun.

An ancient iron sickle. This sharp knife was used for harvesting grain. Sickles are still used in underdeveloped regions of the world.

The Israeli archaeologist Abraham Biran excavated the 4000-year-old site of Tel-Dan. He found a stone inscription which he believes contains the first mention of the royal House of David.

He said to her, *"All you have done for your mother-in-law is known to me. God will reward you for your kindness."*

Boaz soon married Ruth, and she gave birth to a son named Obed, who was the father of Jesse, who in turn fathered David, who became the king of Israel.

Akdamut

A special prayer chanted in traditional synagogues on Shavuot is called *Akdamut*. It is a hymn of praise, thanking God for giving us the Torah.

Confirmation

A Shavuot custom that has grown up in many Conservative and Reform synagogues is that of Confirmation. Because the Jewish people received the Torah on Shavuot, this holiday has become the season for the beautiful ceremony in which boys and girls are confirmed, or initiated, into the fellowship of our people.

Youngsters who have attended religious schools and completed the course of study take part in this religious graduation exercise. They are now considered to be full-fledged sons and daughters of the Jewish faith who have become responsible Jews, just as our ancestors were initiated into freedom and responsibility at Mount Sinai.

Shavuot Taste Treats

Shavuot calls for eating blintzes (a kind of small rolled pancake stuffed with cheese), cheese cake, and other dairy delicacies. The custom of eating dairy foods symbolizes the fact that the Torah is likened to "milk and honey."

And so, with Shavuot, the happy holiday season ticked off for us by the Jewish calendar comes to a close. The wheel has come full circle, and we can echo the words of King Solomon, who wrote in Song of Songs:

For lo, the winter is past
The rain is over and gone,
The flowers appear on the earth
The time of singing has come . . .

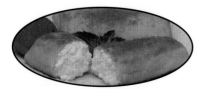

A plate of cheese blintzes

The cycle of Jewish holidays is over. Rosh Hashanah, Sukkot, Chanukah, and all the others have come and gone, bringing in their train joy and solemnity, prayer and family fun.

Laws for the Needy

The story of Ruth and Naomi illustrates the concern of ancient Jews for the needy in their midst. When the shepherds of Abraham and Lot quarreled, Abraham gave Lot his pick of the land. He wanted to provide Lot with the means to make a living.

Among no people of old was there so much concern shown for those in want as in Israel. In the ancient Hebrew state, the poor were assured of a living by the rights in the harvest which the Bible gave them. These rights were five in number.

1. *Pe'ah* ("Corner"): The poor had the right to anything that grew in the corners of the field.
2. *Leket* ("Gathering"): The poor had the right to anything dropped on the ground when the grain was being picked.
3. *Peret* ("Gleaning"): The poor had the right to isolated grapes that fell off the vine.
4. *Olelot* ("Young Clusters"): The poor had the right to grapes that were not perfect.
5. *Shikchah* ("Forgetfulness"): The poor had the right to sheaves of grain that were forgotten by the farmer.

All these parts of the harvest belonged to the poor. The farmer was not allowed to gather them, and all needy people-the poor, the widow, the orphan, and the stranger (whether Jew or non-Jew)-were entitled to them. There was also a special poor tax known as the *ma'aser oni,* or poor tithe. Twice in seven years the Jewish farmer had to set aside one-tenth of the harvest for this purpose and take it to a special storehouse in the district where the poor tithe was kept for distribution.

Modernistic Israeli stamp showing Ruth gleaning in the fields. The caption from the Book of Ruth reads: "and came to a people you had not known before."

Tishah B'Av

AV						אָב
Sun.	Mon.	Tues.	Wed.	Thur.	Fri.	Sat.
			1	2	3	4
5	6	7	8	9	10	11
12	13	14	15	16	17	18
19	20	21	22	23	24	25
26	27	28	29	30		

The Hebrew word *tisha* means nine. The holiday of Tishah B'Av is commemorated on the 9th day of Av.

Although Judaism is not a religion that emphasizes deprivation and self-punishment, there are several fast-days on the Jewish calendar. These have been set aside to recall tragic events in the history of the Jewish people.

The chief of them, Tishah B'Av, falls on the ninth day of the summer month of Av, and has a strange and tradition-filled background.

Tishah B'Av is the saddest day of the Jewish year. The word *tishah*, indicating the day of the month, means "nine," and Av is the ninth month of the Jewish year. On this day, many Jewish historical tragedies took place.

The First Temple Is Destroyed

On the ninth of Av in 586 B.C.E., Solomon's beautiful Temple in Jerusalem was destroyed. Nebuchadnezzar, the king of Babylon, sent his army to conquer the kingdom of Judah. His chariots, battering rams, and well-trained soldiers easily defeated the Jews. Zedekiah, the last king of Judah, was captured and forced to watch his children being murdered. Then he was blinded, put in chains, and marched off as a captive in Babylonia.

The victors destroyed Solomon's Temple and set fire to the rest of the city. After 400 years, the House of David came to a tragic end. Most of the leaders and teachers were put to death or deported to Babylonia. There, far from their homeland, they lived in the Babylonian Exile.

The Second Temple Is Destroyed

Six hundred years later in 70 C.E., on the very same day, the Second Temple was destroyed.

In 63 B.C.E., Pompey's Roman legions overran Judea and after a three-month siege captured Jerusalem. Although

This miniature from a 14th century French Bible shows the blinded king Zedekiah being led into captivity. Zedekiah's desperate rebellion against Nebuchadnezzar led to the Babylonian invasion of Judah in 587 B.C.E.

Rome seemed all-powerful, the Jews never gave up the dream of independence. Jewish rebels called Zealots formed guerilla bands and attacked Roman patrols and outposts. Finally, in 66 C.E. the people of Judea rose up in revolt against Rome, and after much fierce fighting regained control of Jerusalem. The following year, a well-equipped, powerful Roman army invaded Judea. In 70 C.E., the Roman general Titus began the siege of Jerusalem. On the ninth of Av, the Romans stormed the Temple and destroyed the city. More than a million Jews died in the war and tens of thousands were marched into exile and slavery.

Bar Kochba is Defeated

About 60 years later, Hadrian became emperor of Rome. He decided to rebuild the Temple as a place of worship for Rome's pagan gods. Determined to destroy Judaism, he outlawed the study of Torah and many other traditional religious practices.

Hadrian's decrees triggered a new revolt. In 132 C.E., under the leadership of Bar Kochba, the people of Judea defeated the Roman garrison and drove it into Syria. The Jews enjoyed two short years of freedom.

Hadrian sent Severus, his best general, to crush the revolt. One by one, the Jewish strongholds were destroyed. Bar Kochba and his soldiers made their last stand in the mountain fortress of Betar. On the ninth day of Av in 135 B.C.E., Betar was overwhelmed and the defenders were massacred.

The Jews of Spain

Jews first settled in Spain in Roman times. When the Arabs conquered part of Spain in 755 C.E., thousands more emigrated from North Africa. The Arab rulers welcomed the Jews and used their commercial, political, and professional talents for their own advantage. The period from the ninth to the twelfth century, during which the Jews of Spain lived in relative freedom and prosperity, was called the Golden Age of Spain.

The Marranos

Under Arab rule, Jewish poets, scientists, teachers, merchants, and politicians were welcome in Spanish society. Jews freely practiced their religion and built beautiful synagogues and schools of learning.

The fortress of Masada was built by King Herod. It has been excavated and a large part has been reconstructed.
In 73 C.E., after a long siege the Romans overran Masada. When they entered the stronghold they found the bodies of the defenders. The Jews had killed their families and themselves, rather than be captured by the Romans.

The Romans celebrated their triumph over the Jews by erecting the Arch of Titus in Rome.

A copy of the carving on the Arch of Titus, showing the Menorah and other furniture of the Temple being carried in triumph through the streets of Rome.

Isabella and Ferdinand witness the conversion of a Jew. Note that the kneeling Jew has crossed his arms into the shape of a cross.

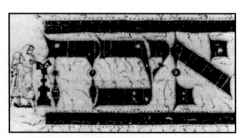

This painting from a German manuscript of 1344 decorates *Eycha*, the first Hebrew word in the Book of Lamentations. It shows a Jew, wearing a *tallit*, preparing to read the text. The Book of Lamentations was written in response to the destruction of the First Temple. On Tisha B'Av, it is read in the synagogue in a sad chant.

Things changed when the Christians reconquered Spain. Jews were now seen as interlopers. The Inquisition was set up to force them to convert to Christianity. Thousands of Jews converted, but many of them continued to practice Judaism in secret. Those who lived as Christians before the outside world but as Jews in private were called Marranos. Many of them were arrested and tortured by the Inquisition police.

Under pressure from the Inquisition, King Ferdinand and Queen Isabella ordered the Jews of Spain to convert or leave the country. Hundreds of thousands chose to leave. The expulsion from Spain took place on the ninth day of Av in 1492. By sea and by land, scores of thousands of Jews sadly departed from their homeland, a place where their ancestors had lived for many centuries.

The Lamentations of Jeremiah

Lamentations, a sad book of the Bible, is read as part of the synagogue service on Tishah B'Av. It describes the sorrow of the prophet Jeremiah, who lived through the destruction of Jerusalem by the Babylonians. As Jeremiah looked upon the ravaged city, he compared its sorrow and desolation to that of a woman mourning her husband's death:

How lonely sits the city that was full of people,
How like a widow she has become.
She that was great among the nations,
Has become a vassal.

Not only are the words of Lamentations sad, but the trope, or chant, in which it is recited aloud has a sad and mournful sound. In some temples, on Tishah B'Av, the worshipers sit on backless benches or on the floor as a sign of mourning.

Some traditional Jews observe the nine days before Tishah B'Av as a mourning period. During this time they do not buy new clothes, have their hair cut, swim, or eat meat.

And Close with Hope

The Sabbath following *Tishah B'Av* is called *Shabbat Nachamu*. On it we read the fortieth chapter of Isaiah, which contains a dream of hope and comfort: "Comfort ye, comfort ye, my people, Saith your God . . ."

The Fast of the Seventeenth of Tammuz

On this day Roman soldiers broke through the walls of Jerusalem leading to the destruction of the Second Temple in 70 C.E. According to tradition, it was also on this day that Moses broke the first set of the tablets of the Ten Commandments.

The fast of the seventeenth of Tammuz begins the three weeks of mourning which conclude on the ninth of *Av* with Tishah B'Av.

Tzom Gedaliah

The Fast of Gedaliah falls on the day after Rosh Hashanah. Gedaliah was the governor appointed by Nebuchadnezzar to rule the Jews of Palestine. On this day Gedaliah was assassinated, and Nebuchadnezzar ordered reprisals against the Jews.

Asarah B' Tevet

On the tenth day of the winter month of Tevet, Nebuchadnezzar began his siege of Jerusalem. Deprived of food and supplies, the populace grew weaker, until at last Nebuchadnezzar was able to storm the city and destroy the First Temple in 586 B.C.E.

Tishah B'Av in Israel

In Israel on Tishah B'Av, many people gather at the Western Wall in the Old City of Jerusalem. This wall is all that remains of the Second Temple destroyed by the Romans so long ago. Here people pray and hope that Israel today will have the strength to withstand all of the enemies that seek its ruin.

This 15th–century French painting shows Pompey and his soldiers desecrating and looting the Holy Temple.

The Synagogue

According to the Torah, God wanted to dwell in the midst of His people. So God gave Moses detailed instructions how to build a portable tabernacle in which God would reside. This is an artist's rendering of the tabernacle. The outer court of the tabernacle was 175 feet long and 90 feet wide.

Archaeologists have unearthed the stone relief of the Holy Ark in the ancient synagogue in Capernaum. The original Holy Ark was built by Moses, and was carried from place to place before being permanently enshrined in the First Temple.

Since every Jewish festival and fast is observed in the synagogue with special services and ceremonies it is time to focus our spotlight on the Jewish house of worship. The best way to begin is to walk into your synagogue or temple. The building may be new, but the synagogue itself is the oldest of Jewish institutions.

It was in Babylon, some 2,500 years ago, that the synagogue was born. Our ancestors had been exiled from the Holy Land to Babylon in 586 B.C.E. The First Temple in Jerusalem had gone up in flames. Did this mean the end of Jewish worship and prayer? The captives in Babylon did not think so.

Though far from their native land, they gathered, perhaps at first in private homes, to listen to words of encouragement from their spiritual leaders. They remembered the Temple ceremonies. They recited passages from the Torah or Prophets, observed the national feast and fast days, and sang the Psalms of David. All this held them together as a people and gave them hope that one day they would return to Israel.

Center of Jewish Life

Each of these meetings was called a *knesset*, or "assembly," a word that was translated into Greek many years later as "synagogue." A synagogue was and is more than a place of worship. It is a house of assembly for all Jewish activities: prayer, education, and general communal welfare.

More than a half century after the exile began in 586 B.C.E., Persia conquered Babylon and allowed many of the Jewish captives to return to Judea and rebuild the Temple. This second Temple existed until the Roman general Titus destroyed it in 70 C.E.

Those Jews who remained in Babylonia continued to meet and worship in synagogues. Moreover, even though they had a Temple once again, the Jews of the Second Commonwealth in Judea did not forsake the newly created institution of the synagogue.

So that All Might Take Part

The Temple was the place of worship where sacrifices were offered daily, but in this sanctuary the priests (*kohanim*) were in charge. Since those who were not priests felt that they too should be allowed to participate, the ordinary Israelites in every town were organized into twenty-four divisions called *ma'amadot*. Each *ma'amad* went to Jerusalem to take part in the Temple ceremonies for about two weeks of every year. Those who remained at home assembled in a place in their town especially set aside for worship–in other words, a synagogue.

Originally, the services may have been limited to the Sabbath, when work ceased. Next, they may have taken place on Mondays and Thursdays, the market days when the country folk came to town. Finally, services were held every day.

"When Ten Jews Assemble"

The Talmud refers to the synagogue as *bet am*, "the house of the people." The rabbis declared:

Let a person but enter a synagogue, even stand behind a pillar in the corner, and pray in a whisper, and the Holy One, blessed be God, listens to the prayer. . . . When ten Jews assemble in prayer, the Shechinah, the Divine Presence, is there.

In the town of Betar there were 400 synagogues with elementary teachers and religious schools. The holiness of the house of worship was emphasized in Jewish law, which said that even if a synagogue was in ruins, one was not permitted to destroy it.

The beautiful frescoes and inscriptions in the remains of ancient synagogues such as the one at Dura–Europos in Syria dating from the third century C.E., show how much the people loved and cared for their houses of worship.

The Ark in the land of the Philistines. Taken from the fresco in the synagogue at Dura-Europos, 3rd century C.E.

A reconstruction of Solomon's Temple.

131

The remains of the synagogue at Capernaum on the shores of the Sea of Galilee.

A medieval painting of a Hebrew teacher and his young pupil. Note the whip and the hourglass. Germany, 13th cent.

A reconstruction of the synagogue in Kaifeng, China. The synagogue was built in 1173 and was rebuilt by the Jewish Mandarin Chao Ying Chen.

"Miniature Temple"

The synagogue was often called a *mikdash ma'at*, a "miniature temple."

One of the largest synagogues of ancient times was in the Egyptian city of Alexandria. It had two rows of massive columns on either side of the great hall, and in the middle was a huge wooden platform, or *bimah*. The building was so big that the *chazzan*, or reader, had to give a signal by waving a cloth in order to have the congregation answer amen to his prayers. In this synagogue the congregants were always seated according to their trades: blacksmiths, goldsmiths, weavers, and so on, each in their own section.

When the Second Temple was destroyed in 70 C.E., the many synagogues in Jerusalem also went up in flames. By this time, hundreds of other synagogues existed wherever Jews lived, in Asia, Africa, and Europe. And as Jewish merchant ships opened new roads of commerce the construction of synagogues increased. They were built in countries as far east as China and as far west as Italy, Spain, France, and Germany. German Jews, fleeing from pogroms, brought the synagogue to Eastern Europe. Refugees from the Inquisition in Spain and Portugal came to Holland, and built houses of worship where they prayed in the Sephardic or Spanish tradition.

In the Middle Ages

In the Middle Ages, Jews were often forced to live in separate areas of the town called ghettos. They led a communal life of their own which was culturally rich and had its happy side. The most important institution in the Jewish community of those days was the synagogue.

The synagogue building stood in the center of the ghetto. Here people came for religious services, study and discussion, celebrations and meetings.

The Three Names

Because of its many functions, the synagogue was known by three names: *bet ha-tefillah*, or house of worship; *bet ha-midrash*, or house of study; and *bet ha-knesset*, or house of assembly.

On Sabbath and holiday afternoons the rabbi of the community would speak to the congregants. Teachers and preachers from foreign countries brought news from abroad. A messenger from Palestine would sometimes bring news of the Holy Land to the community. The weary traveler came to the synagogue to find lodging and our custom of reciting the *Kiddush* on Friday night in the synagogue is a result of that age–old practice of hospitality.

Children were given their names in the synagogue and bridegrooms came there to offer prayers on the Sabbath before their weddings. It is still customary to express sympathy for mourners by turning toward them with words of comfort as they enter the synagogue on Friday night.

Adult Education

The synagogue was the world's first school of adult education. As the Talmud says:

> *Upon returning home from the field in the evening, go to the synagogue. If you are used to studying the Torah, study the Torah; or if you are accustomed to studying the Mishnah, study the Mishnah.*

It was also in the synagogue that children began their religious studies, first by accompanying their parents to services, and later by attending its religious school.

The Talmud advised that Torah study should begin at the age of four, the study of Mishnah at the age of ten, and Talmud study at the age of fifteen.

Home of the *Cheder*

The synagogue housed both the *cheder*, or school for children, and the higher school of learning, or *yeshiva*. The synagogue was a true community center, a places where town meetings were held, and where charity was collected and distributed. The synagogue was a shelter for travelers as well as for students. When disputes arose they were settled at trials in the synagogue. Friends met in the synagogue and used its library for reading and study. The officers of the synagogue were also the leaders of the community.

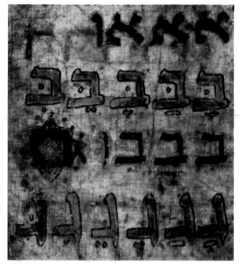

This book was produced in 10th century Egypt to teach the *alefbet* to young Hebrew students. This page was found in the Cairo Genizah.

"The Cheder," by Moritz Oppenheim, 19th century. Young pupils who have just started to study wait their turn to recite the Hebrew *alefbet*. Notice the student standing on a stool as he recites.

The Jews in this Polish synagogue are wearing fur hats called *streimels* that were worn on holidays and special occasions. This rabbi and his disciples are praying in front of a desk called a *shtender*. The texts are located on shelves above them. The Yiddish word for "standing" is *shtayt*, hence the Yiddish word *shtender*.

The Mill Street Synagogue of the Shearith Israel Congregation of New York, erected in 1730.

This chart for counting the Omer between Passover and Shavuot was used in the synagogue.

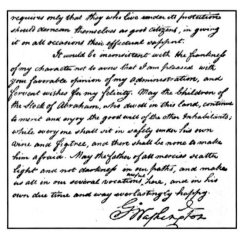

George Washington's famous letter to the Jews of Newport, admiring their expression of faith in American democracy.

When Tyranny Failed

As the Jewish people settled in various countries, the local governments often sought to curb Jewish life by issuing decrees against building new synagogues or making them taller than the mosques or churches.

The history of the Jewish people is portrayed in the role of the synagogue. Sometimes it even served as a fortress, as in France and Germany during the Crusades, or in Poland during the Chmielnicki pogroms of 1648. During the period of the Inquisition in Spain, the Marranos, who were forced to pretend that they were Christians, made their synagogues in cellars or caves so that spies would be unable to overhear the prayers and inform the police.

Always the Same Purpose

At the dawn of modern times the ghettos vanished and many Jewish communities built synagogues of beauty and grandeur. But the chief purpose of every synagogue, whether it was majestic or humble, was the same: to provide a place where people could worship God in the tradition of their ancestors.

The Synagogue in America

A little over three hundred years ago, a vessel containing twenty-three men, women, and children fleeing from persecution in South America sailed into what is today New York harbor. They settled in New Amsterdam, soon to be renamed New York. These twenty-three pioneers formed the first Jewish community in America.

First American Synagogue

Soon after they had landed, these early settlers formed a congregation named Shearith Israel, which means "Remnant of Israel." Peter Stuyvesant, the Dutch governor, did not permit them to build a synagogue, so they held services under the trees, in homes, and in a rented one-room building in what is now the heart of New York's financial district. A map of Manhattan Island from 1695 indicates a Jewish synagogue on the south side of Wall Street near Beaver Street.

In 1730 the congregation built the first synagogue in North America, the Mill Street Synagogue, which remained in use for almost a century. Today, Congregation Shearith Israel, also known as the Spanish and Portuguese Synagogue, faces Central Park in Manhattan. It proudly observed its own three hundredth birthday during the American Jewish Tercentenary celebration.

That first synagogue on Mill Street was 35 feet square and 21 feet high. From 1730 to 1825 all of New York's Jews worshiped in it. Until 1850, when the first synagogue was opened in the then independent city of Brooklyn, Jews would row across the East River to spend the Sabbath with their brethren in Manhattan.

The Ark of Congregation Beth Elohim, Charleston, South Carolina, is a replica of the one destroyed by fire in 1838. The original Ark was built in 1799.

Serving New Communities

In the meantime, however, other houses of worship were being built to meet the needs of Jews arriving in America. In Newport, Rhode Island, where religious freedom was offered to all, the Touro Synagogue was dedicated in 1763. Jews came to Savannah, Georgia in 1734, and organized a congregation within a month of arriving. In 1745 religious services were first held in Philadelphia. Five years later, a synagogue was built in Charleston, South Carolina. And in 1790 a sixth organized Jewish community took shape in Richmond, Virginia. To these congregations, President George Washington sent letters which are still quoted today because they so strongly champion tolerance and understanding.

An American Historical Monument

The Touro Synagogue is now a United States National Monument. In the year 1658 fifteen Jewish families of Spanish-Portuguese stock settled in Newport. They were attracted to Rhode Island because in this colony founded by Roger Williams, all people, regardless of nationality or faith, were granted religious freedom. In Newport the Jews felt they could live a fruitful life without fear of persecution.

Interior of the beautiful Newport synagogue, the first permanent synagogue in the New World. Named *Yeshuat Israel*, the congregation and its building was supported by Judah Touro for many years.

For one hundred years the town's Jewish residents worshiped in private homes. In 1763 what is now the oldest synagogue building in the United States was dedicated.

Peter Harrison, a famous English architect, was chosen for the work. Reverend Isaac Touro, the father of the American Jewish philanthropist Judah Touro, was the rabbi of the Newport congregation and dedicated the synagogue building which is today a national shrine.

Advertisement (1850) for denim work clothes produced by Levi Strauss & Co.

Painting depicting the stream of numbed immigrants and their back-breaking labor in the sweatshops. Albert Einstein, in front, with the white hair, was one of them.

The Statue of Liberty was a beacon of hope and freedom for all immigrants.

The synagogue, a brick building, is at a sharp angle to the street, so that the Ark can face the east, toward Jerusalem. The bricks–196,715 in number–were imported from England. No nails at all were used in the structure, only wooden pegs, possibly because no iron tool was used in building the Temple in Jerusalem.

A Torah from Holland

One of the prized possessions of the Touro Synagogue is a Torah scroll that was brought from Amsterdam, Holland. It is at least 400 years old. The silver bells which adorn the scroll were made by the early American silversmith Myer Myers and are an outstanding example of craftsmanship.

The Escape Passage

A feature of great interest is the underground passage. The opening to the passage is in the floor of the *bimah*. At one time the tunnel had an exit to the street at the side of the synagogue. The underground passage was probably built because the early settlers wished to have a symbol by which they could remind their children of the persecution they had suffered in Europe. Secret passageways in synagogues were a feature of Marrano life in Spain. They served as hiding places or as escape exits in times of danger.

George Washington and the Jews

In 1780, a meeting of the General Assembly of Rhode Island was held in the Touro Synagogue. In 1790, George Washington wrote a letter to the warden of the synagogue, Moses Seixas, in which he stated, "happily the Government of the United States . . . gives to bigotry no sanction, to persecution no assistance." A copy of this letter is on the west wall of the synagogue.

Influx of Newcomers

Until 1815, most of the Jewish settlers who came to this country were descendants of Jews from Spain and Portugal. Then, as the American frontier swept westward and southward, as railroads spanned the country, as steamer passage across the Atlantic dwindled to nine or ten days, general population figures skyrocketed, and the Jewish population in the United States grew from 3,000 to 250,000.

Most of the newcomers came from Germany, eager to flee the anti-Semitism that was widespread in that country at the beginning of the nineteenth century. In the United States, they laid the cornerstone of American Reform Judaism and founded many religious and philanthropic organizations.

America had firmly established itself as a symbol of freedom and equality. When new waves of persecution battered the defenseless Jews of Eastern Europe in Russia, Galicia, and Romania, they turned to the "golden land," and America opened its heart to them. Among the immigrants who poured into eastern ports between 1880 and 1920 were two million Jews.

There were three great periods of Jewish immigration to the United States. The first brought the Sephardic Jews; the second, the German Jews; and the third, the Eastern European Jews. Each group was different and brought its own Jewish traditions to the New World. The immigrants were of all possible types—merchants, peddlers who traveled with packs on their backs, factory workers toiling in sweatshops. All of them contributed in their own way to America and to American Jewish life.

Building the Community

In the early years of American history it was the synagogue that held the Jewish community together. The *shochet* who slaughtered meat according to Jewish ritual was paid by the congregation. Matzah making was in the hands of the religious community. Every poor person, every needy widow and orphan, was helped through the synagogue.

The Three Branches

As the country grew and as its Jewish population developed, the synagogue remained a vital part of the American Jewish community. The Reform, Conservative, and Reconstructionist movements grew up alongside of traditional Orthodoxy. Each branch of the Jewish faith gathered followers and strength.

Jewish centers of learning, such as Hebrew Union College–Jewish Institute of Religion, the Jewish Theological Seminary of America, the Reconstructionist Rabbinical College, and Yeshiva University, undertook the task of preparing American young people to be rabbis in our synagogues.

Solomon Schechter

In 1861 Rabbi Sabato Morais and his associates founded the Jewish Theological Seminary. It was first headed by the scholar Solomon Schechter. He gathered an impressive faculty and gave form to the Conservative movement. The Jewish Theological Seminary ordains Conservative rabbis and graduates Jewish scholars and educators.

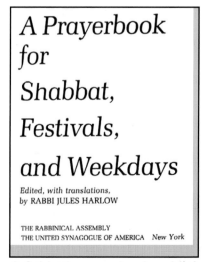

A Prayerbook for Shabbat, Festivals, and Weekdays

Edited, with translations, by RABBI JULES HARLOW

THE RABBINICAL ASSEMBLY
THE UNITED SYNAGOGUE OF AMERICA   New York

A Sabbath prayerbook published by the Conservative movement.

In 1873, Rabbi Isaac Mayer Wise founded the Hebrew Union College in Cincinnati, Ohio. It was the first American institution of Jewish higher education and for the training of Reform rabbis. Today the HUC–JIR has branches in New York, Los Angeles and Israel. The HUC–JIR is a powerful voice for Reform Jewry.

Aerial view of the Hebrew Union College in Cincinnati, Ohio. The complex includes a synagogue, library, and rabbinical school.

GATES OF PRAYER

The New Union Prayerbook

—————

Weekdays, Sabbaths and Festivals
Services and Prayers
for Synagogue and Home

—————

Central Conference of American Rabbis

This Sabbath and Festival prayerbook is published by the Central Conference of American Rabbis [Reform].

Under their guidance, the synagogue has become more and more a center of Jewish activities and social life. It is the modern version of the *bet ha-knesset* of old, offering religious services, a Jewish library, classes, and a place for family celebrations.

A House of Study

In America today, the Jewish community is truly synagogue-centered. Today, we find more and more children in synagogue classrooms. In America today, incidentally, there are more than 2,000 Jewish schools, many of them holding sessions in temples and synagogues. There are congregational schools sponsored by the synagogues they serve. Other kinds of Jewish schools in America are the yeshivot and all-day schools, which are the fastest-growing type of school today, and the Talmud Torah, supported by the community as a whole.

Education in temple and synagogue continues into the evening, for it is there that parents come to participate in adult education classes. The grown-ups study everything from Jewish history to arts and crafts, from Jewish literature to Jewish dance.

A House of Assembly

The synagogue today is host to many groups that foster neighborliness, goodwill, and patriotism. Jewish War Veterans, B'nai B'rith, Boy Scouts and Girl Scouts, men's and women's clubs meet within its friendly walls. Fund raising drives support the Community Federation, the UJA, Israel Bond campaigns, and the rabbinical schools.

Thus the American synagogue today fulfills its ancient threefold calling: to be a house of worship (*bet ha-tefillah*), a house of study (*bet ha-midrash*), and a house of assembly (*bet ha-knesset*).

Talking of Numbers

As new congregations form they usually join one of the three national synagogue organizations. The membership rolls of these groups offer a picture of the synagogues in our land. The Union of Orthodox Jewish Congregations numbers 950 congregations; the United Synagogue of America (Conservative) has a membership of 875 congregations; the Union of American Hebrew Congregations (Reform) has 850 congregations and the Reconstructionist Movement has 100 congregations. There are many synagogues that do not officially belong to any of these bodies.

From that single hard-won synagogue in early New York there are now over 3,000 congregations. Within the borders of North America, the synagogue has taken root and flourished as the heart of Jewish life.

Sacred Objects

In our synagogues and temples we find many sacred ceremonial objects. They are symbols of our faith, hallowed by custom and tradition. They have graced our houses of worship for many centuries. To know about them is to have more respect for them, for they are a bond connecting us with our faith, our history, and our people.

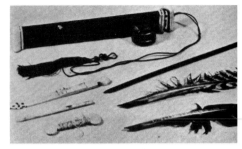

These tools are used in writing a Torah scroll. Here you see the inkwell, the reeds and their case, quills, and sinews (of kosher animals) for sewing parchment sheets together.

The Torah

What is the most precious object in every synagogue? The Torah scroll, of course. Just as we have kept the Torah sacred for thousands of years, so has it kept the Jewish people alive during all that time. The Torah—the word itself means "teaching" or "law"—is a scroll made of specially prepared parchment. The Five Books of Moses that it contains may be written only by hand and without punctuation or vowel points. For the purpose of Sabbath reading, the Torah has been divided into fifty-four *sidrot*, or portions.

Writing a *Sefer Torah*

The *Sefer Torah* must always be written by hand. Today, as for countless past generations, the Holy Scroll is prepared with painstaking care by a *sofer*, or scribe, specially trained in Jewish law and traditions for his sacred task.

Siddur and *Machzor*

The *Siddur* is the prayerbook for weekdays and Sabbath; the *Machzor* is used on festivals. The prayerbook contains passages from the Bible and from the Talmud, as well as selections written by rabbis and poets through the Middle Ages. The *Siddur* is mostly in Hebrew, but some of its prayers are in Aramaic, the language Jews used in everyday life in Babylonia. The *Kaddish*, for example, which is a hymn of praise to God and is

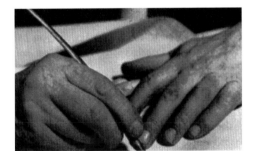

A *sofer*, writing a Torah in the traditional way with a feather pen and special ink on parchment. In Babylonia , the Torah was divided into 54 sections called *sidrot*, so that the entire Torah could be read completely in one year. Some synagogues read the Torah in a triennial cycle and complete the Torah reading in three years.

A *tallit*. The fringes called *tzitzit* are knotted in the four corners of the *tallit*.

said as a prayer for the dead, is still repeated in its ancient Aramaic. Prayers such as the *Shema* and the *Amidah*, and beloved hymns like *Adon Olam* and *Yigdal*, are found in the pages of our prayerbook.

Tallit

The *tallit* is the prayer shawl traditionally worn by men and boys at the morning services on weekdays, Sabbaths, and has now been adopted as well by some women in the liberal branches of Judaism. It recalls the style of the upper garment worn in ancient Israel. When Jews went to other lands, the *tallit* came to be used only for religious services. The *tallit* is fringed at each of its four corners in accordance with the specifications given in the Bible:

Make a fringe upon the corners of your garments so that you may look upon it and remember the commandments of the Lord. Numbers 15:38

Up above the *Aron Ha-Kodesh* hangs a light which is never permitted to go out. The *ner tamid*, the "eternal light" is the symbol of the presence of God among us. In the days of the Temple, a lamp containing pure olive oil burned continuously before the Ark.

Aron Ha–Kodesh

The *Aron Ha–Kodesh,* or Holy Ark, is a wooden chest or cabinet on the *bimah*, often beautifully decorated, in which the Torah scrolls are kept.

Ten Commandments

Above the Ark are two tablets with Hebrew letters on them, usually abbreviations of the Ten Commandments, which are found in Exodus 20:2–14 and Deuteronomy 5:6–18. The Ten Commandments tell us to worship God and be kind and honest to one another. They are the highest laws in Judaism and the basis of the moral law of humankind.

Menorah

The menorah reminds us of the golden seven-branched candelabrum that stood in the Holy Temple. The light it sheds stands for the brightness of Torah.

Ner Tamid

Up above the *Aron Ha–Kodesh* hangs a light which is never permitted to go out. This is the *ner tamid*, the "eternal light," a symbol of the presence of God among us, of happiness, of the light that the synagogue gives. In the days of the ancient Temple, a lamp containing pure olive oil burned continually, illuminating at all times the *aron* holding the Ten Commandments. When a new synagogue is dedicated, the most important ceremonies are the placing of the Torah scrolls in the ark and the lighting of the *ner tamid*.

Bimah

The *bimah* is the raised platform on which the desk stands for the reading of the weekly portions from the Torah and the Prophets. The *bimah* is sometimes placed in the center of the synagogue, where it represents the altar that once stood in the middle compartment of the Temple, and sometimes at the front of the synagogue.

Tzedakah Box

The Temple in Jerusalem had a charity box. Contributions were used for Temple repairs and to help the poor. The custom has remained with us, for we all know that giving charity is one of the finest things we can do. Often there will be a little sign on a charity box in a synagogue stating the purpose for which the money is to be used. It may be for clothing the poor, extending loans to the needy, or for some other worthwhile cause or institution.

A charity collection box from a synagogue in Bohemia, 19th century. The top hebrew line reads *matan b'sayter,* meaning "giving charity secretly." According to Maimonides this type of giving is one the highest form of charity.

Synagogue Duties

Over the centuries, certain synagogue duties have been performed by persons specially trained in Jewish law, customs, traditions. Here are a few of the offices of the synagogue, brief descriptions of their history and the role they play today.

Rabbi

The title rabbi, which means "my teacher," is given to a religious leader and teacher. The title was first used during the time of the destruction of the Second Temple (70 C.E.). Today, rabbis are ordained by the rabbinical seminary from which they were graduated.

The duties of a rabbi are to serve as religious leader of the congregation, make decisions on practical questions of Jewish law, conduct services, and preach on Sabbaths, holy days, and festivals, teach Judaism to children and adult groups, and officiate at important events in the lives of the congregants (such as circumcision, marriage, and burial). In the past only

A Jewish soup kitchen in London's East end, 1879.

141

A bearded cantor and his choir. Italy ca. 1470.

men could be rabbis. Today, in the Reform, Conservative, and Reconstructionist movements, women also serve in this role.

Chazzan

In the days of the Mishnah and Talmud, the *chazzan* was a caretaker of the synagogue and an official at religious ceremonies. Today the term *chazzan*, or cantor, designates the person who chants the religious services in the synagogue. In the Reform, Conservative and Reconstructionist movements, but not in Orthodox Judaism, women often serve as cantors.

Shammash

The *shammash*, or sexton, has had a role in synagogue life for many centuries. In early times and in the medieval period he stood ready to carry out official synagogue decisions. He was the superintendent of the synagogue, and in East European towns, would call the congregants to services at daybreak. Sometimes, the duties of the *shammash* were so numerous that he was given assistants to help. In many synagogues today, the *shammash* is well-versed in Jewish learning and often reads from the Torah.

Ba'al Koreh

The *ba'al koreh*, or "master reader," chants the portions (*sidrot*) from the Torah. Long ago, this was one of the functions of the *chazzan* and later of the *shammash*. When the duties of the *shammash* became too heavy he had the right to hire a *ba'al koreh* to help him.

Gabbai

The *gabbai's* title comes from the Hebrew word for "to raise" or "to collect," and in medieval times he was a very important congregational official, for he was the treasurer of the synagogue. Today, the *gabbai* is often a congregant who is given certain synagogue duties to perform, such as maintaining order during services, collecting dues, keeping records, and the like.

Ba'al Toke'ah

The *ba'al toke'ah* is the "master blower" whose honor it is to blow the shofar when synagogue services require it.

Synagogue clock, Bohemia, ca. 1870. This unusual clock has settings for the daily and Shabbat prayers. The clocks on the right are set for the morning, afternoon and Friday night services. The clocks on the left are set for the morning, afternoon and evening services for the Sabbath.
The center clock is for the regular time of day.

Ba'al Tefillah

The *ba'al tefillah* is a person (other than the *chazzan*) who leads the congregation in prayer. A *ba'al tefillah* who leads the morning service is called the *ba'al shacharit*; one who leads the additional service is called the *ba'al musaf*.

This is the synagogue, its background, its role, the meaning of its ceremonial objects. No one can deny that the history of the synagogue truly records the preservation of the Jewish people. Without this ancient institution, the Jews could not have endured hardship and suffering, nor continued in our devotion to Torah, to learning, and to social justice. The synagogue and temple of today remain the echo of the past and the sounding board for current needs.

A young *ba'al tefillah* leads the congregation in prayer.

The Torah

Moses and the Torah

After the Israelites left Egypt, they camped around Mount Sinai. Moses ascended the mountain and remained there for forty days and nights. Then, amid thunder and lightning, he descended and presented the people with the Ten Commandments. According to some traditions, he gave them the entire Torah. Torah is the Hebrew name for the first five books of the Bible. In Hebrew it means "teaching" and "law."

While the Israelites wandered through the desert for forty years, Moses instituted the practice of reading sections of the Torah on Sabbaths, festivals, and Rosh Chodesh.

The Torah in Israel and Babylon

Long afterward, during the Babylonian Exile, Ezra the Scribe and the Men of the Great Assembly ruled that a specific *sidrah*, or portion, from the Torah was to be assigned to each Sabbath, so that all five scrolls (the Five Books of Moses) could be completed in one full year. They divided the Torah into 54 *sidrot* according to the number of the weeks in a leap year, when an extra month, Second Adar, is added. In a normal year, when there are only 52 weeks, the two extra *sidrot* are read on special Sabbaths.

The rabbis in ancient Israel disagreed with their colleagues in Babylonia. They divided the Torah into 155 smaller portions so that it would take three years to read the whole Torah. This system is called the triennial cycle, and it is now followed in Reform, Reconstructionist and many Conservative congregations.

Ezra also instituted the reading of short sections of the Torah on Mondays and Thursdays and Saturday afternoons. Mondays and Thursdays were market days when farmers came to the city to sell their produce and purchase supplies.

The imposing heights of Mount Sinai.

Ezra recognized that these days were opportunities to assemble a group and teach Torah.

Today, Orthodox and Conservative synagogues continue the practice and read short sections of the Torah on Mondays, Thursdays and Saturday afternoons.

The systematic reading of the Torah has had an extraordinary educational and spiritual impact on the life of Jews throughout their history. The Torah is not just read, it is studied and explained; and its ethical lessons are applied to the daily life of Jews no matter where they reside. The Torah is the cornerstone of the Jewish religion and has had a profound effect on Jewish survival.

Judaism is religion centered on this sacred document. Every synagogue and temple enshrines at least one Torah scroll. The Torah scroll is beautified with adornments which are draped on and around it.

The *Haftarah*

A portion from the Prophets called the *Haftarah* is also read on each Sabbath. The *Haftarah* always has a thematic relationship to the weekly *sidrah*. The custom of reading the *Haftarah* was instituted during the occupation of ancient Israel by the Greek conquerors. The Greeks forbade the reading of the Torah, so the rabbis cleverly substituted the reading of a selection from the Prophets. Today, both the *sidrah* and the *Haftarah* are read on Sabbaths and holidays.

The *Trope*

The Torah itself is handwritten on parchment with a feather pen using a specially prepared black ink. As in the ancient Torah that Moses presented to the Israelites there is no punctuation and no vowel symbols. In the synagogue the Torah is chanted with special musical notes called the *trope*.

The *Ba'al Koreh*

Even Jews who cannot read the Torah want to participate in the reading. This is made possible by calling people to the pulpit to recite special blessings before and after each of the Torah readings. These people are said to have had an *aliyah*.

In ancient times each person who was called to the Torah would read a portion to the congregation. Today, the

The *sofer* uses a special script. The decorative little crowns on the top of some letters are called *tagin*. These crowns may only be used on only seven letters. The *sofer* may not write from memory and he must pronounce each word before writing it.

These are the Hebrew names and symbols of the trope used in chanting the Torah.

A *ba'al koreh* reads the Torah

The honor of lifting the Torah and showing it to the congregation is called *hagbah*.

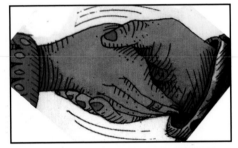

ALIYAH CONGRATULATIONS
After an *aliyah* the honoree is congratulated by shaking his or her hand and saying "*Yashar Koach*" "May you be strengthened."

A Keter Torah

A *sofer* attaching the Torah parchment to the *atzei chayyim*.

Torah reading is performed by a master reader called a *ba'al koreh*. The *ba'al koreh* or the helper, called a *gabbai*, calls individual members to witness and participate in the Torah reading. This honor is called an *aliyah*.

The Order of the *Aliyot*

The first *aliyah* goes to a *kohen*, a person who is descended from the priestly family of Aaron, the brother of Moses. The second *aliyah* is assigned to a *levi*, a descendant of the priestly tribe of Levi. The next five *aliyot* are reserved for Israelites, who are the majority of the Jews. Many synagogues do not assign the first two *aliyot* to a *kohen* and *levi*, because they feel that these divisions are outdated: today all Jews are equal and should be treated equally.

The *Ba'al Maftir*

In addition to the seven Torah *aliyot*, there is the honor of reading the *Haftarah*. The person who reads the *Haftarah* is called the *ba'al maftir*. The reading of the *Haftarah* is preceded by and ends with special blessings.

The Honors

Several other honors are distributed during the Torah service. The honor of opening the Ark and taking out the Torah scroll is called *petichah*, meaning "opening." The honor of lifting the Torah scroll and showing it to the congregation is called *hagbah*. Another honor is called *gelilah*; the honoree ties and dresses the Torah before it is returned to the *Aron Ha–Kodesh*.

Atzei Chayyim

The wooden rollers (*atzei chayyim*, or "trees of life") on which the Torah scroll is wound are made of hard wood and have flat round tops and bottoms to support the edges of the rolled-up scroll. The Torah itself is called an *Etz Chayyim*, the "tree of life."

Keter Torah

Over the upper ends of the *atzei chayyim*, we place the *keter Torah*, the "crown of the Torah." It is usually wrought of silver and adorned with little bells, and is one of the scroll's chief ornaments.

Mantle of the Law

The Mantle of the Law covers the holy scroll when it is not in use. It is usually made of embroidered silk or satin. Old worn-out mantles, like old scrolls and all other objects associated with it, are stored away, for they are too sacred to be discarded or used for anything else.

Choshen

When the Torah is taken out of the Ark, we see its beautiful breastplate, or *Choshen,* suspended by a chain from the top of the rollers. In the center of the breastplate there is frequently a tiny Ark whose doors are in the form of the two tablets of the Law. The lower part of the breastplate has a place where small plates may be inserted. The name of one of the Jewish festivals is engraved on each plate, to be displayed on the holiday or Sabbath on which the scroll is used.

Aron Ha-Kodesh

We keep the scrolls of the Torah in the *Aron Ha-kodesh,* or Holy Ark. This chest or closet is named after the *Aron Ha-Brit,* the Ark of the Covenant, which held the tablets of the Ten Commandments when our ancestors crossed the desert. The *Aron Ha-Kodesh,* is placed against the synagogue wall facing east or toward Jerusalem.

Parochet

The Children of Israel, while wandering in the desert, hung a curtain before the Ark of the Covenant, and we follow their ancient example in many of our synagogues today. The *parochet,* or curtain, is made of fine material and hangs in front of the *Aron Ha-Kodesh*; it is often embroidered, usually with a rendering of the Ten Commandments.

Yad

The pointer of silver or olive wood which is used to guide the reading of the Torah is called the *yad,* or "hand." Shaped like a staff its end is narrow and in the form of a closed fist with the forefinger outstretched. When the Torah scroll is rolled, the *yad* is hung by a chain over the *atzei chayyim,* and rests on the silver breastplate.

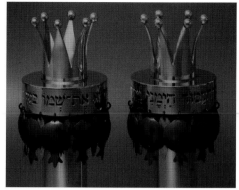

Rimmonim meaning "pomegranates" are ornaments for the top of the Torah.

An **Aron Ha-Kodesh**

A **parochet**

Bar and Bat Mitzvah

The head-piece has the letter *shin* stamped on it; the knot of the arm-piece forms the letter *yud*. The strap of the head phylactery is tied in back into a knot shaped like a *daled*. The three Hebrew letters spell *Shaddai,* "Almighty."

The insides of the *tefillin* contain handwritten strips of parchment on which are inscribed passages from the Torah.

Bar or Bat Mitzvah is a great moment in the life of every Jewish child. It means that the child has become a "son or daughter of the commandments." The celebration, the excitement, the joy that surround the ceremony of Bar and Bat Mitzvah lives on forever in the child's memory. The study and preparation, reading from the Torah and the Prophets, putting on the *tallit*, or prayer shawl, on Sabbaths and holidays—all this begins when a child reaches this shining milestone on the road of life.

Tefillin

From the age of thirteen, Jewish boys and sometimes Jewish girls as well, begin putting on *tefillin* (phylacteries) during morning weekday prayers. The custom arises from the biblical commandment:

And you shall bind them for a sign upon your arm, for frontlets [or head garments] between thine eyes.

Each of the two *tefillin* is a little square box made of parchment with a long strap, or *retzuah*, attached. One box, called the *shel rosh*, is worn above the forehead, and the other, the *shel yad*, is worn on the left arm. Both contain handwritten strips of parchment on which are inscribed passages from the Bible. Orthodox and Conservative Jews observe this commandment.

Tallit

The prayer shawl recalls the upper garment worn in ancient Palestine. When Jews settled in other lands, they began wearing the *tallit* only at or during religious services.

The Bible tells us: *Make a fringe upon the corners of your garments . . . that you may look upon it and remember the commandments of the Almighty.*

148

In olden times, these fringes were worn on the outer garments in daily use. The *tallit* is worn at morning prayers on weekdays, Sabbaths, and festivals.

The *Drashah*

The speech, or *drashah,* which some children deliver at their Bar or Bat Mitzvah celebration is an old Jewish custom dating back to the learned oration on some topic which a yeshiva student would present at his Bar Mitzvah and at his wedding.

Maftir and *Haftarah*

Bar and Bat Mitzvah means that a child is entering the period of youth. To mark this change with an appropriate ceremony, the child is called up to the Torah when the last section of the portion of the week, the *maftir,* is read from the Holy Scroll. Afterwards, he or she chants the *Haftarah,* or selection from the Prophets. From the Bar/Bat Mitzvah Sabbath on, a child may enjoy the privilege of being called to the Torah and be counted as part of a minyan, the quorum required for religious services.

Cantillation

When we read aloud from the Torah we use a special chant based on musical notes. These notes are called the trope, or *ta'amei neginah.* According to tradition, we follow this system in order to read the Scriptures as they were read in the days of Ezra and Nehemiah.

How Old Is Bar/Bat Mitzvah?

How old is the Bar/Bat Mitzvah ceremony? Scholars have shown that a ritual of this kind existed as early as the sixth century C.E. in Palestine. One source tells us that a great Babylonian sage rose to his feet when his son was called to the Torah for the first time and recited the benediction: "Blessed be God, Who has relieved me of the responsibility for this child."

Much later, in the Middle Ages, the Bar Mitzvah ceremony became quite elaborate. The boy, who by now had been studying Jewish subjects intensively for several years, was expected to deliver a lecture on a difficult point in the Talmud or other rabbinic learning.

The *tallit* is the prayer shawl worn by some congregants during the morning prayer on weekdays, Shabbats and festivals. The band on the upper left of the *tallit* is called the *atarah*. The *tzitzit* are attached at the four corners. Four threads are drawn through a corner hole making eight strings, and they are knotted and wound in a special way. The eight threads correspond to the eight days that passed between the day the Hebrews began the Exodus from Egypt and the day they sang the victory song at the Red Sea. The five knots correspond to the Five Books of the Torah. There are a total of thirty–nine windings of the *tzitzit*. Thirty–nine corresponds to the numerical value of the phrase "God is one." The four corners ensure that a person will see this reminder of God's presence wherever he or she looks.

A Bat Mitzvah reading her Torah portion.

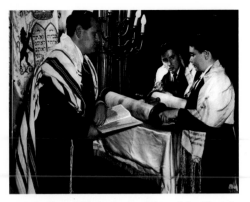

A Bar Mitzvah reciting his Torah portion.

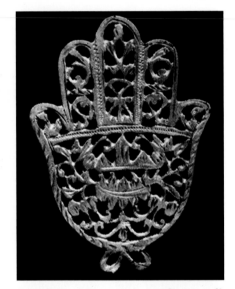

Amulets are used against evil powers. In Morocco the *Hamsa* is very popular. It is shaped like the palm of a hand and is reputed to ward off the evil eye.

A Sephardic Bar Mitzvah ceremony at the Western Wall. The young man is carrying a Torah.

Finally, in the twentieth century, as the idea of treating boys and girls equally gained acceptance, the ceremony of Bat Mitzvah was introduced for girls. It is now fully accepted in Reform, Reconstructionist, and Conservative Judaism as a ceremony in which girls, like boys, are called to the Torah at services in the synagogue. While this is not permitted in Orthodox Judaism, some Orthodox congregations have other ceremonies for marking the Bat Mitzvah of girls.

Bar and Bat Mitzvah have become one of the great occasions in Jewish life. As the observance spread, it took on different forms and features in accordance with the culture of the lands in which it was adopted. Here are some unusual Bar Mitzvah customs practiced in faraway lands.

Morocco

When a boy reaches twelve his father or teacher prepares him to deliver a talmudic lecture with rabbinical commentaries. When the boy becomes thirteen, the rabbis examine him at length. After the examination they all go to a family feast in honor of the Bar Mitzvah.

On Thursday morning family and friends congregate at the home of the Bar Mitzvah for morning prayer. The rabbi binds the *tefillin* armpiece on the boy's arm, and the father binds on the headpiece. This is done to the accompaniment of song and choir. The Bar Mitzvah is called to the Torah.

Soon after the Torah scroll is returned to the Ark, the Bar Mitzvah delivers his speech, translating it himself into Arabic so that the women, too, may understand. When he finishes the rabbis engage him in questions and discussions. Afterwards, the listeners congratulate the boy, saying: "Be strong and blessed! May you grow up to spread and strengthen Torah."

On the following Sabbath the Bar Mitzvah is called on to chant the *Haftarah* in the synagogue.

Other North African Countries

On the Sabbath before the Bar Mitzvah, which is called *Shabbat Tefillin*, the relatives gather for a party which lasts until early Sunday morning. That afternoon the womenfolk, dressed in holiday clothes, visit friends, acquaintances, even

150

the boy's friends, and invite them to the celebration held in the evening of the same day. When they all gather together they bring along a barber who cuts the hair of the Bar Mitzvah. Those who are present contribute a coin to the barber in payment for his work.

Monday morning, the rabbi and the teacher proceed to the home of the parents. They wrap the Bar Mitzvah boy in a *tallit* and crown him with *tefillin*. Then they lead him to synagogue in a candlelit procession to the accompaniment of songs.

In the synagogue, the father, members of the family, and the Bar Mitzvah are called up to the Torah. The rabbi blesses the boy, who then presents his address. This is followed by the distribution of charity to the poor by the members of the family.

After the service everyone accompanies the boy to his home, where the guests are fed a festive meal. In the afternoon the Bar Mitzvah, wearing *tallit* and *tefillin*, and accompanied by his friends, calls on the women of the family. Every relative unwinds the *tefillin* straps from around his arm and presents him with a coin.

In some Sephardic communities boys begin to put on *tefillin* a year (in the case of an orphan, two years) before the age of thirteen, and the parents hold a big family feast.

On his thirteenth birthday, the Bar Mitzvah boy carries his *tallit* and *tefillin* all through the day. At the family festivities the boy is permitted to invite his friends to a feast. The following Sabbath, the Bar Mitzvah is privileged to march around the synagogue carrying the Torah scroll. He is followed by boys of his age who snap their fingers in rhythm.

Bar Mitzvah in Yemen

Since in Yemen even children who are not of Bar Mitzvah age are called up to the Torah, the calling up to the Torah is not as special a ceremony as elsewhere.

On the morning of his Bar Mitzvah day, the son accompanies his father to the synagogue, where he puts on the *tefillin* under the supervision of his teacher. The Bar Mitzvah chants the Torah portion of the week before the congregation. After the service the boy is led home like a bridegroom, with song and dance. At home a big feast awaits the company.

A silver on wood Torah case. The upper section of the silver case is inscribed with biblical passages. This type of Torah holder is typical of Sephardic synagogues.

A *cheder* was a school in Eastern Europe. In Yemen it was called a *khutab*. The Jews in Yemen were very poor and could not afford individual texts for each of the children. The students sat around a single text and learned to read backwards and sideways. Notice the children seated around the books.

A Bar Mitzvah reads his Torah portion.

Bar/Bat Mitzvah Today

Although Bar Mitzvah has gone through many changes in its development through the centuries its original meaning remains simple and beautiful. On this day, the child who has come into possession of the religious heritage of Judaism has for the first time the right to lead a congregation in prayer, the duty to recite a passage when called to the Torah, the privilege of being counted as a member of a minyan, and the opportunity to thank God for being a member of the Jewish people.

The Jewish Home

The Jewish home has kept our people alive through the ages. It is at home that we practice the customs and ceremonies we learn in school. In the home we absorb ideas which will mold our thinking, our attitudes, and actions.

One of the basic ingredients of the Jewish home is a collection of appropriate ceremonial objects and the observance of certain customs. For all Jews celebrate the same holidays and cherish the same Torah. Despite differences in culture, these things provide a common bond. They give us a sense of unity not only with fellow Jews in other lands but with the generations of Jews who have preceded us on this earth.

A Richer and Brighter Home

What are some of the objects and observances which we may expect to find in the Jewish home which makes it a brighter place to live in? When we have them we add a link to the golden chain of tradition forged by our ancestors.

Mezuzah

When we move into a new home the first thing we do is fasten a mezuzah to the upper part of the right doorpost of each room. By doing this we announce that we are proud members of the Jewish people and aware of our long and honorable heritage. The word *mezuzah* means "doorpost" in Hebrew.

The *mezuzah* consists of a small case of metal or wood containing a roll of parchment. Upon the tiny scroll we find two biblical passages, Deuteronomy 6:5–9 and Numbers 11:13–21. They are in Hebrew, written in the manner of Torah script.

The first is the famous passage known as the *Shema*, which begins: *"Hear, O Israel, the Lord our God, the Lord is One."*

The Rothschilds rose from being moneychangers in the Frankfurt ghetto to become a financial dynasty. This painting shows the family at prayer in their home, in their own private synagogue.

A *mezuzah* parchment is handwritten by a *sofer* and contains the *Shema*. The *Shema Yisrael* ("Hear, O Israel") is Judaism's confession of faith, proclaiming the absolute unity of god. It consists of two quotations from the Bible.

153

The decorative cases for *mezu-zot* come in a variety of materials and designs.

In religious homes, it is customary to decorate the eastern wall with a *mizrach*. The Hebrew word *mizrach* means "east." Placing the *mizrach*, enables the owners and guests to recite their prayers facing east, toward Jerusalam. Many of the plaques have the word *mizrach* etched into the design. In many cases, the design also includes Kabbalistic inscriptions or drawings of holy places.

Wine cup and challah.

Through a small opening in the upper part of the *mezuzah* case is seen the Hebrew word *Shaddai*, meaning "Almighty."

Mizrach

We face east when we pray in order to remind ourselves of the importance of the Land of Israel in our spiritual history. And that is why many Jewish homes have a plaque with the word *mizrach*, meaning "east," on a wall facing eastward. The *mizrach* is decorated with beautiful flowers and designs. The members of a household turn toward it when they pray, so that they may face the Land of Israel, the ancient home of the Jewish people, and its capital, Jerusalem, where the Temple stood.

Sabbath Candles

Of all the lovely Jewish customs one of the most beautiful is the lighting of the Shabbat candles. When a family member says the blessing over the glowing candles, they cover their eyes, so that they can concentrate on the prayer. Before the ceremony, the children drop coins in the *tzedakah* box for charity. Afterwards, the parents bless their children and pray to God that they may grow strong and healthy and wise.

Wine Cup

A beautiful silver wine cup is used on the eve of Sabbaths and other holidays, except fast-days, when reciting the *Kiddush* prayer that ushers in the festival.

Havdalah Candle

When three stars appear in the sky it is time for the *Havdalah* service which marks the close of a Sabbath or festival. *Havdalah* means "separation," and the ceremony emphasizes the difference between the holy day and the weekday. The family says a blessing over wine, spices, and light. The blessing over the light is to remind us that light was the first thing God created.

The *Havdalah* candle usually has three wicks which provide a brilliant and strong light. The three wicks represent the three classes of Jews: *kohanim* (priests), Levites, and Israelites. Individually they cast a dim light. However, when

154

they cooperate, they emit a very strong and intense flame. The same can be said for the Jewish people. When they act as one they are strong. When they are not unified, they are weak and have no power.

An ornate spicebox.

Spicebox

The box containing *besamim,* or sweet-smelling spices, is used during the *Havdalah* service. The spices have replaced the burning of incense which was customary on festive occasions. Spiceboxes often are made to resemble towers. These are called by the Hebrew word for "tower," *migdal.*

Chanukiah

The *chanukiah,* or Chanukah candelabrum, waits from Kislev to Kislev to be put into use. It is the "star" of the Chanukah celebration, but it adorns our home with equal grace the rest of the year. When we see it, we know that this is of a home that is proud of the traditions of the Jewish people.

Seder Plate–*Karah*

The Seder plate is used on the first and second nights of Passover. The Seder plate itself, through inscriptions and decorations, tells the story of Pesach. It is the duty of the Seder plate to bear the foods that symbolize the sorrow and joys of Passover. Usually it is divided into sections, and each section is marked in accordance with the food that is placed into it: *matzot,* shankbone, roasted egg, bitter herbs, *charoset* and *karpas.*

A traditionally designed *chanukiah* manufactured in Israel.

Jewish Books

Every Jewish home should have a Jewish library, bookshelves showing that the family members accept our people's age-old ideal of learning. A Jewish library should contain a Bible, a prayerbook, books on Jewish history, and poetry books by famous Jewish authors. There are also many books of Jewish paintings, and volumes especially written for boys and girls which deserve a place in your Jewish bookcase.

The Dietary Laws

Judaism is a religion which has often been described as a way of life. This means that it embraces all aspects of life. One important area of our religion is that of the dietary laws. The

A modern–design Seder plate

155

Bible contains the basis of our regulations about food.

The laws in the Bible were discussed, explained, and expanded by the sages of the Talmud, by philosophers like Maimonides, in codes of Jewish law like the *Shulchan Aruch*, and in other works.

Today the laws of *kashrut* are observed in the traditional form by Orthodox Jews, and in a somewhat less stringent form by Conservative Jews. Reform Judaism does not require observance of the dietary laws, but some Reform Jews have adopted some of the principles of *kashrut* in their personal lives. Some present-day Jews argue that dietary laws for the modern world should prohibit meat, or at least meat of animals raised under inhumane conditions, and thus should emphasize vegetarianism.

Why Are These Laws Important?

According to the Bible we were given dietary laws to make us pure and holy. The Bible lists those animals, fowl, and fish which we may eat and those which are forbidden.

For many the dietary laws are a mark of Jewish loyalty and identity. Over the centuries, many Jews gave up their lives rather than allow themselves to be forced to eat forbidden foods.

What Is Permitted and What Is Forbidden

All fruits and vegetables may be eaten; and so may all dairy foods, as long as the milk is from a kosher animal.

Winged and creeping things are not to be eaten. Kosher fish must have fins and scales. All shellfish are forbidden.

Mammals which have cloven hoofs and chew their cud are permitted. This includes meat of cows, sheep, and goats, but not that of pigs.

The Bible enumerates all the fowls which may not be eaten. Among the permitted are chickens, ducks, and turkeys.

Most of the forbidden animals and birds are creatures that prey on other creatures.

Dairy and Meat

Mixing meat and dairy foods is strictly forbidden by Jewish religious law. The Bible says: "You shall not cook the kid in its mother's milk." This regulation was applied to all manner of

Shechitah ("slaughtering") of animals is carried out in accordance with humane Jewish laws. Only a properly qualified person called a *shochet* may perform *shechitah*. The meat is then inspected and certified as kosher. The kosher stamp shown here was used in a European Jewish community in the 19th century.

meat and dairy products. It was extended to utensils. Every kosher home has two sets of dishes, pots, and other food utensils. In order to make the distinction between meat and dairy clear, observant Jews wait six hours after eating meat before eating dairy food.

Attaching the *mezuzah*.

Kashrut and *Shechitah*

Kosher meat must be carefully supervised from the moment the animal is slaughtered to the time it reaches the table. Only a *shochet,* a learned and pious person who is thoroughly trained, is permitted to slaughter a kosher animal.

Shechitah, the act of slaughtering, is a religious rite; the rules must be observed strictly.

After *shechitah,* the *shochet* examines the animal carefully to see that it has no disease or other flaw which would render it unfit. The carcass is inspected by a *mashgiach*, who stamps it with an official seal. Kosher retail meat markets are supervised by a *mashgiach,* too, to ensure proper handling and care. Kashrut has been considered a foundation-stone of the Jewish religion for centuries upon centuries. It is still observed with scrupulous attention by a significant proportion of the Jewish people.

Chanukat Ha-Bayit

The home is the vital center of Jewish life and we cannot leave it without mentioning the custom of *Chanukat Ha-Bayit* ("dedication of the home" or house-warming). When a Jewish family moves into a new dwelling, they invite relatives and friends to celebrate the occasion.

The ceremony begins with the fastening of a *mezuzah* on the doorpost. At the same time the benediction is said: *Blessed are you, Almighty Ruler of the universe, Who has made us holy with mitzvot and commanded us to fasten the mezuzah.*

Bread and salt, ancient symbols of life and happiness, are brought into the house. Refreshments and good cheer are, of course, the order of the day. The *Chanukat Ha-Bayit* is actually a prayer dressed as a pleasant ceremony, a prayer to God for good health and a good life under a new roof.

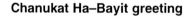

Chanukat Ha–Bayit greeting

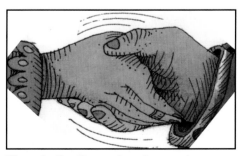

The dedication of a home is a very happy occassion for the whole family. You congratulate them by wishing them *"Mazel Tov"* meaning "Good Luck".

The World of Jewish Books

For centuries, Jews have been known as the People of the Book. True, this phrase refers to the Bible, our Book of Books, but it also indicates our love for books in general. From the days when books were published in manuscript form and were considered rare treasures until our own time, books have always been among the Jew's dearest possessions.

An old legend tells us:

When Adam was driven from Eden, he was sorrowful. God pitied him and said: *The Tree of Knowledge did not make humans wise, nor did they eat their fill of the Tree of Life. What shall be their fate?" And God created the book and said to it: "Go forth and accompany humans. Be a friend and companion to them, comfort them, teach them, and gladden their hearts."*

Importance of Books

Can you imagine life without books? Would there be schools, or libraries, teachers, or physicians? Would there be any learning without books?

For our people, as for every other, books have been a vital force for growth.

In the very beginning, the Jewish people came into existence because of a book. The Bible tells us that before Moses died, he "wrote the words of this Torah in a book."

The Origin of "Book"

When we use the word "book," we mean a printed volume, made up of a number of sheets printed on both sides and bound together and provided with a cover.

In ancient times, however, a book was any single manuscript work. It was only after the introduction of printing, in the fifteenth century, that the word "book" came to mean a

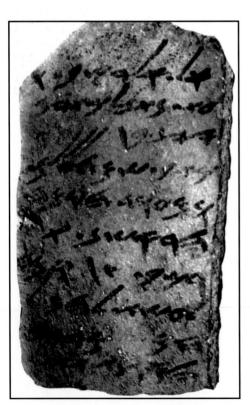

This potsherd containing *daatz* writing comes from Arad, First Temple. This ancient *alefbet* was replaced by the Aramaic system of writing because of its simplicity.

printed volume. In the middle of the fifteenth century movable type was invented. This is the dividing line in the history of books. Before this time all books were in manuscript (which means handwritten); after this time all books were printed.

Two Manuscript Periods

The manuscript period is also divided into two: (1) the period when books were written on clay tablets and papyrus rolls, and (2) the period when parchment manuscripts were bound together in a form that looked like a modern book.

The earliest Jewish records do not mention clay tablet "books" or papyrus rolls, such as other nations used. Instead, they speak of scrolls written on the skins of animals. These hides were not bound together like books of today but were laid end-to-end and rolled up into a scroll that looked very much like the Torah scrolls in our synagogues and temples.

Since each scroll had to be written by hand, books were extremely scarce and most of the early books were either read aloud or recited from memory to whole groups of people by wandering storytellers. A book in ancient times was to be heard rather than to be read silently to oneself.

Thus the Bible tells us that King Josiah of Judah called "all the men of Judah and all the inhabitants of Jerusalem with him, and the priests, and the prophets, and all the people, both small and great: and he read in their ears all the words of the book of the covenant which was found in the house of the Lord."

Later, when the Jews returned to Israel from their exile in Babylon, their leader, Ezra, read them the book of the law, or Torah.

As time went on, however, more and more scrolls were written and circulated among the common people. We know, for example, that messages from the prophets and government proclamations were recopied by hand and distributed among the people.

And, of course, the Torah, which became more and more important in the synagogue service, was constantly copied and recopied. To this day, the Torah scrolls found in our temples must be written by hand on animal skins according to rules laid down by the rabbis in still another Jewish book, the Talmud.

A *sofer*, or scribe, writing a Torah in the traditional way with a feather pen and special ink. In Babylon, the Torah was divided into 54 sections called *sidrot*, so that the entire Torah could be completely read in one whole year. In traditional synagogues the Torah is read on Sabbaths, holy days, and Monday and Thursday mornings.

Modern Hebrew	Old Hebrew	Phoenician	Early Greek	Later Greek	Latin	English
א	ꓱꓱꓱ	ꓘ	A	A	A	A
ב	𐤂𐤂	ꓱ	ꓶꓮ	B	B	B
ג	ꓶꓶ	ꓶ	ꓶ	ꓶ	C G	C G
ד	ꓷ	ꓷ	ꓷ	ꓷ	D	D
ה	ꓱꓱꓱ	ꓱ	ꓱ	E	E	E
ו	ꓬꓬꓬ	Y	ꓶ	ꓶ	F V	F V U
ז	ꓲꓲꓲ	ꓲ	I	I	...	Z
ח	ꓱꓱꓱ	ꓱ	B	B	H	E H
ט	ꓫ ꓫ	⊕	⊗	⊗	...	TH PH
י	ꓓꓓꓓꓓ	ꓱ	ꓱ	ꓱ	I	I
כ	ꓳꓶꓷ	ꓱ	ꓱ	ꓱ	...	K KH
ל	ꓲꓲꓲ	ꓶ	ꓶ	ꓶ	L	L
מ	ꓵꓵꓵ	ꓵ	ꓵ	ꓵ	M	M
נ	ꓵꓵꓵ	ꓵ	ꓱ	ꓱ	N	N
ס	ꓱ ꓱ	ꓱ	ꓱ	ꓱ	X	X
ע	ꓳ	ꓳ	ꓳ	ꓳ	O	O
פ	ꓱ	ꓱ	ꓱ	ꓱ	P	P
צ	ꓱꓱ	ꓱ	ꓱ	ꓱ	...	S
ק	ꓱ	ꓱ	ꓱ	ꓱ	Q	Q
ר	ꓱ ꓱ	ꓱ	ꓱ	ꓱ	R	R
ש	ꓪꓪ	ꓪ	ꓱ	ꓱ	S	S
ת	ꓴꓴꓴ	X	ꓴ	ꓴ	T	T

Table showing how the Hebrew and Phoenician letters passed through Greek and Latin forms to their present English forms.

The Dead Sea Scrolls are the oldest Hebrew manuscripts in existence. They are housed in the Shrine of the Book in the Israel Museum, Jerusalem. The scroll of Isaiah is displayed fully opened around a drum.

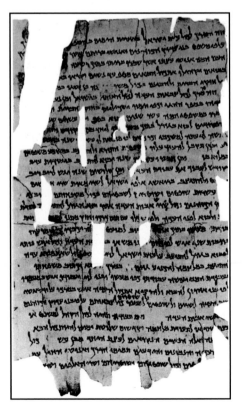

The first page of an Essene scroll found at Qumran. The scroll is entitled Community Rule.

The famous Dead Sea Scrolls, discovered in Palestine in 1947, consist in part of biblical books copied down by an unknown Jewish scribe for use in religious study.

Changes are Made

In time, wooden rollers were placed on the ends of some of the larger scrolls to make them easier to handle.

Soon, other changes came into use. Paper replaced parchment as the writing material and then someone came up with a brand-new idea–putting the pages of a manuscript one on top of the other and binding them together in modern book form instead of rolling them up into a scroll.

By the Middle Ages most Jewish books were in modern form and only those used in the synagogue service were still in scrolls.

The early manuscripts in book form were extremely large compared with present-day books. Some of them were so big, in fact, that it took two people to handle them. The reason for this was that books were still scarce, so, by making them large, several people could read them at the same time.

Illustrations in Books

Since they were written by hand, many of the early books were works of art as well as literature. The scribes who copied the books would often illustrate them richly and in many colors. Since the rabbis forbade any illustrations in the Torah, scribes would save some of their richest illustrations for the Passover Haggadah.

The Invention of Printing

Late in the fifteenth century the invention of printing changed the form of the Jewish book for all time.

The first Jewish book to come off a printing press was an edition of Rashi's commentary on the Bible, printed in Italy in 1475. From Italy the art of Hebrew printing spread to Spain and Portugal. After the Spanish Inquisition in 1492, the art of printing moved, along with the Spanish Jews, to all the countries of the world in which Jews lived.

The introduction of printing had a powerful effect on Jewish life. Books decreased in price and very soon, almost everyone could afford a *siddur* or some other sacred book. Now a copy of the Bible could be found not only among the rich but in practically every Jewish home.

The books most frequently printed by Jews at first were, of course, religious books. As time went on, however, story-books, books of legends, schoolbooks, and books only meant for entertainment were widely circulated among Jews.

More and more Jewish books were printed every year, and the quality of the printing, which had been poor at first, became better as the years went by. By the nineteenth century, Jewish books in Hebrew, Yiddish, Ladino, and other languages were published and distributed on a worldwide scale.

The Greatest Jewish Books

Of the many volumes on the Jewish bookshelf, the greatest of all are three: the Bible, the Talmud, and the *siddur*. Without the first, there would be no Jewish people; without the second, there would be a vast gap in Jewish scholarship and learning; without the third, there would be no bridge of prayer uniting many centuries of Jewish happiness and despair, fears and hopes.

The Bible

Our most cherished possession, the Bible, has been translated from Hebrew into over a thousand tongues; it continues today, as in ages past, to help people lead a good and righteous life. The Bible tells us that there is One God; it teaches us to honor our parents; it urges us to tell only the truth. The Bible contains the world's most wonderful stories—about heroes like Moses, Joshua, and Samson; about thrilling events like the Flood and the Exodus; about stirring prophecies like those of Isaiah and Jeremiah.

The Bible—our Torah—has been the very center of Jewish spiritual life. Study it over and over again, said the rabbis, for all knowledge and wisdom may be found in it.

The Bible consists of twenty-four books divided into three sections: the Torah, the Prophets, and the Writings.

The Sanhedrin

In Judea itself, the people continued to live peacefully, abiding by the laws of the Torah as explained by the high priest and by the members of the Great Assembly. The Torah was the law

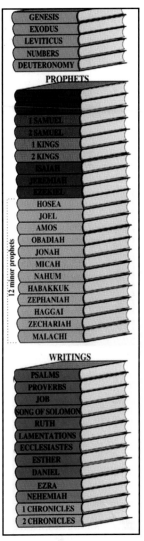

THE TANAK (BIBLE)
The complete Hebrew Bible is called TaNaK. It is divided into three divisions; *Torah* (Five Books of Moses), *Neviim* (Prophets), and *Ketuvim* (Writings).
The name Tanak comes from the first letters of each of the three divisions. *T* is for *Torah*, *N* is for *Neviim* and *K* is for *Ketuvim*.
There are a total of 24 separate books in the Tanak. The Torah consists of 5 books, the Prophets 8 books, and the Writings 11 books.
The chapter divisions and the numbering of the verses were introduced into the Tanak to make quoting from it much easier.
The language of the Tanak is Hebrew except for portions of the books of Daniel and Ezra, which are in Aramaic.

An engraving in a Hebrew-Latin edition of the Mishnah (1744). It illustrates a session of the Sanhedrin.

We are told that Ptolemy II, in his huge library at Alexandria, possessed all of the world's great literature except the Five Books of Moses. He sent a request to the High Priest at Jerusalem, asking for a copy of these books and permission to translate them into Greek. When they arrived, the king invited 70 Jewish sages to Alexandria and set each scholar to work by himself on the translation. The 70 sages had no contact with each other. Yet, when their work was finished, all 70 translations were identical. We do not know whether this story is fact or legend, but this first Greek translation of the Bible came to be known as the *Septuagint*, meaning the translation "by these 70." The Septuagint created a stir in the ancient world. By that time Greek had become the official language throughout the ancient world. Jews who knew Greek, but no longer knew Hebrew, were now able to read their own Torah. In addition, the Septuagint translation also enabled non-Jews to read the Bible. This is a page from Codex Sinaiticus, a manuscript of the Septuagint which was found at the Catherina Monastery.

and the way of life for the entire nation. Almost all Jews could read and write, and beginning in the time of Ezra, the Torah was studied by people of every background–farmers, shepherds, merchants and artisans.

When necessary, the Great Assembly interpreted the laws of the Torah to fit new conditions and situations. This body, also known as the Great Synagogue and as the Sanhedrin, was a legislature, a court, and a national council. In addition, it served as a training ground for the leaders who went out to teach in the synagogues of Judea's towns and villages.

The Bible is Compiled

Around 200 C.E. the scribes collected and carefully examined all the holy writings of the Jewish people. These were put together in the great collection of sacred literature that eventually came to be known as the Hebrew Bible. Among the writings they included were: the Five Books of Moses, or Torah; the books of the prophets; historical works like the books of Samuel, Kings, Chronicles, Ezra, Nehemiah, Esther, and Ruth; and philosophical and poetic works like Psalms, Lamentations, Ecclesiastes, Job, and Proverbs.

The Bible was the repository of the Jewish historical and religious experience until that time, the highpoint of ancient Hebrew literary achievement, and the foundation of Judaism. In addition to the writings gathered in the Bible, many other books were written in Hebrew throughout this period. Some of them were lost with the passage of time. Others were preserved in later collections, such as the Apocrypha.

The Apocrypha

The Apocrypha are a group of books that tell us much about the social and religious life of the Jewish people during the period of the Second Temple. The word Apocrypha, in Greek, means "hidden away." Because these books were not included with the twenty-four books of the Hebrew Bible, they were regarded as hidden away.

All of the apocryphal texts are said to have been written after the fifth century B.C.E. They are referred to in Hebrew as *ketuvim acharonim* ("later writings") because they were composed after the time of Ezra the Scribe. Among the Apocrypha are the books of the Maccabees, which tell us much about the revolt against the Syrian Greeks, including the story of Hannah and her seven sons. Another important text is the Wisdom of Ben Sira, which contains a collection of proverbs.

Mishnah

After the second revolt against Rome, led by Bar Kochba, Rabbi Yehudah Ha-Nasi, the most important rabbinic leader, feared that the collection of oral teachings on the Torah had grown so large that no one could possibly remember it all. With the assistance of his colleagues and students, Yehudah Ha-Nasi systematically organized the entire Oral Tradition.

This work was called the Mishnah. The Mishnah, written in Hebrew, is divided into six main divisions, each one dealing with a different area of life.

The *Yeshiva* in Yavneh

After the destruction of Jerusalem, General Vespasian granted Rabbi Yochanan ben Zakkai permission to set up a *yeshiva* in the coastal town of Yavneh. As soon as the academy opened, Rabbi Yochanan re–established the Sanhedrin. This Jewish court consisted of 71 scholars who would decide questions of Jewish law and Torah scholarship.

Rabbi Yochanan also instituted the practice of appointing rabbis to serve as teachers who would continue to strengthen the long, unbroken chain of Jewish tradition.

The Talmud

Choni ha-Me'aggel once saw an old man planting a carob tree. He asked him when he thought the tree would bear fruit. "After seventy years," was the reply.

"Do you expect to live seventy years and eat the fruit of your labor?"

"I did not find the world empty when I entered it," said the old man, "and as my fathers planted for me before I was born, so do I plant for those who will come after me."

This legend, which you read earlier in connection with Tu Bi-Shevat, is taken from the Talmud and is one of the hundreds of stories to be found in its pages; yet no one would call the Talmud a storybook. The Talmud contains all our religious

The interior of the Yochanan ben Zakkai Sephardic Synagogue in the Jewish Quarter of Old Jerusalem. It is one of the oldest synagogues in Meah Shearim. In the 1948 the synagogue was destroyed by the Arab Legion. It was rebuilt in 1972.

This page is from a manuscript of the Mishnah written between the 12th and 14th centuries.

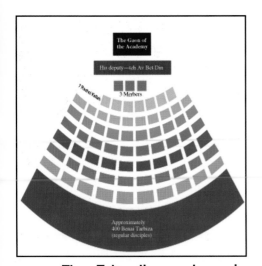

The Talmudic academy in Babylonia was headed by a *gaon*. The academy consisted of 70 sages whose places in the hierarchy were fixed. The sages closer to the *gaon*, were generally the more advanced.

A page from tractate *Ketubot*. The Mishnah is in the center. To the right is the commentary of Rabbi Obadiah Bartinura, who lived in Italy and then in Jerusalem in the 15th century. To the left is the commentary of Rabbi Yomtov Lipman Heller of the 17th century.

laws; but it is more than a law book. It tells us much about our history; still, it is certainly not a history text.

The Talmud (from the Hebrew word *lomed*, meaning "study") has often been called a sea of learning. This is an apt comparison: like a sea, it has boundaries which we can measure; and yet, like a sea, it has depths which have never been completely plumbed.

The Babylonian Talmud

In the generations after the time of Yehudah Ha-Nasi, the rabbis of Israel and Babylon compiled Aramaic commentaries on the Mishnah which are known as the Gemara. The combination of the Hebrew Mishnah and the Aramaic Gemara is called the Talmud.

The forty-odd volumes of the Talmud contain no punctuation. One word may express the meaning of a whole sentence. There are no question marks to guide the reader. The Talmud has remained an open book to the studious because of the commentaries on its text.

All of these works–the Mishnah, the Gemara, and the commentaries–make up the Talmud as we know it today. The 2.5 million words of the Babylonian Talmud are one of the greatest achievements of the Jewish people. Its 6,000 pages, containing the contributions of over 2,000 scholars, form an encyclopedia of Jewish culture. Built upon the solid foundation of our Torah, the Talmud sums up a thousand years of religious and social thought of the Jewish people.

Generations of our ancestors were nourished on its wisdom; thousands upon thousands of Jewish youths pored over its leaves; to become a rabbi and spiritual leader, a Jew must still, as in days past, devotedly study the Talmud.

Whenever persecution lashed at the Jews, the Talmud, too, suffered the fury of the persecutors and was burned. However, like the Jewish people, it always survived the foe. Today, it enriches our institutions of learning and libraries as well as many Jewish homes and continues to cast its light into every corner of every Jewish community in the world.

The *Siddur*

The prayerbook, or *siddur*, is like a skyscraper of the spirit which was built very slowly, brick by brick. Gradually, over the centuries, the prayers in the *siddur* changed and were added to. At last the *siddur* became a rich collection of Jewish literature. Its passages show the development of Jewish life: the *Shema Yisrael* of the Bible, the *Hallel* from King David's Psalms, the *Ani Ma'amin* of Maimonides. The *siddur* also contains the religious poetry and prayers of known and unknown authors. Their words so touched the hearts of our people that they found their way into the *siddur*. For over 1,000 years, the *siddur* has graced Jewish homes in every corner of the globe.

These eternal masterworks of Jewish learning and literature have helped us survive hardships and persecution and, to stay united as a people.

Other Great Jewish Books

There are many, many other great Jewish books and great Jewish authors. In the following pages, you will meet but a few, all of which had enormous influence upon Jewish life and literature.

Works of Maimonides

Rabbi Moses ben Maimon, usually called Maimonides or Rambam (from the initials of his name) lived from 1135 to 1204. He spent much of his early life wandering from place to place because of religious persecution. At last he settled in Cairo, Egypt, and became the court physician of Sultan Saladin.

Maimonides had a brilliant mind and despite hardship, studied Talmud, logic, mathematics, medicine, astronomy, and the other natural sciences. He wrote works which have influenced Judaism to our own day. His commentary on the Mishnah was written between the ages of twenty-three and thirty-three. The *Mishneh Torah* is a summary of material in the Bible, the two Talmuds, and the legal writings of the rabbis up to Rambam's time. Here we find Maimonides' famous "Eight Degrees of Charity."

As a leader of the Jewish community, Maimonides knew that people are often embarrassed when they need assistance and receive it publicly. To guide his fellow Jews in the practice of *tzedakah*, he formulated a "ladder" known as the "Eight Degrees of Charity." The first degree is the best way to give charity; the second is the next best, and so on.

A Talmud class at the Reconstructionist Rabbinical College in Wyncote, Pennsylvania.

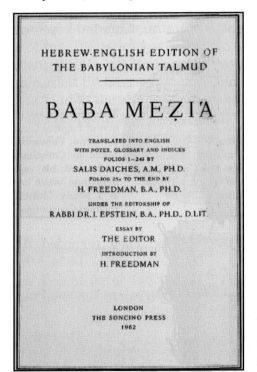

Several editions of the Talmud have been translated into English. This is one of the title pages of the Soncino edition, published in England. In 1923 Rabbi Meir Shapiro decided to found a course of Talmud study which he called *Daf Yomi*. The word *daf* means "page" and *yomi* means "daily." Rabbi Shapiro's plan envisaged the study of all 2711 pages (*dapim*) of the Talmud in seven and a quarter years. Today, many people all over the world participate in the *Daf Yomi* program. Some study the Talmud individually, some in groups which use both the original and the English translation. There are *Daf Yomi* groups in Hollywood, the Senate in Washington, and the board rooms of Wall Street.

A drawing of Rabbi Moses Maimonides. His Hebrew name was Rabbi Moshe ben Maimon. We lovingly call him Rambam. The name Rambam comes from the Hebrew letters R-Rabbi, M-Moshe, B-ben, M-Maimon.

The autograph of Maimonides.

An Illustration from the *Mishneh Torah*. The *Mishneh Torah*, also known as the *Yad Ha-Hazakah*, "Strong Hand," was the most important rabbinic work of Moses Maimonides. It consists of 14 volumes, and catalogues the subjects of all religious and legal regulations in talmudic literature.

Guide for the Perplexed

Another of Maimonides' works is the *Guide for the Perplexed*, a treatise which gave Rambam a respected reputation among the philosophers of world history. It was written in Arabic to make it accessible to as many people as possible. Maimonides, scholar, rabbi, philosopher, and physician, was one of the most remarkable men of all time.

Rashi's Commentaries

Rabbi Shlomo Itzchaki, better known as Rashi (an abbreviation of his name), was born in Troyes, France in 1040 and died in his native city in 1105. As a young man he felt that not enough people understood the meaning of the Bible, and he decided to write a new explanation. Throughout his life, he wrote commentaries on nearly all the books of the Bible and on most of the Talmud. His commentary on the Torah was the first Hebrew book to be printed (in 1475). And more than a hundred commentaries have been written on his commentary.

Rashi's greatness lies in his ability to open the difficult books of the Bible and Talmud to everyone who wants to drink of their wisdom. To explain the things he discussed, Rashi studied the subjects thoroughly. When he dealt with talmudic laws concerning illness, he studied medicine; he also learned the craft of the shoemaker, the smith, and the shipwright. The rabbis of the Middle Ages honored Rashi by calling him *parshandata*, "Interpreter of the Law." He made our ancient heritage live, not for the scholar alone, but for the Jewish people as a whole.

The *Shulchan Aruch*

In 1492, when Joseph Karo was four his family fled the Spanish Inquisition, taking the lad to Portugal. When Joseph was eight his family was driven out of Portugal; this time they went to Constantinople. Young Karo studied there and moved on; in 1536 he settled in Safed, Palestine. His fame rests on the *Shulchan Aruch* (which means "The Prepared Table"), published in Venice in 1565. This work is a guide for the observance of traditional Judaism. (Karo's book was popularized by an abridgment known as the *Kitzur Shulchan Aruch*, written by Rabbi Solomon Ganzfried in the nineteenth century.)

The author of the *Shulchan Aruch* studied all the discussions of problems of Jewish law and presented the decisions. In the *Shulchan Aruch* we learn the laws about benedictions (blessings), about charity, about building a family, about judges and courts, and so on. There was no problem of religious Jewish life up to his time that the *Shulchan Aruch* does not touch on. In many Jewish homes, the shorter version of Karo's work (the *Kitzur*) came third, after the *siddur* and the *Chumash* (Five Books of Moses).

Rare Treasures

Most old Jewish books, including some rare and ancient editions, have come down to us because Jews have always loved and treasured books. Jews were among the first people in the world to collect books and form their own private libraries. Such libraries were founded all over the world, old books were saved so that we might have and enjoy them today.

As for old holy books, they have come down to us because of an ancient Jewish law which forbids the destruction of any book that has the name of God in it.

When such books grew worn and old, they were not thrown away but were stored in a special room of the synagogue called a *genizah*. By searching those old storehouses of books archaeologists have been able to come away with some rare finds.

During World War II the great Jewish publishing centers of Europe were either destroyed or damaged beyond repair. The Nazis, who hated the freedom that the Jewish book represents, held public book burnings at which they destroyed books that Jews had treasured for centuries.

Books Today

Although there are still many Jewish books published in Europe, the United States, Israel, and Argentina have become the Jewish book–publishing capitals of the world. Thousands of books dealing with Jewish history, religion, public affairs, and literature are published in this country every year. Some of these books are written in Hebrew or Yiddish, while most are in English.

The Rashi chapel in the city of Worms, the synagogue where the great commentator worshiped and taught.

Portrait of Chaim Nachman Bialik, 1873–1934, painted by L. Pasternak. He was the greatest Hebrew poet of modern times. Bialik supported himself as a businessman, teacher and publisher. Today in Israel, Bialik is considered the national poet.

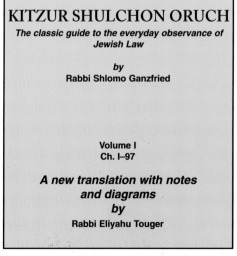

KITZUR SHULCHON ORUCH
The classic guide to the everyday observance of Jewish Law

by
Rabbi Shlomo Ganzfried

Volume I
Ch. I–97

A new translation with notes and diagrams
by
Rabbi Eliyahu Touger

English tranlation of the *Kitzur Shulchan Aruch.*

The Genizah was usually a room in a synagogue where books and ritual objects containing the name of God was stored. According to Jewish law, these books and objects must not be destroyed. In ancient times holy books were buried next to a coffin of a community leader or a scholar. The best known genizah was discovered by Solomon Schechter at the Ezra Synagogue in Cairo, Egypt. In 1896 Prof. Schechter traveled to Cairo and after prolonged negotiations was allowed to remove over 100,000 pages which he took to the University of Cambridge, in England. Among the dusty and torn pages were important letters, documents and parts of holy texts. Among the literary treasures were letters from Maimonides. This is a photo of Schechter examining the fragments in his office.

Today, with thousands of years of Jewish literature behind us, with the growth of the Jewish communities in the United States, Israel, and elsewhere, we may look forward to yet another golden age of Jewish writing. And today every one of us can do easily what our ancestors could only dream of doing; we can read and own many books.

By this time, you may know why an ancient Jewish sage once said: "A book is a good companion."

Among the Jewish people it was always felt that nothing could add more to the beauty and warmth of a home than a collection of Jewish books, carefully chosen and always increasing. Moses ben Jacob Ibn Ezra, a famed Jewish poet and philosopher of twelfth-century Spain, declared:

A book is the most delightful companion. If you wish entertainment, its witty sayings will amuse you; if you want advice, its words of wisdom will gladden you. Within its covers it holds everything: what is first and what is last, what is gone and what still is. Although it is not alive, it talks about things both dead and living.

Jewish Nobel Prize Winners for Literature

Nobel Prizes are awarded annually to men and women who have "rendered the greatest service to mankind." Since the establishment of the prize in 1899, it has been awarded to the following Jews or people of Jewish descent for their contributions to literature.

1910 - Paul J. L. Heyse
1927 - Henri Bergson
1958 - Boris Pasternak
1966 - Shmuel Yosef Agnon
1967 - Nelly Sachs
1976 - Saul Bellow
1978 - Isaac Bashevis Singer
1981 - Elias Canetti
1987 - Joseph Brodsky
1991 - Nadine Gordiner

In all fields of endeavor–World Peace, Literature, Medicine, Chemistry, Physics and Economics–Jews have been awarded more than 100 Nobel Prizes. Jews are less than 1% of the world's population, yet they have made up more than 15% of all recipients.

A rabbi and his students.

American Jewish Writers

Jewish writers have become a powerful force in American fiction, poetry, drama, and criticism. The following is just a few who came to be published, read and acclaimed. Some did not write about Jewish subjects and did not deal with their ethnic experience. In addition to Saul Bellow, Norman Mailer, Bernard Malamud, Arthur Miller, and Philip Roth, there are a whole host of important writers such as: Meyer Levin, Elie Wiesel, Isaac Bashevis Singer, Chaim Potok, Irwin Shaw, Cynthia Ozick, Jay Neugeborn, E. L. Doctorow, Arthur Cohen, Bruce Freedman, Grace Paley and Stanley Elkin. The list is endless and keeps growing.

Of course the lists does not include the thousands of Jewish professionals, politicians and intellectuals who write books about their particular institutions, occupations and their scientific and technical specialties.

Norman Mailer, U.S. novelist and essayist. His two years with the U.S. Army in the Pacific theatre during World War II provided him with the background for his best--selling novel "The Naked and the Dead." Norman Mailer has won many literary awards and the Pulitzer prize.

A poster promoting Jewish Book Month. Each year the Jewish Book Council provides information, sponsors and coordinates Jewish book fairs in the United States and Canada.

Every year during Hebrew Book Week, every large Israeli city turns its empty spaces into book markets. All publishers cooperate and sell their books at bargain prices.

Israeli stamp issued in honor of the 1965 Israeli International Book Fair.

The Cycle of Jewish Life

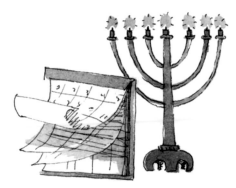

BABY–NAMING SERVICE
At the baby–naming service the rabbi recites a *Mi–Sheberach* prayer, meaning "may God bless." In this prayer the parents as well as the newborn baby are blessed. After the blessing the baby is given its Hebrew name. The happy parents have wrapped the child in a *tallit*.

From birth to death we are wrapped in Jewish custom and tradition. For, as has often been said, Judaism is more than a religion. It is a way of life. Because it is that, a wealth of observances have clustered round the great events of birth, Bar and Bat Mitzvah, marriage, and death.

A Child Is Born

In ancient times, a large family was considered a great blessing. The Bible says: "Be fruitful and multiply." When a child was born a messenger was sent at once to bring the news to the father. "A child is born to you!" he would cry, and there would be great rejoicing.

In biblical days, a child was given a name that had a definite idea behind it. Joseph was so named because his name is derived from the Hebrew word meaning "to add," and his mother said, "The Lord added to me another son." Sometimes a child was named for a living creature or a plant. Deborah means "bee"; Tamar means "palm-tree."

Today, a Jewish child is usually named after a dear one who is dead, in order to keep the name alive and remembered in the family.

Circumcision

On the eighth day after his birth, a baby boy undergoes the rite of circumcision, or *Brit Milah*. A symbol of Jewish allegiance, *Brit Milah* has been practiced by our people for some 4,000 years.

It began in the days of Abraham. The book of Genesis tells us: *This is My Covenant, which you shall keep, between Me and you and your seed after you. Every male among you shall be circumcised. . . . And Abraham was ninety years old and nine, when he was circumcised in the flesh of his foreskin.*

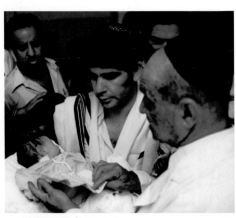

A circumcision ceremony. Family and friends share the parents' joy.

The Torah tells us exactly when a Jewish male shall be circumcised: *And in the eighth day the flesh of his foreskin shall be circumcised.*

Just before the child is circumcised he is placed upon Elijah's Chair, a seat reserved for the prophet Elijah. Tradition says, that this is to make the child develop into a healthy grown-up.

Boys are named at the circumcision ceremony, girls receive their name in the synagogue when the parents are called to the Torah on the Sabbath following birth. A new ceremony has been developed to celebrate the birth of a daughter. It is called *Simchat Bat (*daughter's joy).

The infant is carried to the circumcision by a woman who is given the honor. The godfather or *sandak* (holder) holds the baby during the circumcision. In the 18th and 19th century, synagogues often had special thrones for *sandak*. Some had two seats, with the second reserved for the prophet Elijah who was believed to protect newborn children. The back of this throne is ornamented and has selections from the circumcision service.

Pidyon Ha-Ben
At the end of his first month of life a firstborn boy takes part in yet another ceremony, that of *Pidyon Ha-Ben*, or redemption of the firstborn. The reason for this custom is that in olden days firstborn males were dedicated to the service of God, to act as priests, musicians, and servants in the Temple. Later, the tribe of Levi was appointed to officiate in the Temple. The book of Numbers tells us: *And, behold, I have taken the Levites instead of every firstborn; and the Levites shall be mine.*

From then on, every firstborn male child was freed or redeemed from service by paying the amount of five *shekalim* (about $2.50) to the *kohen* or *levite* who served in his place.

Today a *kohen*, or descendant of the priestly tribe, is invited to the *Pidyon Ha-Ben* ceremony. After receiving the five *shekalim*, he usually turns the money over to a charitable Jewish cause. A new ceremony has been created, very much like the *Pidyon Ha-Ben*. It is called *Pidyon Ha-Bat*, redemption of the firstborn daughter.

Bar Mitzvah and Bat Mitzvah
The customs and traditions of Bar and Bat Mitzvah are fully discussed in the chapter devoted to this great event in a Jew's life.

Marriage
The Jewish boy and girl have grown up and are now ready to take the most important step in their lives: marriage.

"A Jewish Wedding" by Moritz Oppenheim, 1861. Painting of a German marriage ceremony, showing a *tallit* serving as a *chuppah* canopy.

171

A *ketubah* (marriage contract) written in Italy, 1838. This document, listing the obligations of the bridegroom toward his bride, is written in Aramaic and must bear the signatures of two witnesses.

This musical number dates back to 1900. The word *choson* means "bridegroom" and the word *kale* means "bride." *Mazol tov* means "good luck."

A happy bride and groom display their *ketubah*.

Because this is such a decisive moment in the life of any individual, many laws, customs, and traditions have been handed down to Jewish parents and to their children who are about to take the holy vow of matrimony.

The first guide, as usual, is the Bible. There you will find a description of the first known Jewish wedding, that of Isaac and Rebekah. What does this wonderful story teach us? For one thing, you learn that even in those days Jews, did not marry people who were not Jewish. Second, you learn that a young man asked the girl of his choice for her consent before he sought the approval of her parents. Third, you learn that young people looked for signs of good character in their prospective mates before "taking the plunge."

In Jewish tradition, the engagement played a very serious role. An engagement party was held at which the betrothal or engagement was declared. A document bearing the formal terms of the forthcoming wedding was signed (and in some Orthodox families it still is), and the approximate date of the marriage was set. Then it was time for a toast of *Le–Chayyim!* and *Mazel Tov!* to the future bride and groom, and for merry-making by all the guests.

Today, in most cases, the formalities of the betrothal are disposed of immediately before the wedding ceremony itself.

June Brides

In the Orthodox tradition, Jewish weddings may not be held between Passover and Shavuot (except on Lag Ba-Omer and Rosh Chodesh Sivan), for this is a time of mourning. Nor may a marriage be solemnized during the Three Weeks before Tishah B' Av, or on Sabbaths and holidays. Any other time is considered a fine time for a wedding, though the month of June is a favorite with brides everywhere.

On the Sabbath before the wedding, the bride (*kallah*) and groom (*chatan*) are called to the Torah in the synagogue. If possible, their families are present on this happy occasion. There is an interesting reason for the tradition of "calling-up," or *Aufruf*, as it is known in Yiddish.

According to the Talmud, King Solomon had a special gate for bridegrooms built in the Temple, where the inhabitants of Jerusalem would gather on the Sabbath to congratulate the fortunate young men. After the destruction of the

172

Temple, this was no longer possible. Instead, the sages ordained that the bridegrooms should go to the synagogue so that their friends and neighbors could see them and congratulate them.

A happy bride and bridegroom under the *chuppah*. The banner on the *chuppah* reads "a voice of happiness and a voice of joy."

Harei At Mekudeshet . . .

The day of the wedding is here. Invitations have been sent, The wedding may take place in a synagogue, in a hotel ballroom, or in the quiet of a rabbi's study. It is the solemnity and sacredness of the event that counts, not the surroundings.

The bride and groom stand under the *chuppah*, or marriage canopy, which represents the litter in which the bride was transported in long-forgotten days. The bride wears white, a symbol of purity and, according to tradition, a touch of mourning (for white is the color of the burial shroud) for the destruction of the Temple. For this last reason, the groom sometimes wears a white robe (*kittel*) when he stands under the *chuppah*.

The groom is led under the *chuppah* by his parents, followed by the bride escorted by her father and mother. The assembled guests hear the blessing over wine and, if they are close enough, observe the groom slip the wedding ring (which must be smooth with no ornamentation, to ensure a smooth and unbroken married life) on the forefinger of the bride's right hand. At some weddings, called double-ring ceremonies, the bride also presents the groom with a ring. As they perform this act, the bride and groom recite the ancient vow, *Harei at mekudeshet li be-taba'at zu ke-dat Mosheh ve-Yisrael* ("You are hereby betrothed to me by token of this ring in accordance with the laws of Moses and Israel").

An outdoor wedding, blessed by the sun under a *chuppah* made from a *tallit*.

Following this, the *ketubah*, or marriage contract is read aloud. The *ketubah*, written in Aramaic, details the rights and responsibilities of husband to wife in wedded life. It is the duty of the wife to preserve this document. In the very late Middle Ages and in early modern times, many beautifully illuminated and decorated and illustrated *ketubot* were prepared for wealthy families, and they may be seen in museums and private collections.

Next, the Seven Blessings are recited. One of them, translated into English, follows:

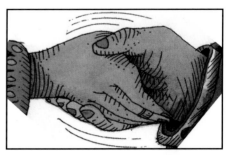

WEDDING GREETINGS
After the wedding ceremony you wish the bride and groom and members of the family *Mazel Tov* "good luck."

173

Crushing the wine glass.

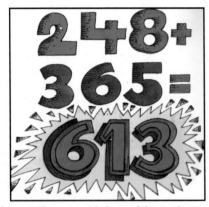

According to Maimonides, there are 613 *mitzvot* in the Torah. The Hebrew letters whose numerical value equals 613 spell out the word *taryag mitzvot*.There are 248 yes–do *mitzvot*. These are mitzvot that God wants us to do, such as praying and honoring our parents. In Hebrew these are called *mitzvot aseh*. There are 365 *mitzvot* that are the don't do kind. These are called *mitzvot lo ta' aseh*. Do not steal and do not kill are just two examples.There are *mitzvot* associated with every part of your life: how you behave in school and how you play sports, how you treat your friends and family. *Mitzvot* are a part of the cycle of your Jewish life: birth, Bar Mitzvah/Bat Mitzvah, wedding, and death.There are *mitzvot* about the food you eat and how you will act as a grown-up in business or in your profession.

Blessed are You, Almighty our God, Ruler of the universe, Who has created joy and gladness, bridegroom and bride, mirth and exultation, pleasure and delight, love, brotherhood, peace and fellowship. Soon may there be heard in the cities of Judah and in the streets of Jerusalem, the voice of joy and gladness, the voice of the bridegroom and the voice of the bride, the jubilant voice of bridegrooms from their canopy, and of youths from their feast of song.

Blessed are You, Almighty, Who makes the bridegroom to rejoice with the bride.

The ceremony closes with the crushing of the wine-glass under the bridegroom's heel. The reason is to provide still another reminder of the destruction of the Temple in Jerusalem, thus demonstrating that even in times of the greatest personal happiness we pause for a moment to recall the sorrows of our people.

With the stamp of the shoe and the crunch of the glass, the wedding ceremony is over. The new husband and wife retreat from under the *chuppah* to cries of *Mazel Tov*, and the guests are welcomed to the wedding feast.

These are the essentials of a Jewish wedding. The age-old customs and traditions are basic and they have served to maintain the solidity and unity of our people throughout the centuries.

Tzedakah

Tzedakah is not an event or occasion in the life of a Jew. Yet it is so much a part of our collective and personal existence, and has permeated the consciousness of our people to such an extent, that a discussion of the cycle of Jewish living would be incomplete without it.

To be a Jew means to understand the concept or idea of *tzedakah*, to support it, to pass it along to our children. It is a golden thread in the rich fabric of our heritage. It is part and parcel of Jewish life.

From earliest times, *tzedakah* has meant the act of sharing what we have, being kind to the poor, and doing good deeds. The best one-word translation of the Hebrew term *tzedakah* is "righteousness," and that is what it has signified throughout the ages.

Tzedakah in Bible Days

The Bible gives us our first lessons in *tzedakah*. Abraham was practicing righteousness when he invited the three strangers to come in out of the midday sun and break bread with him. He was not giving charity; he was sharing what was his with those who possessed less.

Because our ancestors were a farming nation, the Bible gave them many special regulations so that they could perform deeds of *tzedakah* in the daily routine of living. When the harvest was reaped, a portion had to be left for the unfortunate. The corners of the field and the fruit and grain which the farmer forgot were to be left untouched after the harvest. "You shall leave them for the poor and for the stranger," says the Bible.

Every seventh year was called *Shemitah*, and for those twelve months the land was to lie fallow, or unworked. Whatever happened to grow of itself during the year belonged to the needy—the stranger, the fatherless, the widow.

Tzedakah in the Talmudic Period

The people that had been given the Torah carried its teachings everywhere. When we had our Temple in Jerusalem, there was a room in it known as the *Lishkat Chasha'im* ("chamber of secrets"). It was purposely kept very dark so that well-to-do persons might leave *tzedakah* donations unobserved and the poor might take as much as they needed without being seen. The earliest synagogues adopted the practice and had similar private rooms.

Leaders of the community were chosen to be in charge of relief work. There were *gabbaim tzedakah* who collected and distributed funds to the poor. They followed a *tzedakah* system that had been used in the days of the Second Temple. Every town had a community-chest, or *kuppah*. Each Friday, the poor would receive money for meals for the whole week and for clothing. There was also a charity-bowl, in which food was kept for the hungry, a clothing fund, and a burial fund. The rabbis said that a city that had no charity-box was not worth living in.

The most important rule our ancestors followed was that no one should be put to shame for receiving *tzedakah*. For that reason it was a custom to set aside special buildings open

In many Jewish communities there were voluntary societies (*havurot*) which were devoted to Jewish education and charity for the needy. Two major functions of these societies was the charity fund and the soup kitchen. The fund provided financial assistance to the poor and the kitchen supplied food and meals to the poor.

This illustration from the *Golden Haggadah* shows a Jewish volunteer distributing food to the poor.

The Jewish community was touched by the drowning of Ida and her husband the beloved philanthropist Nathan Straus. In the highest act of *tzedakah* they gave their seats in a lifeboat so that two other people could live.

The tradition of *gemilut chasadim* (free loans) is an ancient and honorable one. *Gemilut* means "doing kindness." This Jew in pre-Holocaust Poland is shown borrowing money from a free loan society.

HIAS is the acronym for Hebrew Sheltering and Immigrant Aid Society. Its object is to assist Jewish immigrants coming to the United States. After World War I and II a network of agencies were established in Eastern Europe and millions of Jews were helped in their journeys to safety to other countries. HIAS is active in over 50 countries and is also active in Israel.

HIAS is a *tzedakah* institution which has supported the poor, helps the aged, helps refugees and ransoms political prisoners.

on all four sides, where the poor might enter and eat their fill without begging.

The Community in Europe

When the Jewish people were driven into exile, there was more need than ever for deeds of kindness. Many Jews wandered from place to place unable to establish a permanent home. Communal life often had to be built in an atmosphere of persecution and intolerance. The Jewish family had to care for its own, because no one else would undertake the task.

In the Middle Ages, *tzedakah* societies existed all over Europe. They undertook many important assignments. They supported and clothed the poor; they educated the children of the poor and contributed to wedding funds for poor girls; they educated orphans, visited the sick, sheltered the aged; and provided burials for those who could not afford it. They ransomed prisoners who had been kidnapped for the purpose of extorting money. This last mission, called *pidyon shevu'im*, was one of the most vital acts of *tzedakah* in medieval times.

During the centuries of Jewish life in Europe, many customs arose which were designed to mask the face of charity and make it appear like anything but that. In order to protect the poor from being embarrassed, messengers were sent from house to house with a sack. Those who could, put something into it; those who needed aid, helped themselves from the sack, and no one was the wiser.

Hachnasat Orchim

As means of communication developed, one city was able to learn of the achievements of another, and communities taught each other new ways to practice *tzedakah*. In our great-grandparents' time, there was no Jewish settlement without a *hachnasat orchim*, or lodging-house for the wayfarer. This institution exists to our very own day.

In fact, wherever there was a synagogue no one had to go hungry. There a person in need could obtain money for food, find a place to rest, even be put up overnight. And which well to-do *ba'al ha-bayit,* or head of a family, would not bring with him a poor stranger on Friday night when he returned home from the synagogue?

When parents blessed their children, they would add: "And may you have a hospitable table, and extend a warm welcome to the needy."

Tzedakah Today

The Jewish tradition of righteousness, of *tzedakah*, stands us in good stead today. For never has *tzedakah* been so important as in our own times. And never has it been needed on so large a scale.

In our own communities, we are called upon to practice *tzedakah* all the time. When we contribute to the Community Chest we are aiding those less fortunate than we. That is *tzedakah*. When we provide the Jewish Federation in our community with the means to support Jewish education, to cure the sick, assist the aged, and protect the homeless, that is *tzedakah* in its finest form.

Tzedakah Agencies

Although *tzedakah* begins at home, it does not end there. When World War II wiped out six million Jews, we in North America who were more fortunate were faced with the staggering task of helping those who survived to rebuild their lives. Through such agencies as the American Jewish Joint Distribution Committee, the United Jewish Appeal, and the United Palestine Appeal, we did our utmost to help the remnant of European Jewry regain its strength and to create a strong and flourishing State of Israel.

And that is how we will fulfill the same age-old, time-honored mission in the twenty-first century. In these ways we practice *tzedakah*, a mitzvah as old as the Jewish people.

The Meaning of Death

All living things–human beings, beasts, insects, flowers–must one day die. To be alive means to bear within oneself the seeds of death. To avoid death means not to have lived at all.

Judaism teaches us to face this final event in the cycle of life with strength and fortitude. Our sages have pondered the meaning of death and have taught us the lesson of continuing to live and to serve God and humanity despite the loss of our loved ones.

The Joint Distribution Committee is the most remarkable and far-reaching of all private philanthropies, feeding, rescuing, training, and resettling persecuted Jews all over the world. The amount given by Jews in democratic countries for JDC activities has increased as the need has grown greater.
JDC programs supply kosher food to local canteens in Eastern European countries so elderly Jews can live out their remaining years in dignity.

The American Jewish community has created many organizations to provide help for Jews around the world. These groups serve all Jews regardless of background or beliefs. The leading Jewish communal organization is the Jewish Federation. Their fundraising campaign is called the United Jewish Appeal (UJA). There are other important Jewish organizations that have arisen to fulfill the mitzvah of helping all people. This photo was taken at the 92nd Street Y in New York. The largest and most famous community center in the world and a member agency of New York's Federation of Jewish Philanthropies. The Federation aids Jewish education, hospitals, and other Jewish activities.

Those who prepare a body for burial are members of an organization called *chevra kadisha,* an Aramaic term meaning "holy society." Any Jew can join a *chevra kadisha* and be trained in the mitzvot of *chesed shel emet.* The first known *chevra kadisha* society is from 16th century Prague. By the 17th century it had set regulations regarding burial fees, graves, and rules for erecting tombstones. What makes this particular society interesting is that Rabbi Judah Loew ben Bezalel (1525-1609), known by the title Maharal, established the rules. In addition to being a rabbi, he was a mathematician and philosopher.

THE *YIZKOR* PRAYER

The *Yizkor* prayer is recited on Yom Kippur, Shemini Atzeret, Passover and Shavuot. The recitation of the *Yizkor* prayer helps the family members to remember their loved ones and their way of life. It is also customary to light a *Yahrzeit* candle on the anniversary of the loved one's death.

The Jewish religion teaches us first to honor and respect our parents when they are alive, as it is written in the Ten Commandments. Only after we have attended to this *mitzvah* can we honestly revere the memory of dear ones when they are dead.

Reverence for the dead was displayed by our forefather Abraham when he bought a burial place for his wife Sarah. The Cave of Machpelah became the burial ground for Abraham and Sarah, Isaac and Rebekah, Jacob and Leah.

This attitude of respect and reverence has been handed down from generation to generation. Today we still observe annual memorial days (*Yahrzeit*), hold memorial services (*Yizkor*) in the synagogue or temple on major holidays, and visit the graves of loved ones at certain seasons of the year.

All the Jewish rites and traditions surrounding death, burial, and mourning are designed to honor the memory of the departed and to help those who remain behind to carry on their lives with dignity and courage.

The Funeral

When a person dies, the first words said by those who hear the news are *Baruch Dayan Emet,* "Blessed be the True Judge." For, while death is tragic, we accept it as the decree of an all-wise and all-understanding God, Who rules the world in mercy and wisdom. Close relatives of the deceased make a slight tear in their clothing, called *keriah,* as a symbol of mourning which they will display for one week.

The funeral procession is simple and dignified. The procession halts briefly at the synagogue which the deceased attended, where a prayer is recited. The burial takes place in a Jewish cemetery, often called the *bet chayyim,* the House of Eternal Life. Often a little sack of Israeli soil is placed in the grave, for our ancestors considered it a great mitzvah to live and die in Eretz Yisrael, and if they could not do so, at least they might have a bit of Holy Land soil with them on the final journey.

When the coffin has been covered with earth, spaded in by family and friends, the famous prayer *El Moleh Rachamim* ("O God, Full of Mercy") is recited, and then the *Kaddish* is said by the sons and daughters of the deceased.

The *Kaddish* speaks of the greatness of God and of the everlasting peace that will prevail in the messianic era at the end of time.

Sitting *Shivah*

When the mourners return home, they are given a hard-boiled egg, symbol of life in the midst of death. The bereaved sit on low stools for the mourning period known as *Shivah*. During this period relatives and friends come to visit and to console the mourners. Services are conducted in the home during the *Shivah* period, and *Kaddish* is recited by the children of the deceased at each service, as it will be for the next eleven months. During this eleven-month period the mourners will refrain from pleasures and amusements. Orthodox and Conservative Jews sit *shivah* for seven days. Reform Jews sit *shivah* for three days.

About one year after the death of the loved one, a tombstone is unveiled, and relatives and friends assemble once again to pay honor to the dead.

The *Yahrzeit*

Every year thereafter, the death anniversary, or *Yahrzeit*, is observed at home and in the synagogue. A memorial candle, usually set in a glass, is lit at sunset; it will not go out until the next sunset. *Kaddish* is recited in the synagogue. Many visit the grave on the day of *Yahrzeit*. Memorializing the dead is one of the most widely observed Jewish customs, crossing the boundaries separating Reform, Orthodoxy, Conservatism and Reconstructionism.

Aside from *Yahrzeit*, memorial services called *Yizkor* are held for all Jewish dead on the holidays of Yom Kippur, Shemini Atzeret, the last day of Passover, and Shavuot. Each person silently reads several *Yizkor* prayers, inserting the names of the deceased.

Old Jewish cemetery, Prague, Czechoslovakia.

SHIVAH ETIQUETTE
As you enter the house you will notice that the mourners are seated on low stools or benches. After you express your condolences and are ready to leave, it is customary to say *HaMakom yenachem etchem* "May God comfort you."

A *Yahrzeit* light.

A Final Word

The mourning customs, while they vary from land to land, from community to community, and even from family to family, all serve a threefold purpose: to fill our lives with the dignity and self-respect of honorable human beings; to show our attachment to our faith and our people; and to express our belief in the goodness and wisdom of an Eternal, All-Knowing God.

In truth, that is the purpose underlying all our holidays, customs, and ceremonies.

And, by knowing and learning these things, are we not learning our Jewish heritage?

INDEX

181

PHOTOGRAPHIC CREDITS

PHOTOGRAPHERS: Bill Aron, Hank Azzuto, Jack Hazut
SPECIAL PHOTOGRAPHERS: Carol Attia, Debbi Cooper, Michael Loeb, Steve Henry Woodcraft, Chapel Hill, NC.
INSTITUTIONAL PHOTOCREDITS: AMERICAN FRIENDS OF THE HEBREW UNIVERSITY, New York City: AMERICAN JOINT DISTRIBUTION COMMITTEE, New York City: BEIT MIDRASH, Jerusalem, Israel: BEIT HAT-FUTSOTH, Tel Aviv: BEZALEL NATIONAL MUSEUM, Jerusalem, Israel: BIBLE MUSEUM, Amsterdam, Holland: BIB-LIO THEQUE NATIONALE, Paris, France: BODLEIAN LIBRARY, Oxford, England: BRITISH MUSEUM, London, England: BREIT, J., New York City: DEPARTMENT OF ANTIQUITIES, Jerusalem, Israel:HEBREW UNION COLLEGE, Cincinnati, Ohio: HEBREW UNIVERSITY,Jerusalem, Israel:ISRAEL GOVERNMENT PRESS OFFICE, Jerusalem, Israel ISRAEL STAMP OFFICE, Jerusalem, Israel: ISRAEL STATE ARCHIVES, Jerusalem, Israel; JEWISH NATIONAL FUND, New York City: JOINT DISTRIBUTION COMMITTEE, New York City: LOEB, MICHAEL MUSEO de PRADO, Madrid, Spain; ORIENTAL MUSEUM, Chicago, Ill: PALESTINE ARCHEOLIGICAL MUSEUM,Jerusalem, Israel: PALAIS de LOUVRE, Paris, France; RECONSTRUCTIONIST RABBINICAL COLLEGE, Wyncote, Pa. TOURO SYNAGOGUE, Newport, Rhode Island: WOLFSON MUSEUM, Jerusalem, Israel: YAD VASHEM, Jerusalem, Israel YESHIVA UNIVERSITY, New York City: YIVO INSTITUTE OF JEWISH RESEARCH, New York City: